# IN THE COURT OF DEADLY ASSUMPTIONS:

*ANOTHER WRONGFUL CONVICTION,*

*ANOTHER MURDERED GIRL ABANDONED?*

By
*George Sherwood*

## The Colder Case Series
### by George Sherwood

*Uncivil Twilight:*
*1920s Death Sentence that Left a Serial Killer Free to Stalk and Kill Children in 1937*

*Colder Case:*
*How California Executed the Wrong Man and Left a Serial Killer Free to Stalk Children* (the 1937 case)

*Abandoned Justice:*
*The Cold Case of Ten-year-old Virginia Brooks* (a similar 1931 case, still unsolved)

*In the Court of Deadly Assumptions:*
*Another Wrongful Conviction, Another Murdered Girl Abandoned*

*Lynch Him!*

"It was a revolting crime and one over which indignation against the perpetrator rises as the evidence is read, but yet legal judgment must be kept in the balance and the case examined to determine whether the defendant's life has been forfeited by our rules of law" - Court of Appeals of the State of New York.

# Court of Appeals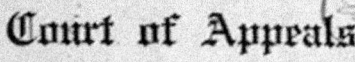
### OF THE STATE OF NEW YORK

THE PEOPLE OF THE STATE OF NEW YORK,
*Respondent,*

against

SAMUEL ELMORE, alias SIMON ELMORE,
*Defendant-Appellant.*

## RECORD ON APPEAL

PETER F. GULOTTA,
WILLIAM C. CASEY,
*Attorneys for Defendant-Appellant,*
Office & P. O. Address,
25 Hyatt Street,
Borough of Richmond,
City of New York.

FRANK H. INNES,
*District Attorney of Richmond County,*
*Attorney for Respondent,*
Office & P. O. Address,
County Court House,
St. George,
Borough of Richmond,
City of New York.

## TABLE OF CONTENTS

Missing **1**

People's Opening Address. **1**

Motion for Withdrawal of Juror **74**

Proceedings at Scene of Crime **95**

Motion to Dismiss. **193**

Defense **195**

Motion to Dismiss **269**

Summation by Mr. Gulotta--For Defendant. **270**

Summation by Mr. Innes--For People **303**

Exhibits **316**

Court of Appeals of the State of New York. **338**

COMMUTATION **339**

APPENDIX **340**

    CRIMINAL LAW AND ITS ADMINISTRATION IN THE STATE OF NEW YORK. **340**

MISSING

Joan Kuleba was only 4-years-old. She went to the beach with her two cousins, just as she had done many times before. This time would be different. Her Aunt Lesandi gave permission for the three children to go to the beach, saying she would join them soon. When Aunt Lesandi got to the beach and asked, "Where is Joan?" her daughter answered, "Mother, she was just here, I don't know." Joan's aunt was not frantic yet. Her niece was probably behind the bungalow they had let for the summer in South Beach, Staten Island. "Bungalow Town" they called where they were staying. There was a pond behind the bungalow and Joan liked to catch killies and put them in a jar of water. She wasn't there. A slight sense of urgency likely trespassed on Aunt Lesandi's vacationing mind but she knew Joan was probably at a friend's a few bungalows away. No, not there. There was no place else little Joan would likely be, and now Aunt Lesandi was worried. From a little after 11:00 A.M. to about 12:25 P.M. on that Thursday, August 12th, 1937, Aunt Lesandi and her children with about 30 other people searched all along the beach, the South Beach boardwalk, and all over Bungalow Town for little Joan Kuleba, to no avail. She vanished.

It was at 12:25 P.M. that one of the searchers called the police for Aunt Lesandi, according to her testimony, and an officer arrived within 10 minutes. Grace Lesandi's was the most important testimony of the trial, yet it was glossed over despite its determining value. It was similar to the efforts of Mrs. Buss in 1925, when she doubted the police theory, as did the parents of the Everett sisters in 1937. The family of victims, it seems, had an uncanny knack of knowing when the authorities were accusing the wrong man.

Of course, everyone kept searching. At about six or seven that evening two detectives found sandals near an overturned boat on the sand, and the detectives took the shoes to Aunt Lesandi for identification. They were Joan's. Now it was assumed she waded out into the water and drowned.

During Samuel Elmore's trial for First Degree Murder, Mrs. Lesandi would, without prompting, testify that the sandals were not wet when they were returned to her. This was of vital import because wet or dry is matter of fact, like forensic science, and the claim that they were dry would contradict in a concrete fashion the theory of the prosecution. How could the little girl walk through the marsh in her shoes without them getting wet? Why were the bottoms of her feet clean? Prosecution testimony claimed the sandals were wet, but the little girl's aunt, the one who wanted justice the most, took it upon herself to point out the little shoes were dry. No one seemed to notice. In fact, none of the science supported the confession. It contradicted it.

The next day, Samuel Elmore was going crab fishing with pots to catch crabs when he observed a body in an abandoned bungalow in the marshes about half mile from Crane's Hotel, South Beach, nearest where the children were playing. He circled the bungalow getting different views from a basement window and the cellar doorway looking down. From there he went to some houses nearby and told a man he needed a phone to call police. Maybe he said there was a little girl's body in the basement of the bungalow and maybe he said the body of a child was there; maybe the father of two girls could tell the gender of a nude body laying on her stomach, maybe not, but the police came either way. Elmore was held in a police car for a couple of hours then taken to the police station. Multiple newspaper stories stated Elmore was grilled continuously for over 24 hours before he confessed. Some reports went so far as to state Elmore was purposely detained and kept from arraignment, because arraignment would obviously interrupt the interrogation. The law in New York at the time required the police to arraign a suspect before a court without delay, and the suspect would then be turned over the sheriff's custody. That obviously meant the police could not grill the suspect as long as they wanted. Newspapers gave the plan away.

For example, the New York Times on Aug 15, 1937:

"Painter, 57, Admits Killing Girl of 4.
"WPA Worker, Who 'Found' Body of Staten Island Child, Breaks After 24-Hour Questioning.
"Trapped by a Chauffeur: Latter Tells of Seeing the Prisoner Walking Along the Beach With Victim. "

The story claimed Elmore had a grasshopper in a bottle and that is how he lured the child away from the beach. The prosecution would argue this throughout the trial despite knowing the confession contradicted it. In typical dramatic structure the story built a fictional narrative, stating Elmore said he told the girl he would take her "to a place where grasshoppers did all sorts of wonderful things."
"Joan took his hand confidently and he led her to a tumbled-down house in a near-by marsh. They stood together in the basement, little Joan looking up at him to hear what the grasshoppers did in that house. He strangled her, attempted a criminal attack on her, tossed her body to the floor by the cellar door, dropped a fifty-pound clump of brick on her back and then when home to lunch."

Some of this is true. There was an "attack" and there was a fifty-pound piece of a brick wall on her back; and her body was on the cellar floor near the door by the steps of the cellar. But what Elmore said to little Joan about grasshoppers and her reply is pure fiction, because Elmore did not take her.

Also of vital importance in the article was the quoting of Chief Inspector John J. Lyons:

"Chief Inspector John J. Lyons said that although

Elmore had confessed, he would not be booked until 12:30 P.M. today. The purpose of deferring the formal charge, according to Mr. Lyons, was to enable the authorities to hold him over the weekend for further investigation.

"The chief inspector explained that if Elmore were booked last night, he would have to appear today in Magistrate's Court for arraignment and then be turned over to the Richmond County Sheriff, who would lodge him in the county jail. By booking Elmore after the Magistrate's Court closes today, the chief inspector pointed out, the police could hold him until after his scheduled appearance in the line-up and Manhattan headquarters tomorrow morning."

The significance of this will become clear. As you read the trial transcript and proceedings, it will become obvious that Elmore was legally innocent and probably factually innocent. Indeed, if the news report is accurate, the law required a notice to the jury that any confession under those circumstances was suspect. New York had laws to help prevent false confessions and the police ignored those laws and got false confessions anyway. Could this story be why the judge so carefully directed the jury to ignore newspapers?

The story then claims Elmore was "drawn irresistibly to the scene of the crime and 'found' her' the next day." It is possible that without tunnel vision the police may have investigated someone else who was near the scene of the crime and was perhaps keeping an eye on it in an unusually defensive manner. An important witness, who happened to be keeping an eye on the abandoned shack, claimed he saw Elmore walking around it, and that Elmore approached him, told him he needed a phone to call the police because there was the body of a girl in the bungalow.

If the child is face down, even if nude, how could

someone know if it was a boy or a girl? The prosecution took full advantage of this statement, but on cross examination the witness was tripped up and ended by saying Elmore said "girl" or "child" or "both" girl and child. Whatever was said, the witness went to get the police while Elmore waited. Upon his return with the police, as he testified,

"Mr. Elmore was standing there where I left him. I said, 'Where is she?'"

So if "returning to the scene of the crime" indicates criminal guilt, and if knowing the victim was female was so suspicious, why wasn't this witness suspicious? This is similar to the claim that Albert Dyer knew the three girls from Inglewood were dead because he was ordered to look for bodies on the Monday they were found. That trial was national news at the time and it was alleged Dyer was a "pied-piper" that led the children to their deaths. Were those news stories influencing memories? (See *Colder Case*.)

In *The Third Degree* author Manuel H. Lavine describes police procedure as it was back in the day. To be specific, his book was published in 1930. There was a bit of a reform movement then because *Convicting the Innocent* was published two years later. It wasn't until 1937 that the U.S. Supreme Court ruled that torture of a prisoner was forbidden during interrogation.

Lavine goes so far as to say the third degree was simply part of police procedure, no more unusual than buses passing on the street. In this New York case, the attention is drawn to the other side of the country, to the east coast, to Staten Island. Could a serial killer operate in California and New York? Why not? Rail lines were near in these cases. But again, as pointed out in my previous books, when the wrong person is convicted of a child's murder, it could potentially leave a serial killer free to go on killing. For that reason, the third degree used on the innocent was the serial killer's friend. How common was it? Lavine explains:

"The law very specifically states that a prisoner must be arraigned at the earliest possible moment, before the nearest magistrate, in the court nearest the scene of his arrest. Night courts are provided so that prisoners arrested after the closing of the afternoon session can be arraigned for all misdemeanors. Felony cases are not brought to Night Court. Those accused of felonies are held prisoner so that if they fail to obtain bail they can be taken to Police Headquarters for the line-up.

"Before the passage of the Baumes Law, well-known offenders made every effort to obtain bail in order to beat going to the line-up. There was always the danger that some complainant might pick them out. Besides that, one gave too many detectives attending the performance an opportunity of becoming familiar with one's features. A criminal is rather sensitive about haring people gaze upon his physiognomy.

"Such is the theory. What is the practice?

"Whack—whack—whack! 'If you don't tell me where Jim the Lug is, I'll kick your brains all over the room.' And the whamming continues, constitutional rights or wrongs. The only time I have heard the legal warning given was when the confession was being repeated for the edification of the Assistant District Attorney assigned to the case.

"The prisoner had either been cajoled into 'coming clean' with his confession, because the big-hearted detective had promised to get him a suspended or light sentence, or he had been so badly kicked and cuffed about that he decided to admit his part in order to avoid further punishment.

"If he had demurred in the presence of the Assistant District Attorney and protested about the manner in which the admission had been obtained, that learned legal luminary would have decided that he wanted to leave the room and smoke a cigarette. He would be afraid that the smoke might irritate the prisoner's eyes.

"When he returned, the prisoner inevitably would in a very docile manner admit anything that was demanded of him."

Why does this matter so much after all this time? Always, there is more at stake than the immediate suspect, his family, the victim, her family, and the others affected. It is not hard to guess how devastated Joan Kuleba's aunt was, along with Joan's parents.

[Ed. Note: The Kuleba's. Joan's mother was already ill and now she is ill and devastated. This picture was not in evidence.]

The crime undoubtedly left a black hole in their hearts that could never heal in the sense of becoming whole again. There is also the risk that whoever killed little Joan, and no one doubted there was a brutal murder of the worst kind, there was the risk the killer will kill again. Most murderers have a very low recidivism rate, but some killers live to kill.

There is a long jump in distance from the crimes of California reported in the previous books in The Colder Case Series to this one in New York. How could there be any connection?

    1. Newspapers reported that a "peculiar knot" was used to tie the cord that strangled little Joan Kuleba. Strange knots were used in the previously reported cases in *Colder Case*. The knots were so unique that some investigators quizzed navy experts about the "sailor" knots.
    2. Children were usually taken from well-populated areas, suggesting the killer was able to blend in, meaning a very non-threatening in appearance.
    3. Prepubescent children were the victims, always girls, except for a young boy.
    4. "Attacks" on girls from "the front and the back" were in evidence unless decomposition was too advanced to determine that evidence.
    5. There was another murder of a little girl in New York and the girl's body was put in the gunnysack like the body of Virginia Brooks in San Diego, and the cord that killed Joan Kuleba was from her own clothing, in the same manner used by the killer of Virginia Brooks when a garrote using her strap was the murder weapon. (See *Abandoned Justice*.)
    5. There were reports Elmore had a cord in his pocket, like Albert Dyer was accused of having in premeditation in the murders of Melba and Madeline Everett and their friend Jeanette Stephens. (See *Colder Case*. The Albert Dyer trial was at its peak when the murder of Joan Kuleba occurred.)
    6. Around this time, there were two other murders of girls in New York with a cord used as the murder weapon. These girls' bodies were put on baby carriages, like the baby carriage found in the Virginia Brooks case that had Virginia's name on it, "The baby carriage had on it

a slip of paper upon which was written in pencil 'this is the property of Virginia Brooks.'" It remained a mystery then and San Diego authorities could never figure out why someone would put a note on a baby carriage like that. To taunt the police? To make an allusion?

7. Like the Stone and Dyer cases, and the unsolved case of Virginia Brooks, the children's bodies were dumped in desolate and lonely places.

8. Joan Kuleba was not with siblings like the sisters in previous cases, but she was with cousins.

9. In both confessions, 3,000 miles apart, both Albert Dyer and Samuel Elmore blurted out a confession within minutes of the respective District Attorneys arriving at an interrogation of the suspects. How was it known confession was forthcoming?

In the documentary *Paradise Lost*, the defense attorney, during the 1994 trial of Jessie Misskelley, Jr., asks Chief Inspector Gary Gitchell why he showed a crime scene photograph of one of the murdered little boys to the defendant during interrogation. Inspector Gitchell testified it was to "invoke a response". He claimed in his testimony that it worked because the suspect confessed shortly thereafter. "He was scared into making a statement..." The inspector explained that when the suspect is silent or provides no new information for too long, the goal then is to keep him talking.

Elmore was taken to the morgue and forced to view the body the Friday night he found the body. Albert Dyer was taken to the crime scene location where the bodies of the three little girls were found and he confessed shortly thereafter. It helped that he was told he would be taken back to the lynch mob to explain his inconsistencies if not. There was a claim that some of the bones of the Martin sisters were put on the table in front of Stone in 1925. He never confessed. This may work well in truthful confessions, but to keep talking without being repetitive, a suspect has to provide a new scenario that might satisfy his inquisitors. Brandon Dassey in *Making a Murderer* stated it clearly. He guessed, like he guessed when doing his homework. The confession invoked in *Paradise Lost* was a false confession that implicated two acquaintances. Dassey's implicated his uncle.

There were three prime strings that the prosecution claimed tied Elmore to the crime:

1. He "found" the body and knew it was a female.

2. A bus driver claimed he saw Elmore near the crime scene with a child. The location of that alleged sighting was three times the distance from the abandoned bungalow to where the sandals were found, and where was the man and child walking from if doubling back to the crime scene? (The bus driver and the two pedestrians were walking toward the beach, not away from it.) In arguments before New York's highest court (included below), there were sometimes claims by the government that it was Joan Kuleba with him. There was no such testimony and the witness could not identify the girl in the red bathing suit. It was so confusing, that even in the high court's opinion there is a claim, by the author of the opinion, that Elmore and the bus driver knew each other. They didn't, and because they didn't, that made a false identification all the more probable. (The *Innocence Project* found that 70% of those exonerated by DNA were convicted with misidentification evidence.)

3. Elmore confessed. Of course, a confession trumps just about everything and counters everything, including objective evidence like forensic science. For example, there was a bottle found in the bungalow cellar with a grasshopper in it. The defense claimed the police must have mentioned this when questioning the bus driver, and during his testimony the bus driver claimed Elmore had something made of glass in his hand as he drove passed Elmore and the little girl walking on the sidewalk (they were all going in the same direction). On cross examination, the bus driver admitted he didn't know what was in the man's hand, glass or not, wrapped or not, or what the shape of it was. There was a bottle found in

the cellar with the body, probably the clearest piece of evidence down in the crime scene so littered with debris (see the photographs below). The bottle was dusted for prints. Nevertheless, the prosecution never introduced those prints into evidence when submitting the bottle. The defense argued it was because the prints did not match Elmore's. Why didn't the defense ask for the fingerprint evidence? Because they were not ready for that possibility and had not even seen the confessions they were up against until the trial.

Indeed, we can't even tell if a man or a woman was responsible for the terrible crime. According to the confession, there should have been semen, and there was testimony that swabs were submitted for analysis, but that was never introduced either. That would be one certain way to confirm that it was a man, and therefore it could have been Elmore because he was a male. What if there was no semen? What if it was a woman? In the Albert Dyer case, Dr. Wagner, the pathologist who did the autopsy, testified the damage to the girls that caused so much bleeding was first caused by fingers, not attempted penetration. There was the case of the rape by foreign object and murder of 8-year-old Sandra Renee Cantu in California. Such a tragic and heart wrenching case. In that 2009 case the FBI profile singled out men with prior records and never considered a woman until Melissa Huckaby brought attention to herself. She pled guilty. This is not to accuse any woman involved in the Elmore case, but to only to point out the severity of the error in failing in the analysis of the swabs. Or maybe like the fingerprints on the jar, the analysis did not conform with the prosecution's theory and so it was hidden.

There is more revealed below, but even if there is no connection in this case to the California cases, there was another false confession. All the symptoms are there.
1) The confession contradicts the physical evidence instead of revealing new physical evidence the police had not found or was misinterpreted.

2) The interrogation was long and grueling.

3) None of the authorities that testified were there at all times during the interrogation, and so could claim plausible deniability to any Third Degree abuse. For a good primer of the third degree in New York, see *Street Justice: A History of Police Violence In New York City*, by Marilynn S. Johnson.

4) There was an attempt to shock the suspect into confessing.

5) The victim's family disagreed with the police theory.

These cases are not easy to read. Some of the crime scene photos are like getting punched in the gut as are the crime scene photos in *Paradise Lost*. They can be physically shocking. Nevertheless, it is important. As the series *Making a Murderer* astutely makes clear, wrongful convictions not only do harm to the justice system, they leave a killer free to kill again. This is the utmost travesty when it leaves children at risk.

I would take responsibility for all misspellings and typos, but there were undoubtedly many in the original, including the spelling of names. The sum and substance is the same however and there is absolutely no attempt to sway opinion by altering the text other than highlighting the original text in **bold** verbatim and commenting (Ed. Note). It is what it is. It is fascinating to observe the circumstantial wall the prosecution builds in an attempt to make it impenetrable, and to look for the defense effort to punch holes in it. The effort by the state is especially glaring in its brief to the high court, when it is necessary to try to justify an error so flagrant it is probable the conviction will be overturned and a new trial ordered.

PEOPLE'S OPENING ADDRESS.

Court Clerk Kosman : All manner of persons having any business to do with this term of the County Court, held in and for the County of Richmond, draw near, give your attendance and you shall be heard. People against Samuel Elmore.

(Both sides ready.)

(Whereupon the Jury was polled and all Jurors answered present.)

Mr. Gulotta : May it please the Court, at this time I make an application to the Court that the defense be furnished with a daily transcript of the minutes.

The Court : No objection to that.

Mr. Innes : No.

The Court : Both sides will be furnished with a daily transcript of the minutes.

Mr. Innes : May it please the Court, gentlemen of the Jury, a little incident here just upset me a little bit. But, I want at this time to ask your undivided attention while I--

The Court: Mr. Innes, may I interrupt you for just one minute. Will you see that those people are seated and no one standing up. I want no interruptions while counsel is opening or summing up.

( Stenographer repeated : "undivided attention while I?" )

Mr. Innes : --recite the details of probably one of the most terrible crimes ever committed in this community. It devolves upon me under the practice and under the Code at this time to say to you what the People expect to prove to establish the crime charged against the defendant and may I at the outset say, that I have no feeling against the defendant, I am here solely to do my duty.

On the 11th day of August, little Joan Kuleba, was playing on the beach at South Beach. She was staying with her aunt, her aunt at a bungalow, I think known as No. 8 or No. 5 Crabtree Road, Seaside Boulevard, and the aunt, that morning, dressed her in a little red bathing suit, and with a pair of sandals, the little girl was permitted to go on the beach. She was seen there by a lady who was employed at a stand or some concession on the beach at about 12:00 o'clock. She was not seen on the beach after that time by anyone who recognized her and not having returned in the afternoon, the aunt turned her in as a missing person, and an officer was sent to the beach to investigate that complaint.

I think that the officer didn't get to the beach until the following morning and at some time that afternoon or the day after, the little girl disappeared, her little sandals were found at the end of a flat bottom boat which will-- which had been upturned in front of Crane's Hotel.

And the officer naturally thought, as those sandals were there, that the little girl was drowned, and the police began to investigate and in the water dragged for her body.

Now, then, at some time during that forenoon about eleven o'clock, an alarm was spread along the beach that there was the body of--a body in an abandoned bungalow, which stands out in the meadows about 900 or a thousand feet from the nearest street on Olympia Boulevard in that direction and about 1,200 feet from the nearest house on South Beach. The body of this little girl was found in that bungalow dead. She had been raped, backwards and forwards, a string was around her neck which choked her to death. She was laid on her face and a 50 pound weight of bricks put on her back. That was the condition under which that little girl was found at that time, found about 11:00 o'clock or a little after.

The officer who was in charge of the-- and I might say that that officer Cosgrove, Thomas Cosgrove, was on the beach superintending the dragging of the waters to find the body. He was told that there was the body up in the meadow in the basement of this abandoned bungalow, and he went up there. The body was identified, the father had come down from New York. He lived in New York, when his child was missing. He was sent for and he came down, and he identified the body. So much for that feature of the case.

Now, then, Elmore, a W.P.A. painter, a man who worked two or three days a week, or whenever they do work, who on the morning of the 12th went to the Seaview Hospital where he was paid off, came back, was doing certain things around the house, left for South Beach, and met this little girl on the beach at some time after 12:00. He said to her, "Hello, Blondy," and she said, "Hello." "Do you want to take a walk?" She was a trustful little thing. She went with him. They walked up the beach to Sand Lane, up Sand Lane to Olympia Boulevard, which is another name for Old Town Road, or a portion of it, walked over Olympia Boulevard and at the corner of Norway Avenue and Olympia Boulevard, Norway Street, I think it is, a bus of the Staten Island Coach Company came along. The driver of that bus saw this little girl in the red bathing suit and the white sandals and Elmore. He was attracted to that pair. I don't know why, but he said, or he, I expect he will say here, that he was so attracted that he nearly stopped his bus and gave a very good look to the pair. The little girl had her head turned away and he didn't see her except he saw the form and saw the red bathing suit and the white sandals and the curly hair she had. They were on their way towards this bungalow out in the meadows, entirely away, as I have told you, from any habitation.

The defendant Elmore was passing along Olympia Boulevard, picked up a milk bottle near Scott's Place, if you remember, Scott's place is an old place in South Beach, formerly a movie studio in part for wild west scenes. **He picked up a milk bottle near Scott's Place and caught a grasshopper, put it in the milk bottle and there was the lure that the little girl was attracted by in following him along, because he said, "We are going to make grasshoppers do some funny stunts."** [Ed. Note: As seen in the map below, Scott's Place, or Scott's Movie Ranch, is at Old Town Road and Sand Lane.]

Now, then, he went to this bungalow, he took off

the bathing suit this little baby had on, this four year old child, he raped her and then later on he said he bungholed her. Now, if you know what that means, it was a new word, a new expression to me, what it was, when I first heard it. That was, he entered her from the rear to the rectum. She cried and from the straps of that bathing suit that he took off that child, he made a noose and tied it with a **black knot,** which I don't understand, maybe you have heard the expression but I never did before, I don't know what a black knot is, but it is some expression of his and he choked that baby to death, and tied the other part up around a door, a portion of which had rotted out and was, the cross piece around the door, that came up to that cross piece, and then he took this large weight of brick that was cemented together and put on that baby's back.

The baby died. She was dead when she was found the following morning, the 13th.

Now, a most peculiar condition arises here. On the morning of the 13th, Elmore started out, he said, to crab down at South Beach. He stated at one time that he hadn't been to South Beach for five years or more, but he got some fish to put in the crab boat, it was the bait. He started for the beach. He went along this same road, or pathway, to this bungalow. That, you might say, was peculiar. I don't think the human mind has ever been plumbed to its real depths. These gentlemen who claim to be psychologists and students to the human reactions and all that, will tell you that a criminal is attracted to the scene of his crime. He came to this bungalow, said he looked through the window at one side and we will show you the pictures of it to show exactly where he said he was, looking through that window. He could see the feet and legs of that baby as she laid on the floor.

He said he went around to the rear, looked in. He started off away and probably having in mind that if he drew a Scotch Herring over the trail, it might be to his advantage. He gave the alarm. **He said there is a child dead** in that bungalow, to a man who was on or near South Beach. He went down in that direction, went across the creek which is there.

Cosgrove was then sent for. He was the man, if you remember, that was searching for the body of this little girl in the water, and they all came up to the bungalow and Elmore had never been in the bungalow that morning but as he passed this window, he said to Cosgrove, "There she is." There is nothing in the view of

the section of that little girl which would indicate whether it was a boy or a girl, it couldn't be told from just looking in that window. He said, **"There she is**."

[Ed. Note: This is not a picture in evidence below. The body was already removed from the cellar, but it does give a good and clear indication of possible angle of sight and the size of the part of a brick wall or foundation that was weighing Joan Kuleba down. Compared with the actual photo in evidence that includes her body, it may or may not have been possible to determine the gender from this angle. In the photos in evidence, the block appears to have come from the brick column behind it because of the poor quality, but obviously it is intact here.]

Now, that in and of itself, and from other things that Cosgrove learned, caused him to have the defendant brought to the station house for examination and, by the way, after the baby was found, the body was found there, an alarm was given to the police department, an investigation was made, the Medical Examiner or Coroner came there, everything remained as it was until the Medical Examiner arrived. Then the body was taken to the morgue and an autopsy was made, the body was identified, the Medical Examiner will tell you that this little child died of strangulation.

Now, then; the defendant was brought to the 120th Precinct Station House. That was on Friday. He was questioned there, told the story of his being there. A perfect alibi. Just happened to run across the meadows, saw this child there naturally he gave the alarm and that was all he knew about it.

Flick, I believe, the man who was driving the bus saw some pictures in the papers and was attracted because of the fact the crime was committed at or near his route, felt that in the interest of justice that he ought to go to the station house to satisfy his own mind as to whether or not Elmore was the man he saw there.

He came up and he said, "That is the man beyond any question that I saw near that abandoned bungalow within a thousand feet of it on this day in question." And he fixes his run and he fixes the time because he was on time and he was due at the South Beach Terminal of his run at 1:15, and he was leaving at 1:20, and he said it was about 1:12 that he saw the defendant and this little girl about a thousand feet away from this deserted bungalow.

**Elmore, heard and knew that he had been identified as being with the little girl in the neighborhood of the crime**.

[Ed. Note: This was apparently the shock that lead to "breaking" Elmore. While it is true a guilty suspect might realize there is no longer any point in denying guilt, it is also possible the suspect might decide the police are so tunnel visioned that there is no point in arguing with them. Then his faith would turn to the courts to straighten it out, but the courts have faith in the police and the elicited confession unless it is proven to be false.]

I was sent for and I arrived at the station house about a quarter of eight. I had never seen Elmore before. I went in the room on the second floor and Chief Inspector Lyons was there from Manhattan, a cop. He introduced me to Elmore and said, "Now, you must tell the truth. This man is the District Attorney, and he wants to know just all there is about this."

I said to Elmore, "Do you want to say something to me? You know now who I am. If you talk it is something that can be used against you. Now, I want the truth. And he started over on this same line that he crossed the meadow and looked in and saw this body.

I said, "Stop your lying. You know you are lying. Now, I want the truth."

**He said, "Well, I did it."**

There was at least eight police officers there at the time. I don't want to be a witness but I participated in this matter to the extent that I tell you and to that extent only. He then gave us the details and Officer Marrinan, who is a stenographer connected with the Precinct, was present. I don't know whether he took any of this talk down. I don't care, because shortly after that, it was reduced to writing and signed by Elmore.

Now, Elmore said later on that he was treated like a gentleman, there was no violence at all, and he said that within the week to a man whom I sent to the jail to look him over. No violence. No promises. No reason whatsoever to question the credence of that confession and he said when that was shown to him after the papers had been typed by Officer Marrinan, "I haven't my glasses, I can't read."

Lieutenant Gifford gave him his glasses and he put them on and read that confession aloud, and after he read it, he signed it.

That was just a sketchy confession and Gifford, the right type of Cop that he should be, said, "Now, that isn't complete, that babies' feet, as she lay there, were clean, what happened to the slippers that she was wearing?"

"Why," he said, "I took them off in that cellar and I put one slipper in each pocket of my clothes, **coat or pants**, went down to the beach and put them on the sand." He said, "Was there anything near where you put them?" [Ed. Note: Wouldn't Elmore know which it was, coat or pants, if this was from an actual confession?]

He said, "Yes, I put them near the end of that flatbottomed boat, and I threw some sand up on them just to cover up the fact that I had left them there." [Ed. Note: Why? Does this make any sense?]

Now, we didn't know about this thing, that was volunteered by him, and is absolutely collaborated as can be. The fact of the grasshopper in the bottle, we knew nothing about what the bottle was there in the basement, and the grasshopper was in it. All of these things go to absolutely establish the bonafidance of that confession. [Ed. Note: The police of course knew of the sandals and the bottle previous to the confession, but how was it that Joan's feet were clean? There is another explanation.]

Now, then, that isn't all. That was Saturday afternoon. Monday morning, the Grand Jury of this County was convened. This matter was presented to the Grand Jury and an indictment was voted before twelve o'clock that Monday morning after he had confessed on Saturday and had signed the confession.

That was, as I tell you, it was just a one-page, not a full page statement, but enough to show that he was there, was the guilty person. On Monday morning, after he came from line-up, as I remember, he was brought to my office in this building and was there interrogated by my associate, Mr. McKinney. He gave at that time a great deal of detail showing where he was during all that morning, who he met, where he met this little girl, and following along just as I have told you, he gave a full and detailed statement, five pages long and signed every one of those pages and signed it at the end, witnessed by three or four people and by Mr. McKinney, one of whom was the Sheriff of this County. [Ed. Note, this second confession, consisting mostly of contradictions and verisimilitude, if the New York Times are is correct, was obtained illegally. But the first confession was not enough.]

We will show he was calm and self-possessed at that Monday morning conference where that detailed confession was obtained and he is wholly unconcerned. [Ed. Note: Depressed and beaten?]

I don't know how he could be. He was asked over at the station house after he signed his confession, he said he felt better after he made it and signed it, that it was, it had taken something off his conscience. I don't believe he has any. Surely his act as done indicates that he has not.

Now, gentlemen, if we prove all these things to your satisfaction, beyond a reasonable doubt, I say to you that Samuel Elmore has forfeited his life to the State of New York, and I expect to prove everything that I have said in substance substantially the way that I have said it. Thank you.

Peter Gulotta : May it please your Honor, a motion is made at this time to dismiss the indictment against the defendant, on each and every count, upon the ground that that indictment states that a crime was committed on the 12th day of August, 1937, and on the further ground that the bill of particulars states that that crime was committed on the 12th day of August, 1937, between the hours of 11:00 A. M., and 4:00 P. M., whereas, as I understand by the District Attorney's opening., it took place on the 11th. That matter is not included in the bill of particulars. I think that if the stenographer reads that back, I just want to straighten that point out, the 11th is the date mentioned by the District Attorney.

The Court : Well, the District Attorney mentioned the 12th in his opening.

Mr. Innes : If I said the 11th, it was a misstatement. It was the 12th.

Mr. Gulotta : I more particularly say this to your Honor because in view of our defense, we want the records straight, that it was the 12th, and not the 11th.

The Court : The District Attorney stated in his opening it was the 12th and not the 11th and the indictment states that it was the 12th.

Mr. Gulotta : In view of that fact, the objection is withdrawn.

Mr. Casey : Your Honor, I don't think there is any need of our witnesses being here today and will your Honor instruct them to go and have them return, tomorrow morning?

Court Clerk Kosman : All witnesses on the part of the defendant are excused now until tomorrow morning. Defense witnesses come back tomorrow morning.

Mr. Casey : And now, your Honor, I further make a motion that all witnesses be excluded from the court room during the trial.

Mr. Innes : That is discretionary with your Honor. It takes time to get the witnesses.

The Court : You may use the anteroom for the witnesses and have them available. See that the anteroom is available.

Mr. Innes : That is all right, it is discretionary.

Mr. Casey : The only one, Mr. McKitrick, has been subpoenaed by Mr. Innes, and of course, we may need him during the course of the examination so I would like to have him not included.

The Court : Mr. McKitrick will remain in the Court room. The Sheriff will see that the adjoining room is used for the witnesses so they can be called in from that room.

Mr. Gulotta: If your Honor pleases, the defendant waives opening.

The Court : The defendant waives opening.

Mr. Innes : Is Doctor Jacobi here?

Dr. Seltzner?

**Testimony**

DOCTOR JOSEPH P. SELTZER, 16 Island Avenue, Fairfield, Maine, called as a witness on behalf of the People, first being duly sworn, testified as follows :

Direct examination by Mr. Innes:
Q. Doctor, you are now associated with the Staten Island Hospital, are you not? A. Yes, I am.
Q. And you were so associated on the 13th day of August last? A. That is right.
Q. And did you respond to a call to a bungalow in the meadows near South Beach on that day? A. Yes, I did.
Q. About what time did you arrive at that bungalow? A. It was about 12:45 o'clock, that I arrived, yes, I have the record that I made on that day.
Q. Oh, yes, I see, all right. Now, then, did you go in the basement of that bungalow? A. Yes, I did.
Q. What did you find? A. I found the body of a little girl face down on the floor of the basement with a stout cord tied around her neck and the other end of the cord attached to the door knob of the door which was open.
Q. And was that child alive or dead at that time? A. That child was dead.
Q. And are you, from your examination, are you able to state about how long the child had been dead? A. I should say approximately many hours, the body was very cold.
Q. Did you disturb the child at all as she laid there? A. No, I only made a superficial examination to determine whether or not life was present. Q. All right. Your witness.

Cross-examination by Mr. Gulotta:
Q. You say that in your opinion that child had been dead many hours? A. That is right, sir.
Q. Can you give us any more definite opinion as

to the time? A. No, I can't.

Q. In other words, she may have been dead several days so far as you know? A. That is true.

Q. And may only have been dead five minutes so far as you know? A. Not so short a time as that. She was dead many hours.

Q. What is the shortest time that in your opinion she could have been dead? A. About 12 hours I should say.

Q. About 12 hours. But, you don't know over and above 12 hours, it may have been any length of time, is that right? A. Oh, no.

Q. And how long is the longest period of time that she could have been dead? A. Two or three days at the most.

Q. So that in your opinion, this child may have been dead 12 hours to two or three days? A. Yes.

Q. Is that right? A. That is only the result of a very superficial examination.

Q. Now, you said something about a stout cord. Can you more definitely describe what you, what this cord looked like to you? A. Well, it was the kind of cord that is used for wrapping parcels when they are mailed.

Q. Ordinary twine? A. Beg pardon?

Q. The ordinary twine that you get at stores that they wrap parcels with? A. No, it was stronger than that, it would probably be impossible to break by the ordinary person.

Q. Did you, in any way, move the body? A. No, I didn't.

Q. Did you notice that there was something on top of the body? A. Yes, I did.

Q. Did you remove that? A. No, I didn't.

Q. Did you touch the body? A. Yes, I did.

Q. And where did you touch the body? A. I felt it, for the radial pulse, I felt it for the pericardial region, to determine whether or not the heart was beating. I felt the pulse to see whether or not there was--there were any breath sounds.

Q. Now, did you notice how far away the door knob to which the string was tied, how far away from the body that was? A. That was immediately above or almost above the child's neck.

Q. I see. And, for what extent would you say that that string or cord extended from the body to this door knob? A. One and a half to two feet.

Q. One and a half to two feet. And your sole purpose, Doctor, as I understand it, was to go there and ascertain whether this child was dead or alive, am I right? A. That is right.

Mr. Gulotta : That is all.

Mr. Innes : Now, Mrs. Lesandi.

MRS. GRACE LESANDI, 675 Second Avenue, New York City, New York, called as a witness on behalf of the People, first being duly sworn, testified as follows :

Direct examination by Mr. Innes:

Q. Now, Mrs. Lesandi, you are the aunt? A. Yes.

Q. Of this little Joan Kuleba? Right? A. Yes.

Q. And did you have a bungalow at South Beach during last summer? A. Yes, I had it about a block away, called "Bungalow Town".

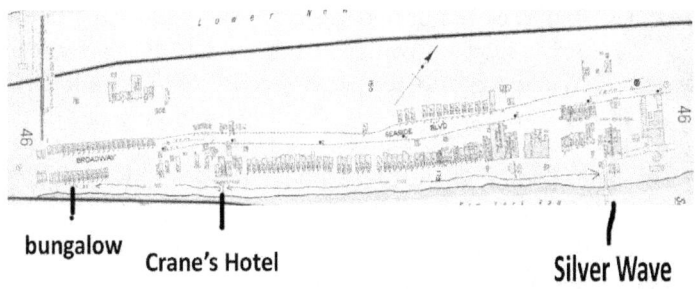

[Ed. Note: It is about 600 feet or one block from bungalow #8 to Crane's Hotel, where the sandals were found. It is another 1500 feet or more than a quarter mile to the Silver Wave Hotel. This map of the boardwalk was not in evidence and is only for the purposes of orientation.]

Q. Bungalow Town. And prior to the--no,--did Joan Kuleba stay with you part of the summer? A. Yes, she was with me all summer.

Q. All summer. Coming down about what time? A. Well, I would say around the 2nd of July.

Q. And she remained with you up to? A. Her death.

Q. The time of her death. Now, then, on the morning of the 12th day of August, did you see Joan Kuleba? A. Yes. I gave her her breakfast and she was playing in the back yard for a little while.

Q. Yes. A. Then I called her in, I put on her bathing suit, she had her breakfast and I sent her with my two little children on the Beach until I got there. That was about ten to eleven or five to eleven, I don't exactly recall. [Ed. Note: Unfortunately, it is not clear how old her children were and when she joined them on the beach. Did she permit them to go to the beach or did she go to the beach at "ten to eleven or five to eleven"?]

Q. Now, when you got to the beach did you see Joan? A. When I got to the beach my two little children were in the water, one of my children was coming out of the water and I asked my little girl, Marion, where Joan is. She said, **"Mother, she was just here, I don't know."** So of course I looked around and I went toward the back, thinking that she was in back of the bungalow which she always does, picking up little Killies and putting them in a bottle with water, so I discovered that she wasn't there. Naturally, I had my children come out of the water and we were looking around for her. We went to Bungalow Town to a friend of mine thinking probably she walked there and she was not there. So then, I did become alarmed because I figured there was no other place for her to be. Well, we made a big search, about thirty people, we went all over.

Mr. Gulotta : That, if your Honor please, is objected to upon the ground that it is not binding upon the defendant.

The Court : Objection sustained, just tell what you did, not what anyone else did, just tell what you did.

A. Well, as we went to a concession, the place called the Silver Wave, there is a young lady there who works for her mother--at this concession. We were there three years ago at this bungalow and she claims--

Mr. Innes : Oh, no, you can't say that.

The Court : Tell what you did.

Q. The other lady is here and-- A. Anyway that is what she told me.

Q. All right. A. Anyway, we couldn't find the child and about 25 after twelve, one of the neighbors called up headquarters and within ten minutes one officer came.

[Ed. Note: This testimony is key. If she looked for Joan for an hour and a half, from 11:00 to 12:25, where was Joan? Did her kidnapper have her? Is that why Elmore was not charged with kidnapping, because this time would have to be accounted for? Elmore was definitely ruled out as being there when Joan disappeared. Indeed, that is when his alibi is tightest. Also, note this comment: "A. Well, as we went to a concession, the place called the Silver Wave, there is a young lady there who works for her mother--at this concession. We were there three years ago at this bungalow and she claims—" The word "claims" strongly suggests this witness, who will testify, did not see Joan at 12:30. So the first crime scene was the kidnapping at around 11:00 o'clock, and Elmore could not have done that. This was never brought out by anyone.

Q. Do you know who that officer was? A. Well, he was a stocky man, I think I would know if I see him.

Q. You have seen him since, have you not? A. Well, I don't remember, I was too hysterical after that, I don't remember.

Mr. Gulotta: I move to strike it out.

Mr. Innes : All right, that is consented to.

A. Well, the officer came and he said, I told the story just how Joan disappeared, and he said, "Well, we are going to be on the look-out." He said "we will look all around". Well, it was three o'clock and no word, so the officer told me to go down to headquarters which is down here. I came here and I spoke to Detective Cosgrove, I think his name was. Well, he said, we will wait until six o'clock, we will wait until six o'clock, he said, and if we don't get no word, we will put it in the missing bureau for her.

Well, I said, "All right". I went back and it was six o'clock, and no word. Then, one of my neighbors called my husband up and the baby's father--

By Mr. Innes:

Q. Now, then, did you, would you recognize that bathing suit if you saw it again, Mrs. Lesandi? A. Yes, I would.

Q. I show you this garment, and ask you if that is the bathing suit? A. Yes, that certainly is the bathing suit.

Q. And you put that on little Joan? A. Yes, I did.

Q. That morning as she was wearing this, the last time that you saw her? A. The last time I saw her.

Mr. Innes: I offer that in evidence, if the Court pleases as evidence.

Mr. Gulotta: The objection is made to it on the ground it is calculated to inflame the minds of the jury.

The Court: Is that the only ground?

Mr. Gulotta : And on the further grounds that there is no basis laid for it, no connection has been made. It is incompetent, irrelevant and immaterial.

The Court: I will mark it for identification at this time and allow you to call the witness back to have him identify it, that it was on the child at that time.

Mr. Innes : Dr. Jacobi could testify to that.

The Court : He said she was dressed in a bathing suit, whether it was one or not. Mark it for identification at this time.

(Whereupon the bathing suit was entered for

identification, as People's Exhibit No. 1.)

The Court: Did I understand you to testify that when the baby left for the beach she had the bathing suit on her?

The Witness : Yes, sir.

The Court : When did you next see her?

The Witness : I didn't see the baby, only in the coffin.

The Court : When did you next see her? Did you see her when the body was found?

The Witness : No, I wouldn't witness it.

By Mr. Innes :

Q. Now, Mrs. Lesandi, what if anything was little Joan wearing on her feet, when you last saw her? A. She wore little white sandals.

Mr. Innes : May I suspend just for a moment?

Q. By the way, Mrs. Lesandi, when did you next see those sandals that little Joan was wearing? A. Well, around five or six o'clock, the detective came with them and found them on the beach and presented them to me.

Q. I see. You saw them that same afternoon between five and six o'clock? A. Yes.

Q. And they were the same sandals that you put on little Joan? A. Yes.

Q. When she left that morning, is that right? A. Yes. And they were not wet, they were dry.

Q. What is that? A. You know, they weren't wet.

[Ed. Note: Here is the other reason Mrs. Lesandi was the strongest witness of the defense. In order for a confession to be valid, there must be corroborating evidence. The prosecution will make these sandals proof of corroboration, as if only the killer could have known where he put them. The contradiction is that if Joan walked to the bungalow with her sandals on, that would explain her clean feet. But they would have to get wet and would not have time to dry. This points strongly to a false confession. The real kidnapper probably left the sandals there when taking Joan.   So how could her feet be clean then?]

Q. He brought them to your bungalow? A. Yes.

Mr. Innes : That is all.

Mr. Gulotta : No questions. [Ed. Note: If this were "Making a Murderer" now would be the time to yell at your screen.]

Mr. Innes : Now, Dr. Jacobi.

The Court : Are you through with this witness?

Mr. Innes : Yes.

The Court : You haven't identified the sandals.

Mr. Innes : Well, hold up, yes, that is right, I asked you if you did recognize those, they are on the way down.

By Mr. Innes :

Q. I show you a pair of sandals, Mrs. Lesandi, do you recognize those as the ones that you put on Joan that morning? A. Yes, I certainly do.

Q. And you say that about the time she left she was wearing them when she left? A. She was wearing them.

Q. And when do you say you next saw them between five and six of that same day? A. Yes, when the detective came.

Q. The 12th of August? A. Yes.

Q. And they were brought to you by a policeman? A. By the policeman.

Q. And you are positive these are the same? A. Yes.

Q. Shoes, sandals that she was wearing? A. Positive.

Q. That morning? A. Yes, positive.

Mr. Innes : I offer those for identification, if the Court pleases.

Mr. Gulotta : Objected to as incompetent, irrelevant, immaterial on the ground the proper foundation has not been laid and on the further ground it is calculated to inflame the mind of the jury.

The Court : Objection overruled. Mark them for

identification.

Mr. Gulotta : I respectfully except.

(Whereupon the sandals referred to were marked People's Exhibit No. 2 for Identification.)

Mr. Innes : That is all, Mrs. Lesandi. Now, Dr. Jacobi.

DOCTOR MENDEL JACOBI, 353 Ocean Avenue, Brooklyn, called as a witness in behalf of the People, first being duly sworn, testified as follows :

The Court : You have held this Court up several times recently when you are called. After this, when you are called as a witness you should try to be on time.
Direct examination By Mr. Innes :
Q. Doctor, you are a practicing physician and surgeon? A. Yes.
Q. And have been how long? A. Since 1925.
Mr. Innes :
Q. Qualifications conceded?
Mr. Gulotta : They are admitted.
By Mr. Innes :
Q. You are also Medical Examiner for the Borough of Richmond, are you not? A. I am.
Q. And you have been such for several years? A. Since 1931.
Q. On the 13th day of August, this year, were you called to an abandoned bungalow in the meadows near South Beach? A. I was.
Q. About what time did you arrive there? A. About one thirty in the afternoon.
Q. And you found a number of officers there? A. I did.
Q. And you also found myself there? A. I did.
Q. Will you describe the place where you found that body? A. That body was in a deserted bungalow situated in a marsh at the end of a street that I was told was North Berger Avenue and which I had considerable difficulty finding.

Mr. Gulotta : I object to that as incompetent, irrelevant and immaterial, not responsive.

The Court : Objection sustained. You did eventually find it, didn't you?

The Witness : I did.

The Court : Just tell us what you found in regard to it.

The Witness : I found a tumbled-down bungalow with a good many people around it. I was directed to look in the cellar.

By Mr. Innes :

Q. Now, then, will you describe that cellar as you remember it? A. As I remember it, the cellar, it was an empty cellar, it looked as if it had been long in disuse, there was a furnace in the back of it, there was a concrete pile or a pile of bricks and concrete that projected up a part as a support from the floor. There was a door leading to the cellar which was approached by two or three steps leading from the ground in the cellar. That door, when I came there, was open against the wall at the right as one looked in, and I found the body lying on the ground on that cellar and as I have described it in my notes. When viewed at the scene, the body was completely nude lying diagonally from the right with the cellar stairs with the feet pointing towards the stairs, a rope was looped tightly around the neck and tied to an adjacent door. The body was lying on its abdomen. There was a large mass of cemented brick lying across the middle of the back. The clothes of the deceased, **a bathing suit, was lying in a nearby corner of the cellar**.

Q. Now, I show you this Exhibit No. 1 for identification. Do you recognize that, Doctor, as the bathing suit that you saw there? A. I do.

Q. And that was near the body? A. That was in a corner near the body.

Mr. Innes : I offer it in evidence now, if the Court pleases.

Mr. Gulotta : An objection is taken to the admission of this in evidence on the ground that there is no proof that it is in the same condition that it was on the day it was found, on the further ground that it is calculated to inflame the minds of the jury, that the proper foundation has not been laid and it is incompetent, irrelevant and immaterial.

The Court : Objection overruled.

Mr. Gulotta : I respectfully except.

(People's Exhibit No. 1 for Identification was received in evidence.)

The Court : Doctor, when you got there were there any police officers present?

The Witness : Yes, a good many.

The Court : If you know, how long had they been there before you got there?

The Witness : I don't know.

By Mr. Innes :

Q. When you investigated, Doctor, had this body and the clothing that was near it been disturbed prior to your arrival there?

Mr. Gulotta: I object to that as not binding upon the defendant.

The Court : Objection is sustained.

Mr. Innes : All right. That is perfectly all right.

Mr. Innes : Did you make an autopsy--no, I withdraw that.

The Court : Mr. Innes, I will withdraw a --I will reconsider my ruling on this bathing suit at this time and deny your motion.

Mr. Innes : All right.

The Court : I will sustain the objection.

(The bathing suit marked in evidence was withdrawn.)

The Court : Doctor, the bathing suit you have seen, you never saw it before?

The Witness : No, sir.

The Court : That was the only bathing suit you saw there?

The Witness : That was the only bathing suit I saw

there.

The Court : At the time you got there, the body was absolutely nude?

The Witness : The body was nude.

The Court : It had no clothes on?

The Witness : It had no clothes on.

By Mr. Innes :

Q. Now, Doctor, what was done or what did you do after you arrived there other than you have stated? A. I examined the body very carefully to decide, to denote the exact state it was in and particularly with reference to the degree and character of rigor mortis.

Q. Yes. Was rigor mortis present? A. It was.

Q. And from your examination are you able to state how long that little girl had been dead? A. With reasonable certainty, yes.

Q. All right, please state it. A. I stated at that time, and state to you now, that that girl had been dead somewhere between 20 and 30 hours with **most likely time interval at about 24 hours from the time I first saw the body**.

Q. I see. Now, then, what was done after that time, Doctor? A. The body, at my direction, was moved to the County Morgue.

Q. And did you, at the County Morgue, make an autopsy? A. I did.

Q. When was that made? A. That autopsy was made at three o'clock on the same afternoon.

Q. And was the body identified for you by anyone? A. It was.

Q. By whom? A. By the father of the deceased, one William Kuleba.

Q. Now, then, tell us what you did at the morgue, what you did with respect to determining the physical condition of that body, upon which you made the autopsy? A. I made a very complete examination of that body, noting all the abnormalities that were present and then proceeded in routine matter to do a complete autopsy, including the head, chest, abdomen.

Q. Now, will you describe, as briefly as you can, what is your regular procedure in making an autopsy? A. Well, first I describe the internal appearance--

Mr. Gulotta : Object to it, if your Honor pleases, as not binding on this defendant, the questioning being what he did on this occasion.

The Court : Don't describe it, tell us what you found, not describing about your notes, but tell us what you found.

Mr. Innes : Yes. A. I found that this child had numerous abrasions of the body, that the child had an abrasion around the neck, the skin and tissues underneath that had little hemorrhages, the covering of the lungs and of the heart had minute hemorrhages in it, that the lungs were over-expanded, that there were several tears around the opening of the vagina and one around the opening of the anus, all three of which were covered with recent blood clots, that the anus was completely relapsed.

Q. Now, then, from the autopsy, are you able to tell this Court and jury the cause of death? A. I am.

Q. Of that little girl? What was it? A. Asphyxia, by strangulation.

Q. When you first observed this cord, was it tightly around the neck? A. It was.

Q. To such an extent to cause strangulation? A. It was.

Q. Now, then, with respect to the ruptures that you say were present at the vagina. Will you describe more particularly what you found on that examination? A. Just above, to the right of the lower portion of the vaginal opening, and just below the lower edge of the right labia majora, that is the larger of the two folds that cover the vagina, and paralleling the lower edge of the right side of the hymen, at a distance of about half an inch from it, there was a linear abrasion through the mucous membrane, that is the covering of the vagina, about 6 millimeters in length, that is about an eighth of an inch and a few millimeters in depth, and that was covered by a few minute recent blood clots. There was a small similar laceration just to the left of the hymen and the hymen itself was not perforated. The skin just to the right of the junction of the rectum and the skin around the anus just at the interior edge of this particular position showed several small abrasions of the skin. That was all.

By Mr. Innes :

Q. Now, then, Doctor, from that examination and your autopsy, are you able to state whether or not there was any penetration of either the organs of this girl or an attempt at penetration? A. I am.

Q. And was there in your opinion? A. There was an attempt in my opinion.

Q. And with respect to the rectum which you describe as the anus, what do you say as to that?

Q. In my opinion there was an attempt at that too.

Mr. Innes : Your witness.

Cross-examination by Mr. Gulotta:

Q. Doctor, is there any question in your mind now as to the cause of death? A. None whatsoever. .

Q. You are certain that this child died by strangulation, is that right? A. Yes.

Q. How long, in your opinion does it take blood to clot? A. That is a variable thing.

Q. You said that rigor mortis has set in for how long? A. I said that rigor mortis had set in, I didn't say how long.

Q. I see. Can you tell us how long? A. No.

Q. Can you tell us how long in your opinion the child had been dead when you looked at her at 1 :30 that day? A. I said about 24 hours.

Q. About 24 hours. And you can't venture any opinion as to how long it would take to form the clots of blood that you described as being around the vagina? A. No, not absolutely.

Q. You can venture no idea at all? A. Yes, I can.

Q. Well, will you venture it? A. It might have taken that length of time although it would probably take time, and then they had persisted.

Q. Doctor, your examination doesn't have

anything to do with the chemical examination of the stomach, does it, does it or doesn't it? A. No.

Q. You didn't make such an examination, did you? A. I didn't.

Q. Would your examination, the one that you made would it be possible that that examination that you made, that it disclosed the presence of semen? A. I don't get that.

Q. The examination that you made. A. Yes.

Q. **Would that ordinarily speaking as a physician, would that examination that you made disclose the presence of semen, if there was any? A. The autopsy that I did, no it couldn't.**

Q. **So that you can't tell us anything about that. A. No, sir, except that I sent some smears from the parietal tissues to our toxicological laboratory for certain examination.**

Q. All right, now you told us, I believe, that the hymen hadn't been broken? A. I did.

Q. And you told us that there was evidence there of an attempt? A. I did.

Q. You said "Yes"? A. I did.

Q. Did you understand my question, what an attempt was? A. An attempt at penetration. There was evidence of trauma in that region.

Q. The penetration, if there was an attempt, would be a very slight penetration, wouldn't it? A. As to that, I can't say.

Q. You said that the hymen was not broken? Did you not? A. I did.

Mr. Gulotta : I think that is all, Doctor.

Mr. Innes : That is all, Doctor.

Mr. Gulotta : One moment. That is all, Doctor, thank you.

Mr. Innes : If the father is here, I just want one question.

WILLIAM KULEBA, 356 East 32nd Street, New York City, New York, called as a witness in behalf of the

People, being first duly sworn, testified as follows :

Direct examination By Mr. Innes :

Q. Now, Mr. Kuleba, just be as calm as you can. Did you see Dr. Jacobi on the 13th of August last? A. Well, not that I know of, you mean at the beach there?

Q. No, at any other place? A. No, I haven't seen him.

Q. Did you see the body of your little girl, Joan? A. I did.

Q. And was the Doctor there, Dr. Jacobi? I think you know. A. Well, I tell you I really wouldn't remember whether he was there or not, because I was so excited I don't remember only a few.

Q. But, you told somebody that was that little girl that was there? A. That is right.

Q. That is all.

Mr. Gulotta : No questions.

Mr. Innes : That is all. Now, Detective Cosgrove.

[Ed. Note: The defense takes every effort to exclude the confessions, and Detective Cosgrove is in the middle of it. Some of this must be in chambers outside the hearing of the jury. Due to this extended war, Detective Cosgrove's testimony is long. Highlights are highlighted below in bold, perhaps with a comment.]

DETECTIVE THOMAS COSGROVE, Shield No. 5389, 9th Detective District, New York City Police Department, called as a witness in behalf of the People, first being duly sworn, testified as follows :

Direct examination By Mr. Innes :

Q. You have been doing plain clothes duty for some time, have you not, in the 120th Precinct of the 9th District? A. I have.

Q. And you were so detailed on the 12th day of August, is that right? A. It is.

Q. Now, at some time that day did you, were you called to South Beach? A. I was.

Q. And on the 12th, about what time was it, what time did you get there? A. Mrs. Lesandi reported Joan Kuleba missing at the station house about three o'clock on the 12th of August.

Q. I see. And did you go with her or did you go to South Beach afterwards? A. Later on I went down to South Beach.

Q. And you got there about what time? A. I got there about four P. M.

Q. And you made certain inquiries there, did you? A. I did.

Q. And did, were you afterwards shown these sandals here? A. I was.

Q. And where did you first see those? A. Detective Bohan was at South Beach in front of Peter Crane's Hotel where he found those sandals on the beach front and they were in the possession --they were given to us by the father of the girl.

Q. Yes. A. The father of the girl and Detective Bohan and Pagano and Hagerty and I were there.

Q. I see. And, did you afterwards cause the police department to make some grappling in the water near there? A. I did.

Q. Now, then, on the 13th of August were you at South Beach? A. I was.

Q. On this same question of the missing little Joan? A. That is right.

Q. And, at some time during the morning was your attention called to, by a Mr. Haff? A. It was.

Q. And without telling us what he said to you, what did you do at that time? A. I proceeded to a department car that was on Seaside Boulevard with Jack McCarthy, William McCrave, Mr. Murphy, and Mr. Haff and we drove to the creek at the foot of Berger Avenue, South Beach.

Q. And who, if anyone, did you see there? A. Samuel Elmore.

Q. Whereabouts was he at that time? A. He was standing by the creek.

Q. Across the creek, or-- A. Across the creek, yes.

Q. Now, then did you have any talk with him at that time? A. Not at that particular time.

Q. Did you shortly after? A. I had a, shortly after, on the way there.

Q. Now, tell us what he said to you and what you said to him? A. **He was walking in the lead with Mr. Haff, through these swamps and marshes, and when we got to the bungalow, we passed a cellar window that wasn't boarded up, and he said, "There she is".**

Q. Yes. A. We then proceeded to the rear of the bungalow and there was the child laying on the cellar floor of the bungalow, **with the bathing suit and cord, bathing suit, straps,** around her neck and he stood up in the rear yard. I then came up--

Q. Did he go in the cellar door? A. He did not.

Q. Did you go in the cellar? A. I did.

Q. Did you touch anything in the cellar at that time? A. I did not, no, sir.

Q. Now, then, what happened after that, Cosgrove? A. I asked him what his name was, where he lived and where he worked. He said he worked in Seaview Hospital. He said he was a painter. I asked him what he was doing here today. He said that his wife asked him to go down and get some clams, that she expected some company. I asked him why he wasn't working today. He said he worked yesterday and this particular day, the 13th, was his day off. I then took the names of the other men and proceeded back and made some phone calls.

Q. Back to where your car was? A. I went to Murphy's home and used his telephone.

Q. I see. Now, then, this particular bungalow, is it near any other building? A. It is not.

Q. And about how far was it from the Murphy's, you say it was? A. Murphy's bungalow, yes.

Q. About how far was it from Murphy's bungalow? A. Oh, I should judge about 2500 feet or more.

Q. I see. And to get to the bungalow did you have to pass through the marshes? A. Marshes and ditches, and little culverts there that were dug out.

Q. I see, did you talk to Elmore about it, how he happened to be there? A. He said his wife asked him to go get some clams down at the beach, that she expected some company.

Q. I see. A. That is the reason for him walking down there, through the marshes, toward the creek to go crabbing.

Q. Did you ask him about any previous times he had been at or near South Beach?

Mr. Gulotta: I object to that as incompetent, irrelevant and immaterial.

The Court : Overruled, part of the conversation, he may repeat the entire conversation.

Mr. Gulotta : I respectfully except.

Q. Yes. A. Later on, when I returned, he told me that he had been there about fifteen years ago, but the location had changed, the swamp lands, since he had been there last.

Q. You mean, that was after you returned making some telephone calls? A. That is right.

Q. And, by the way, where were those calls? A. They were to the police station.

Q. To the headquarters? A. Yes, police headquarters here.

Q. Now, then, did you, you left him at the bungalow while you went down? A. I left him with Haff and the two McCrave brothers, and Murphy came with me.

Q. Then what did you do after that time with respect to Elmore? A. Well, then, the other detectives arrived.

Q. Well, did other detectives arrive? A. They did in the meantime.

Q. About how long after you made the call? A. Why, I, immediately after, I heard the sirens on the way to the place when I was walking back from the swamp.

Q. I see. While you were walking that 2500 feet? A. Yes.

Q. You heard police sirens, did you? A. I did.

Q. And when you came back, were there others there? A. There was patrolman Dahlberg. He was about 500 feet ahead of me walking towards the building through the swamps and marshes.

Q. Was he standing at or near the beach at that time? A. He responded on my 'phone call in the car, I believe.

Q. Now then, you came back and Elmore was still there, was he? A. He was.

Q. Then what, did you have any further conversations with him at that time? A. Well, we then placed him in an automobile and I went down in the cellar.

Q. In whose automobile was he placed, do you know? A. In our Department car.

Q. Then you say you went to the cellar again? A. I returned to the cellar again.

Q. How long did you remain in the cellar? A, Oh, I was there in and out half an hour, maybe an hour.

Q. And other officers came? A. There were, Inspector McGrath.

Q. Inspector Ferre? A. About eight or nine detectives. Inspector Ferre. Later on Chief Lyons, Inspector McNeil, Dr. Jacobi, the ambulance doctor, you, yourself, Mr. McKinney, photographers, and stenographers.

Q. I see. Now then, where did you go after that time? A. I then returned to the beach and made inquiries in the bungalow, seeking for--I later on returned to the police station.

Q. Did you go alone? A. Detective Hagerty was with me.

Q. I see. Now then, you say--did you see that bathing suit? A. I did.

Q. Whereabouts was it when you saw it? A. **It was tied between the door and around the child's neck in a lump.**

Q. I see. You recognize this as the same bathing suit, do you? A. I do.

Q. And the straps were on it? A. It is.

Q. Now then, when did you next see Elmore? A. When I returned to the station house with Detective Hagerty.

Q. He was at the station house at that time? A. He was, yes.

Q. Now then, did you have any talk with him at that time? A. I did, yes.

Q. Tell us what that was? A. I told him that he told me that in a conversation with Inspector Lyons and myself and Elmore, he told me that it was his day off, today, that he had worked yesterday, **and then stated that it was a lie,** that he didn't work the day previous and today was not his day off, that he hadn't worked in a week or ten days.

**Q. That he hadn't worked in a week? A. About that, yes, a week or ten days.** [Ed. Note: The prosecution will claim this is consciousness of guilt, but New York had vagrancy laws and a person could be arrested on the spot. In other word, there are various reasons for him to say he was elsewhere in addition to consciousness of guilt.]

Q. And did you make an investigation to determine whether he had-- A. We later on did, yes.

Q. And you found that he hadn't worked for a week? A. I did, yes.

Q. Now then, did you learn that on the morning of the 12th, did he tell you what he did on the morning of the 12th? A. He said he worked painting the day previous.

Q. I see, but then you say--that was the 12th. He told you afterwards that that was not the fact? A. That was not the truth, yes.

Q. Did he tell you where he was the morning before, the morning of the 12th? A. At first, that conversation, he said he was working but later on he told us the truth about the whole thing.

Q. Well--we will get to that later on. Was anything said about his getting paid on the morning of the 12th? A. Oh, yes. He said he was, at Seaview Hospital and received his pay, $31. and some odd cents, as a painter, that he returned with a man by the name of Barney Siegar in his automobile to Tipperary Corner, that he returned by bus to Concord, that he stopped in an A and P store there for some clams and vegetables for chowder. He then went home, had his lunch. He then stated that he left there and went down to South Beach. Later on he said--

Q. He told you that on the afternoon of that day, or sometime during the day he went? A. That is right.

Q. To South Beach? A. Yes.

Q. Did he at any time tell you that he had been to South Beach on previous days? A. No, he denied that at first, and then he said later on he was there the day previous.

Q. I see. Now then, was Elmore detained in the station house on Friday? A. He was.

Q. He remained there Friday night? A. He was.

Q. And he was there Saturday? A. Yes.

Q. Now then, to your knowledge at any time during Saturday was a man named Flick brought in the room where Elmore was located? A. He was.

Q. And do you know who Flick is now? A. I do now, yes.

Q. Who is he? A. He is a bus operator for the Staten Island Coach Company.

Q. And were you there when a Mrs. Budd was brought in? And saw Elmore? A. I was.

Q. And did you hear what both Flick and Mrs. Budd said in the presence of Elmore? A. I did.

Q. What did they say? A. Mrs. Budd said that she was on the beach the day before, that was the 11th, and that she seen Samuel Elmore on the beach, that she was with her grandchildren on the beach and **she noticed Elmore and her child walking up off the beach, or walking from the beach, that she then ran after her child, took her and looked at Elmore.** She had something on her mind, she said, and when she came to the station house on the morning of the 14th, about four o'clock, Inspector Lyons was there, myself, Inspector

McGrath, she seen Elmore there and she said, that that was the man she seen on the beach the day previous when she was there with her grandchildren.

[Ed. Note: On first reading, the first impression was exactly as intended. Mrs. Budd saved her grandchild from a murderer. This was devious strategy on the part of the prosecution. Elmore may have had a rock solid alibi the day before, but why not charge him with attempted kidnapping and kidnapping of Joan Kuleba? Below you will read that it is standard for the prosecution to charge every count possible, and there were two felony murder charges. Why not add these two and make it four felony murder charges in addition to the two premeditated murder counts? Also, Mrs. Budd in reminiscent of Mrs. MacIntosh, who claimed to see Stone with the two Martin sisters before they were murdered. That was the only evidence linking them that night See *Uncivil Twiligh*t..]

Q. Now then, what, if anything, did you hear Flick say in the presence of the defendant? A. Flick was brought in and he faced Elmore and he said, "That is the man I seen at Norway Avenue and Olympia Boulevard with a child about 1:10 or 1:12, on the day of the 12th of August at Norway Avenue and Olympia Boulevard".

Q. Yes. And was that said in the presence of Elmore? A. It was said--he faced Elmore, he told him.

Q. About what time did Flick come in? A. Flick was there at about 4:30, quarter to five, I believe.

Q. I see. Now then, after that time did you see me at the 120th Precinct Station house? A. I did.

Q. And at about what time, if you remember? A. At about five, fifteen.

Q. And-- A. On the 14th of August.

Q. Did you see or did you hear any conversation between Flick and myself? A. Yes, I heard them tell you that he was--

Q. No, I didn't ask you what he told you, but you heard some conversation? A. I did, yes.

Q. Now, then, where was Elmore at that time? A. He was seated in the matron's room on the second floor of the 120th Precinct.

Q. Now then, did you afterwards see me in that matron's room on that afternoon? A. I did.

Q. And did you hear what Inspector Lyons said to Flick at that time? A. I did yes.

Q. Now, just tell us what you remember.

Mr. Gulotta : I object to that unless it was in the presence--

The Court : In the presence of the defendant.

Mr. Innes : Oh, yes, absolutely. Elmore was there at the time?

The Witness : Elmore was there, Inspector Lyons, Detective Blanke, Detective Schley, myself, Detective Marrinan.

Mr. Innes:

Q. Was Hagerty there? A. Hagerty was there, Inspector Lyons.

Q. And Gifford there? A. Not at that time, not at that particular time.

Q. All right, go ahead. A. Inspector Lyons told Samuel Elmore who you were.

Q. What did he say? A. He said, "This is Mr. Innes, the District Attorney of the County, I want you to tell Mr. Innes the truth about this. " He went on to say something.

Q. Did you hear me say anything to Elmore? A. I did.

Q. Can you remember what that is, or as nearly as you can? A. I think I can. You told him that he was lying, that you wanted him to tell you the truth.

Q. That was after he had made some statement, wasn't it? A. That is right.

Q. All right. A. He then said "I did the deed".

Q. Yes. A. And you said to him what--he said, "I did it", and then he went on to tell us how he had killed the child.

Q. Then I asked him questions? A. You did.

Q. And Inspector Lyons asked him questions? A. He did.

Q. And they all related to this little Joan Kuleba? A. That is right.

Q. Now you say Officer Marrinan was there? A. He was.

Q. Did you afterwards--by the way, Marrinan is a stenographer, is he not? A. He is, he is the stenographer in the Department.

Q. And do you know whether or not he had his note book there at the time and whether or not he took any notes? A. He took Elmore's statement in his short hand book.

Q. Now then, did Marrinan afterwards write out a statement as to the conversation, as to what Elmore said? A. Elmore dictated it to Detective Marrinan, and Marrinan took it down in shorthand and then typed it out.

Q. I see. And after it was typed, what was done with the paper? A. It was shown to Elmore. He said he didn't have his glasses with him, and Lieutenant Gifford gave him his glasses and said, "Can you read it now? " "Yes," "Well read it out loud", so he read it from that story, that paper, and read what he dictated and said that was the truth, that he was glad he got it off his chest, and then he signed it.

Q. I see. Now, I show you this paper and ask you if you recognize that? A. I do.

Q. Is that the paper that Officer Marrinan brought in after he had typewritten it? A. It is.

Q. And is that the paper that was shown to Elmore? A. That is the paper he read from.

Q. And did you hear him read that aloud? A. I did.

Q. You were present all the time? A. I was.

Q. And were several other officers present at the time? A. They were.

Q. After it was read, and as you stated he said it was true, did you see him sign it? A. I did.

Q. And did you sign it as a witness? A. I did.

Q. And who else? A. Lieutenant Howard Gifford,

Detective William Hagerty and Detective John Marrinan.

Q. And were you present at the time Elmore read that paper? A. We were.

Mr. Innes : I offer the papers in evidence.

Mr. Gulotta : Now, if your Honor pleases, the defendant asks at this time for a **preliminary examination** before making any objection.

The Court : All right.

Mr. Innes : All right, you may do that.

Cross-examination by Mr. Casey:

Q. Officer Cosgrove, how long have you been attached to the New York Police Department? A. About 15 years, going on 16

Q. And how long during that time have you been in the Detective Bureau? A. A little over ten years.

Q. Now, on the 13th of August, when you were called to South Beach, Elmore was there? A. I was not called to South Beach on the morning of the 13th.

Q. I mean when you were called down to Haff's house or McCarthy's house. A. I was not called to anybody's house.

Q. Well, you received a message, didn't you? A. I was standing on the beach, and Mr. Haff spoke to me.

Q. I see. And as the result of that conversation, with Mr. Haff, you went to Mr. McCarthy's house, I understand? A. No, I went in my automobile, went in my automobile with these men.

Q. Yes. And from that point you went to the bungalow, is that right? A. That is right.

Q. Now, Samuel Elmore was there, was he not? A. The other side of the creek, yes.

Q. Yes. And he went back to the bungalow with you? A. He was with Mr. Haff and I followed him there.

Q. Now when you--when he was at the bungalow, you had conversation with him? A. I did, yes.

Q. Now, when did you place Samuel Elmore under arrest, at any time that day? A. No.

Q. Did anybody in your presence place Samuel Elmore under arrest? A. No.

Q. And when you, the next time, after you left the bungalow the next place you saw him was at the station house, is that right? A. That is right.

Q. Now, what time did you get to the station house? A. I think about four o'clock that afternoon.

Q. And when you got there, who was present in the room with Samuel Elmore? A. Assistant Chief Lyons, Inspector McGrath, Detective Murphy, Detective Brennan, Sergeant Hildebrant, they were all in and about the office there.

Q. And what office was that in? A. That was in the middle office in the Detective Bureau.

Q. In the Detective Bureau? A. That is right.

Q. That is in the back of the station house? A. In the side, it is not in the back.

Q. Yes, in the side. A. It is in the side, not in the back, facing the street, side street.

Q. And who did the questioning? A. Inspector Lyons.

Q. All the time? A. No.

Q. Who else took any part in the questioning? A. Inspector McGrath.

Q. And anyone else? A. And then I told him about, Inspector Lyons in front of Elmore, the conversation we had at the beach, about him working and it being his day off that day.

Q. I see. And were you there continuously or did you go in and out of the place? A. I was in and out on business.

Q. But, you were there most of the time, were you? A. I was in and out.

Q. How long did the questioning continue on Friday, the 13th? A. Well, we bought him his supper and they spoke to him, **kept talking to him about it, we checked on his story.**

Q. Yes. A. Told us where he had been, we checked on his story.

Q. Well, all this time he was under continuous questioning, wasn't he, by somebody? A. Well, no, he slept. We had a couch there and we let him sleep two or three hours.

Q. Friday night, was he taken anywhere out of the station house? A. He was.

Q. Where was he taken to? A. I was not there but I heard later on.

Q. Well, I don't know, but , he was taken somewhere out of the station house that night? A. Inspector Lyons and Inspector McGrath was with Elmore.

Q. **They took him somewhere and what time did they bring him back again, do you know, pardon me, what time was it that he was taken out? A. It was later on that evening.**

Q. Do you know what time? A. No, I don't, not the exact time.

Q. Approximately, you have no idea of the time? A. Well, it was, it might have been nine or ten o'clock, I don't recall.

Q. I see. And what time was he brought back again? A. I don't know, I was busy downstairs. He was upstairs and I knew nothing about it until later on.

Q. And you said that some time or other he went to bed. What time was that? A. Why, he laid down on the couch and went to sleep around two o'clock.

Q. What time was that about? A. About two or three o'clock.

Q. In the morning? A. Right.

Q. And he had been under continuous questioning from four in the afternoon except for the time that he went out? A. No, he wasn't under continuous questioning, there were lots of times for half an hour, maybe an hour, nobody spoke to him, just sat him over there.

Q. I see. But, all the time these police officers were there, were they, the police officers? A. No.

Q. Were coming in and out? A. No.

Q. And Inspector-- A. Inspector Lyons was there

most of the time and he was the one that was doing all of the questioning of Elmore.

**Q. I see. And, of course, you say you were in and out so you don't know what happened at the intervals while you were out, do you? A. Well, the only time I left was to answer a telephone or call up in answer to some questions.**

Q. Was any representative of the District Attorney's Office there at that time? A. Yes, there was, early that evening.

Q. Who was that? A. Mr. Innes and Mr. McKinney came in.

Q. And did they take part in the questioning? A. Mr. Innes, no, he sat there and listened.

Q. But, he took no part in the questioning at all? A. No, no active part.

Q. Did he at any time or any representative of the District Attorney's office say to Elmore that anything he might say might be held against him? A. They did, yes.

Q. When was that? A. Mr. McKinney, that evening.

Q. That evening, what time? A. About seven or seven-thirty P.M.

Q. On Friday night? A. On Friday the 13th.

**Q. Friday, the 13th. And what time did--what time of the day did they wake him up again for further questioning? A. He woke himself, nobody woke him up.**

**Q. What time was that? A. I wasn't there then.**

Q. You were away so you didn't know the time he got up. A. I don't know what time. I know he was up early.

Q. And what time did you get back to the station house on Saturday? A. Saturday.

Q. What is that? A. I never left there.

Q. Did you sleep in the station house yourself? **A. I dozed off in a chair for about an hour.**

Q. And you don't know what time Elmore got up that day? A. He was up early because we sent out for his breakfast.

Q. I see. What time was that? A. About seven or half-past seven.

Q. And had he been questioned before that? A. Before what?

Q. Before he had his breakfast? A. No.

Q. Sent for his breakfast first, then did the questioning start immediately after that? A. A while later on that morning, they started talking to him again, they told him about his story.

Q. Now, you said something, as I understand it, about some woman being brought in, a Mrs. Budd. What time was she brought in? A. She was brought in around three, half-past three, four o'clock in the morning.

Q. In the morning? A. That is right.

Q. Friday morning? A. The morning of the 14th, that would be early Saturday morning.

Q. Saturday morning? A. Yes.

Q. And on Saturday morning, rather, that would be Saturday, you mean Saturday morning or Sunday morning? A. I mean Saturday morning.

Q. Saturday morning, that is-- A. The morning of the 14th.

Q. Well, then, I thought you said he had gone to bed before two o'clock on that morning? A. He was lying on the couch the day before too.

Q. And he was awakened for this Mrs. Budd? A. That was after four, I imagine that he lay down.

Q. Now, and was there anyone else brought in there to him at that time, at three o'clock in the morning? A. No.

Q. Now, on Saturday, who took part in the questioning? A. Inspector Lyons returned again, Inspector McGrath.

Q. How long did the questioning continue at that time? A. Most of the afternoon we spoke to him.

Q. All morning and all afternoon?

Mr. Innes : No, just let the officer answer.

By Mr. Casey:

Q. Excuse me. All morning? A. No, I said

Inspector Lyons, Inspector McGrath, about from noon on.

Q. From noon on? A. From noon on.

Q. What was Elmore doing from seven o'clock in the morning until about noon? A. Sitting in the office in a chair there, he would get up and walk around.

Q. And nobody questioned him at that time? A. Nobody, **no continuous questioning, no.**

Q. Now, you say you were in and out and there were officers in and out. At any time, did they tell him that they had investigated his story, and that the story was not true? A. They might have, yes.

Q. They continuously did that didn't they? A. **No, they didn't continuously do that at all.**

Q. Didn't they continuously tell him that he was lying? **A. They told him that he was lying, yes.**

Q. **Who did that? A. Well, I think Inspector Lyons did, I told him.**

Q. Yes, and did you tell him that you had investigated the people that he had referred you to, and that they had denied that they had seen him on that day? A. No, I didn't.

Q. Did you investigate the people that he had told you to see? A. He didn't tell me to see anybody.

Q. I see. And now when Mrs. Budd was brought in the station house, there was nobody there except you officers and the defendant wasn't there? A. That is all, Mrs. Budd.

Q. Yes. Now, isn't it customary, officer, in the police department in an important case to have what is known as a line-up for the purpose of identification, for fairness?

Mr. Innes : Oh, I object to that, fairness.

The Court : Objection sustained.

Q. Is it customary to have a line-up of other persons with the supposed defendant? A. Well, if we can get anybody in the line-up, that will--

Q. Well, now, at any time, at any time there were witnesses there, other persons, persons who came in for the purpose of viewing Elmore. Was he ever put in a line of people? A. No.

Q. Now, by line-up, in police circles, is usually meant to line up half a dozen people with the defendants somewhere in it, and then ask the person to pick them out, isn't that correct? A. That is right.

Q. And at no time was that done with Elmore, was it? A. No.

Q. And what time did you say the driver, bus driver, was brought in? A. About a quarter to five. [Ed. Note: This would be later on Sat. the evening of the 14th.]

Q. Quarter to five? A. Four-thirty, quarter to five.

Q. Up to this time had Elmore been arrested? A. No.

Q. You know what the law requires, don't you? A. About what?

Q. Of a police officer on the circumstances of taking a man into custody.

Mr. Innes: I object to that, if the Court pleases.

The Court : With reference to what, Mr. Casey?

Mr. Casey : What?

The Court : In reference to what?

Mr. Casey : In reference to arraigning him before a court.

The Court : He hadn't been arrested up to that time.

Mr. Casey : Well, he was held in custody.

**The Court : He wasn't held in custody, he was there for questioning.**

By Mr. Casey:

Q. Did any of your officers tell Elmore that he was free to leave at any time? A. No.

Q. He wouldn't have been allowed to leave the station house, would he?

Mr. Innes : Oh, I object to that as calling for a conclusion.

The Court : Objection sustained.

Mr. Casey : Exception, your Honor.

Q. And now, when Flick got there, there was no

line-up, was there? A. No.

Q. And that was later in the afternoon? A. Yes.

Q. And it would have been possible to get people in there to form a line-up?

Mr. Innes : I object to that as calling for a pure conclusion.

The Court : Objection sustained.

Mr. Casey : Exception, your Honor.

By Mr. Casey:

Q. Now, this--officer, do you know whether or not the defendant Elmore was taken to the morgue on Friday night or Saturday morning? A. I know now.

**Q. Yes. Who took him there? A. Assistant Chief Lyons, Inspector McGrath.**

Q. But, you were not there when, you didn't go with them did you? A. No, I didn't.

Q. And that was before that alleged statement was signed, was it? A. It was, that was 24 hours or more.

Q. Wait now, what time of the day or night was that? A. What was what?

Q. That he was taken to the morgue? A. It was the night of the 13th, I believe.

Q. And he signed the statement when, according to you? A. He signed the statement on the night of the 14th.

Q. The night of the 14th? A. Well, early in the evening, about a quarter of six.

Q. I see. And what time of the night of the 13th was he taken to the morgue.

Q. Well, I can't say, I am only judging about ten o'clock, maybe before that.

Q. Could it have been later? A. I don't think so.

Q. Well, wasn't it immediately after he was taken to the morgue, that he came back and was allowed to go to bed? A. Not immediately afterwards, no, this is hours later on.

Q. And he was under questioning? A. He laid on the couch, you know, there was a couch in the office and he just set over there.

Q. **Well, he was allowed, he was taken to the morgue and then he was questioned from then until two o'clock in the morning? A. Later than that.**

Q. Three o'clock in the morning? A. Yes.

Q. And then he was allowed to lie down? A. Yes he could lay down any time he felt like it.

Q. **Nobody aroused him. He lay down before Mrs. Budd came in? A. No. He was sitting in a chair smoking cigarettes and drinking coffee.**

Q. I see. Now, to go back to the first day, I understood you to say on your direct examination that Elmore was waiting on the other side of the creek? A. Yes.

Q. And there was no one with him at that time? A. No, no.

Q. He, when you came along, you told him you were a police officer? A. No, I didn't--I did, yes.

Q. Yes. And he accompanied you to that bungalow? A. He walked ahead with Mr. Haff and we followed. They knew the route.

Q. And he stayed at this bungalow all the time that you were there? A. He was told to stay there, and while--

Q. By whom? A. While I made the 'phone call, I called Jack McCrave and his brother to **not let him leave there until I returned from the 'phone call.**

Q. But, you were the only police officer on the job, weren't you? A. I was.

Q. And he pointed out to you the bungalow? A. He came right to the bungalow with us.

Q. Yes, and he stayed there with you all the time, didn't he? A. He did, yes.

Q. Even when you came back from it, from making the telephone call? A. Yes, he was still there.

Q. And when Inspector Lyons and the other officers came there he was still at the bungalow, isn't that correct? A. He was seated in a department car with Detective Murphy and Brennen had him in the car there.

Q. Who was in that car? A. They had him seated in the car.

Q. And who was with them, any one? A. No, they were standing around the car, while he was sitting there.

Q. How long was it that he was there altogether? A. He may have been **there about two hours, a little more than two hours.**

Q. Two hours. And then did he leave for the station house before you did, or not, or who left first? A. I left before he did.

Q. You left before he did? A. I went to the beach.

Q. But, when you got to the station house he was there? A. When I returned he was there.

**Q. All right, now, when was it, officer, that this defendant was finally placed under arrest? A. Sunday, the 15th, about half past twelve.**

**Q. And what time on Sunday? A. About 12:30.**

Q. At noontime? A. Shortly after noon.

Q. And was he taken to Court that day? A. He was not.

Q. There was court in session that day, wasn't there? A. Not in the afternoon, no.

Q. There was a Magistrate's Court open on Sunday, isn't there? A. Not in the afternoon, no.

Q. Well, the Magistrate's Court is open until one o'clock on Sunday, isn't it? A. No, the Magistrate's Court-- when the Magistrate in court finishes his cases he adjourns.

Q. Were you the arresting officer? A. I am.

Q. Did you communicate with the Magistrate's Court?

Mr. Innes : May it please the Court this is possibly cross-examination now, in chief, and it seems is wandering far afield from the question.

**The Court : I will permit it on the question of whether there was duress or not.**

Mr. Innes : All right.

By Mr. Casey:

Q. Did you communicate with the Magistrate's Court? A. I didn't.

Q. So you don't know whether the court was still open or not? A. It wasn't open in the afternoon on

45

Sunday, no.

Q. Did you communicate with the Magistrate? A. I didn't, no.

Q. So you didn't know whether it was open or not, did you? A. I know as a general rule it is not.

Q. Well, you don't know about this particular day of the 13th at all then, what I am getting at. You didn't communicate on the 14th with the Magistrate's Court? A. No, I didn't.

The Court : The 15th.

By Mr. Casey:

Q. Now, you don't know whether it was open or not? A. No.

Mr. Casey : The 15th, excuse me, your Honor, the 15th.

By Mr. Casey:

Q. Now, the court was opened on the morning of the 16th, wasn't it, Monday morning? A. It was.

Q. Yes, and did you take Elmore up to the court on the 16th, to the Magistrate's Court? A. I took him to the County Court.

Q. Don't you know, Officer, that it was your duty to arraign the defendant before the nearest Magistrate on the first opportunity after placing him under arrest?

Mr. Innes : I object to that as incompetent and immaterial.

The Court : Objection sustained, the District Attorney was notified and he turned him over to the District Attorney, it was the District Attorney's duty to--

**Mr. Casey : I beg to inform your Honor the ruling of law is, it is the Officer's duty to take him to the nearest magistrate.**

**The Court : Objection overruled.**

Mr. Casey : Exception, your Honor.

The Court : He said he was arraigned on the 16th, he brought him into the County Court on the 16th.

By the Court:

Q. Did the defendant ask you to have him taken before a Magistrate? A. He didn't.

Mr. Casey : I object to your Honor's questioning.

The Court : At any time did you tell him whether or not there was a telephone available to him?

The Witness : He knew he could use the telephone.

Mr. Casey : I object to that and move to strike it out.

The Court : All right.

By Mr. Casey:

Q. But, you didn't take him to the Magistrate's Court? A. I took him to the County Court.

Q. At what time was that? A. That was after I returned from the Police line-up, having him photographed, probably about eleven o'clock, eleven-thirty, on the morning of the 16th.

By Mr. Casey:

Q. And previous to that you had had him up to the line-up, hadn't you, in Manhattan? A. I did.

Q. So that from the--about four o'clock on the 13th, until about noon on the 16th, he hadn't been near a court, isn't that correct? A. Well, he wasn't placed under arrest until the 15th.

Q. But, he was in custody all during this time? A. He **was not in custody, no.** [Ed: In the Court's charge below, the Judge states he was in custody.]

Q. He was held at the station house? A. He was there for investigation until he was arrested.

Q. Well, now, officer, you just said a little while ago that you told the--some brothers, while you went to telephone, to hold the defendant there? A. Yes.

Q. At the scene of the crime? A. Yes, to keep him there until I returned.

Q. Yes, and you delegated them to take your place in holding the defendant there? A. They didn't hold him there, they just stayed there with him until I returned. He was under no restraint whatsoever.

Q. All right. A. He was walking around.

Q. Then when the other officers came there, he was put in a car, wasn't he, with the other officers? A. No, not with other officers, he was placed in a department car while we were--

Q. And told to stay there. A. We investigated this crime.

Q. And told him to stay there, isn't that a fact? A. Well, there was such a crowd around the place we had to put him some place so we put him in an automobile.

Q. Well, you didn't take Mr. Haff and put him in a car, did you?

Mr. Innes : I object to this.

The Court : Objection sustained.

Mr. Casey : Exception, your Honor.

By Mr. Casey:

Q. Did you put anybody else except Elmore in a car? A. Later on that day, yes.

Q. Yes. A. A man by the name of Terrinova.

Q. Where was he put in custody? In a car? A. On Seaside Boulevard.

Q. At the scene of this crime? A. No, sir.

Q. In connection with this case? A. We picked him up for investigation.

Q. I see. And how long was he held? A. About an hour and a half, two hours.

Q. And then he was released? A. He was.

Q. Now, Officer, when you got to the station house, did somebody lead Elmore in the station house? A. I wasn't there when he was brought in.

Q. Oh, I see, you don't know that. A. I don't know it.

Q. But, when you got to the station house he was already under questioning? A. Yes. Inspector Lyons was talking to him.

Q. And all the time that you say he slept, was there a police officer guarding him? A. One of the detectives, two of the detectives were in the room, the same room where he was lying on a couch.

Q. I see. Now, at any time was he taken in another room for to sleep? That night or the following night? A.

Why, generally upstairs in the front office there is a couch there. The next day we were in the rear, because we were in an office that had to be used, and we moved to the matron's room that was unoccupied.

Q. I see. And did an officer sleep in the bed with him? A. It is just a plain leather couch, roomy enough for one to lay down on. It is not a bed, it is just a leather couch.

Q. And at no time was he placed in a bed with police officers sleeping in the same bed with him? A. No.

Q. Not that you know of? A. I know he wasn't.

Q. Or in a cot next to them? A. No, nobody, he was sitting in a chair.

Q. He was just there alone? A. No, he was there with two or three detectives while they were sitting in chairs, walking around.

Q. And watching him all the time? A. Yes, they were watching him.

Q. Well, now, officer, if this man had attempted to leave the station house, would you have stopped him?

Mr. Innes : I object to that as immaterial.

The Court : Objection sustained.

Mr. Casey : Exception, your Honor. That is all, your Honor.

Mr. Gulotta : May it please the Court at this time the defendant objects to the admission in evidence of this confession on the ground--

The Court : The District Attorney had it--

Mr. Gulotta : I understand he said, "I offered so and so in evidence. "

The Court : But, the District Attorney has the right to reexamine him if he wishes.

Mr. Gulotta : Very well.

Mr. Innes : Very well, I just want to ask one question.

Redirect examination by Mr. Innes :

Q. At any time in your presence while Elmore was

in the station house and before this paper was signed, was there any violence upon him--inflicted upon him, or any threats made to him? A. None whatsoever.

Mr. Innes : That is all. I now offer the papers in evidence.

Mr. Gulotta : Now, if your Honor pleases, the objection is made on the ground that it appears from cross-examination of this witness that the alleged confession or writing was obtained under duress, and that it clearly shows that it is not the voluntary act of this defendant.

The Court : You say you placed the defendant under arrest on the 15th day of August, that was a Sunday, at 12:30.

The Witness : He was booked at the desk.

Examination by the Court:

Q. And at that time the Magistrate's Court was closed? A. It was.

Q. On the next day, which was Monday, the 16th, the defendant was taken down into this building? A. He was, he was first taken to the District Attorney's office.

Q. To the District Attorney's Office? A. Then he was arraigned before your Honor.

Q. Now, at the District Attorney's Office, was that in the morning or afternoon? A. That was in the morning.

Q. What time? A. We returned from the police headquarters shortly before eleven o'clock.

Q. And the Magistrate's Court was in session that day, that Monday? A. It was.

Q. And the County Court was in session that day, that Monday? A. It was.

Q. The defendant was then taken to the District Attorney's Office? A. He was.

Q. At that time did the defendant ask you to be arraigned before the County Court or before the Magistrate's Court?

Mr. Gulotta : I object to that, if your Honor pleases, on the ground that there appears to be under the law, no obligation on the part of the defendant to request that.

The Court : Objection overruled.

Mr. Gulotta: I respectfully except.

A. He didn't.

The Court : All right.

Redirect examination By Mr. Innes :

Q. Now, Officer, at the time when the defendant was arraigned before his Honor, there was an indictment, was there not, against him? A. I was informed when I returned from Manhattan that the Grand Jury had indicted Samuel Elmore for murder in the first degree.

The Court : That is on the 16th, the Monday following the Sunday, the 15th?

A. That is right.

Mr. Innes : Correct.

The Court : Have you finished with this witness?

Mr. Gulotta: Will you note our exception?

The Court : Exception granted. Have you finished with this witness?

Examination by the Court :

Q. Officer, you testified, in answer to Mr. Innes' question that you found the bathing suit around the neck of the girl and that part of it was tied to the door? A. Part of it, one end of the string was tied to the door edge, through where the boards come up, about two or three feet high, the bathing suit was in the middle, and the rest of the cord was around--

Q. What did you mean by the bathing suit was in the middle, was there anything over her body? A. No clothing on the body. [Ed. Note: This is confusing because the doctor previously testified the bathing suit was in a corner of the cellar.]

Q. There was no clothing? A. The child was nude.

Q. The whole bathing suit, or part of the bathing suit was wrapped around which part of the body? A. If you let me have it, I will show you.

Mr. Innes : I offer the statement in evidence now.

The Court : All right, mark it in evidence.

Mr. Gulotta : May we have our exception noted?

(Whereupon the statement referred to was received in evidence and marked People's Exhibit No. 3 in Evidence. )

People's Exhibit No. 3 [The first confession] Read Into Evidence

Mr. Innes : Now, with the permission of the Court, I will read it :

"State of New York, City of New York, County of Richmond. Sworn Statement. 5:45 P. M. August 14th, 1937. Samuel Elmore, being duly sworn, deposes and says : I met the girl down at the foot of the beach, near Crane's, Thursday, August 12th, 1937, about **2 o'clock P. M.** , and took the little girl along for a walk along Old Town Road, just where the bus driver says and fetched the child over to the old shack. I molested her. I put the cord around her neck before I molested her and I had intercourse with her in the vagina and the rectum. **I put the bricks on her back**. I was on the beach Wednesday and the woman that identified me told the truth. I strangled the child about from two to three o'clock. I enticed the child by having a bottle with a grasshopper in it. That is the bottle that you have here. I took the girl from the beach around Sand Lane. I said, 'Come on, you and I take a walk.' I picked up the bottle at Scott's Studio. After I left the shack I came over through the meadows, I went up through Old Town Road, up back of St. Mary's Cemetery to Clove Road and over to my house. I got home around four o'clock. The blood on my shorts was from her and I chucked them in the tub. I stayed home all that night and came back Friday morning to the shack and found the body and notified some people nearby to call the police.

All previous statements made by me have been lies and this statement is the truth. I am making this statement of my own free will and have not been promised any immunity for making this statement. ( Signed) Samuel Elmore. Witnessed by : Det. Thomas S. Cosgrove No. 538,

Lt. Howard W. Gifford, Det. William A. Hagarty No. 665, Det. John F. Marrinan, No. 418. "(Whereupon the stenographer repeated the last question for the Court, as follows : "Q. The whole bathing suit, or part of the bathing suit was wrapped around which part of the body? A. If you let me have it, I will show you. ")

**Mr. Innes : There is another cord which is not evidence at the present time, but I have evidence here to--**

**The Court : Wait.**

**Mr. Innes : Oh, I beg your pardon, I have no right to say that.**

Examination by the Court:

Q. Officer, when you tell us when you first entered the basement, you got there before the Medical Examiner got there? A. I did.

Q. How long before the Medical Examiner got there? A. About an hour and a half.

Q. And you were the first one that entered the cellar? A. I was.

Q. Tell us what condition you found the body at that time in, and the bathing suit? A. The body was laying prone on the stomach, stretched out, the head about the width of your small finger from the floor, the tip, there were some bricks cemented together laying in the middle of the back. The cord, the bathing suit cord, was through the broken panel of the door, around the panel where the door was broken. This was in the middle, and this here part led to the child's neck where this small piece was around her neck, tied around her neck like that. This led to the bathing suit, the bathing suit was rolled up something like this, first, in the middle, and this led to the door. The other end of the string led to the child's neck.

Q. So that her body was bare? A. Yes, with the exception of the bricks on her back, but no clothing.

Q. And the bathing suit was wrapped around with the cord? A. In this position, that end was at the door, this piece led to the child's neck.

Q. And when you got there, you were there when

the Medical Examiner came? A. I was.

Q. Had anything been touched at that time? A. Nobody touched that body but the Medical Examiner.

The Court : All right.

By Mr. Innes :

Q. Officer, I show you a picture and ask you if you recognize that? A. I do.

Q. And what is that? A. That is the bungalow where the child was found murdered in the cellar.

Q. And does it show the window in the side of the bungalow? A. It does.

Q. Towards the front? A. . It does.

Q. Through which Elmore said he looked and saw the body first? A. Yes, that is right.

**Q. And that is the window that he pointed to you and said, "There she is"? A. "There she is. "**

Q. I see. All right.

Mr. Innes: I ask that be marked for identification now at this time, if the Court please.

(Whereupon photograph referred to was marked People's Exhibit No. 4 for identification. )

By Mr. Innes:

Q. Now, officer, after you brought the defendant back from the line-up, you say you took him to the District Attorney's Office? A. I did.

Q. And who did you see there? A. I seen you and Mr. McKinney, Detective Marrinan, Sheriff Dempsey came along later on, and Sheriff Trivisone, and there was another sheriff, I can't recall his name.

Q. And you entered some room there? A. We did.

Q. So far as you know, did you learn that I was before the Grand Jury that morning? A. I did.

Q. Presenting this particular case? A. When I returned, yes.

Q. And the indictment was voted and the jury reported down here about eleven o'clock? A. About that, yes.

Q. Now then, did you see Mr. McKinney in the

District Attorney's office? A. I was directed to Mr. McKinney's office.

Q. Yes. And, did you go there with the defendant? A. I did.

Q. And, did Mr. McKinney ask him some questions there at the time? A. He did.

Q. And, did Elmore answer them? A. **He told Mr. McKinney he was ready to tell him anything he asked him.**

Q. And, so far as you knew, was Elmore under any restraint or anything of the kind? A. He was not.

Q. Were there any threats made? A. No, sir.

Q. Or any promises made? A. No promises.

Q. Now then, while he was there, did Officer Marrinan take down a statement? A. He did, and Mr. McKinney--

Q. Dictated? A. **Asked him the questions and Marrinan took them down, when Elmore answered them.**

Q. Then, afterwards, did Mr. McKinney dictate a paper at that time? A. He did.

**Q. Was it written out by Officer Marrinan? A. He typed it out.**

Q. And, after it was typed, was it brought back into Mr. McKinney's office? A. It was.

Q. Was the defendant there at the time? A. He was.

Q. Was the paper read to him? A. It was.

Q. And what did he say with respect to the truth of the statement? A. He was told that if there was anything that wasn't correct in that statement, to let Mr. McKinney know about it.

Q. Yes. A. It was read to him and we borrowed Sheriff Dempsey's glasses so Elmore could read the statement, and he read it out loud to us and he said, **"That is the truth, and I am glad to get it off my chest."**

Q. Did he, did the defendant sign that paper? A. He did.

Q. And did he sign each page of the paper? A.

Every page.

Q. I show you this paper and ask you if you will be good enough to look at it and tell me if that is the paper that Elmore signed in the District Attorney's office on the morning of, on Monday? A. That is the paper that he dictated in your office.

Q. And was it all prepared prior to the time that he came down to Court and pled before his Honor? A. It was, yes.

Q. And it was afterwards signed by him, I mean after it was read over he signed it? A. Yes, it was read aloud to him and then he was told to read it aloud, he borrowed Sheriff Dempsey's glasses to read it.

Q. I see. And, that is the paper he signed? A. That is the paper.

Q. You recognize it? A. I recognize it, that is my signature.

Q. And, you witnessed it, did you not? A. I did.

Mr. Innes : I offer that in evidence.

Mr. Gulotta : May we examine it, if your Honor please?

The Court : You may.

Mr. Innes : May I be excused for just a moment, if the Court please?

The Court : Do you want a recess?

Mr. Innes : No, you can go right ahead.

Cross-examination by Mr. Gulotta on the Statement:

Q. What time, officer, was it that People's Exhibit No. 3 was signed? A. Which one is three?

Q. That is this statement here? A. Oh, that, just about the time it states there, 5:45.

Q. At what time? A. At about 5:45 P. M.

Q. And, that is on the day of August, 14th, 1937, is it not? A. Right.

Q. Elmore had been taken into custody, some time on the 13th day of August, 1937, had he not? A. He was not taken into custody.

Q. What time did you get down to the scene on August 13th?

Mr. McKinney : If your Honor pleases, at this time I must object to this cross-examination because the purpose of it is only as to this statement.

The Court : Yes.

Mr. Gulotta : Very well, I was going to save my main cross-examination for that.

By Mr. Gulotta :

Q. Now, after that statement was signed on August 14th, how long after this statement was the statement that you now have in your hand signed? A. Well, that was taken on the morning of the 16th.

Q. The 16th? That was two days after this statement was signed, is that right? A. That was after Sunday, and then, when he returned from police headquarters in the line up Monday morning.

Q. And had he been arraigned before that statement was signed? A. He was arraigned after the statement was signed.

Q. After the statement was signed? And, how long a time now expired between the time that he signed this statement and that, in the matter of hours or days? A. Well, about a day and a half.

Q. A day and a half? After he had signed that statement, that is the statement marked People's Exhibit No. 3, he was not arraigned until he had signed that statement, was he? A. He was, he signed this and he was later arraigned.

Q. Yes, but he was not arraigned until he signed the paper that you now hold in your hand, was he? A. That is right.

Q. That is right? And almost two days expired between the time that this was signed and that one that you hold in your hand, is that correct? A. About a day and a half.

Q. Where was he kept during this day and a half? A. He was in the station house and about one o'clock on

Sunday he was booked at the desk and placed in a cell.

Q. Placed in a cell, was he? A. That is right.

Q. And how long did he stay in the cell? A. He stayed in the cell from about one o'clock Sunday until we made the 8 o'clock boat Monday morning for Manhattan, police headquarters.

Q. And was he questioned further before you obtained his signature on that statement, was he questioned further? A. He was not questioned from the time he was booked until he was returned to this office upstairs.

Q. Now, you notice, do you not, that this statement marked People's Exhibit No. 3 is a one-page affair, do you not, officer? A. I do.

Q. And the one you hold in your hand, how many pages is that? A. That is in detail, this one, five.

Q. Why did you wait, if you know, almost two days before you obtained that statement that you have in your hand? **A. I was instructed to do it.**

Q. By whom were you instructed to wait? A. Why, we got that statement and then when we returned here, we got a statement here in the District Attorney's office for the District Attorney.

Q. You stated before, did you not, that he signed this statement, voluntarily, is that right? A. That is right.

Q. Without any duress of any kind, is that right? A. Absolutely.

Q. Without any promise made by the District Attorney or any police officer? Is that right? A. He got no promises.

Q. Right. Did you ask him to sign a lengthy statement at the time he signed this? A. I don't get what you mean.

Q. Did you ask him to sign a statement as lengthy as the one you now hold in your hand in addition to this paper? A. He didn't go any further than that statement and all he spoke of was put on that paper at the time.

Q. At the time he signed this paper, the stenographer took it down, didn't he? A. That is right.

Q. And, that stenographer took it down in short hand, didn't he? A. That stenographer took it just as Elmore said it.

Q. My question is, officer, did he take it down in shorthand? A. I am saying he did.

Q. Yes. And then it was transcribed into a one-paper document. Is that right? A. Just what he said, it just made a page.

Q. All right, now you hadn't asked him to make any additional statement at the time, had you? A. No.

Q. You were content that he had said as much as he said in this paper, is that right? A. After he had told his story to the District Attorney and Inspector Lyons and myself and Marrinan, that is what it amounted to.

Q. You had no idea of obtaining a larger statement, had you, officer? A. Not at that time.

Q. Well, didn't you tell us that you were told particularly not to ask the defendant to sign? A. No.

Q. That statement? A. I did not testify to such at all.

**Q. Well, you didn't? Didn't you say to me before, a few minutes ago, as to why you didn't get that long statement, you said I was asked not to get it? A. No, I didn't testify to that at all.**

Q. When were you asked to get this statement? A. I was never asked to get this statement.

Q. Were you there when it was taken? A. I was.

Q. And who else was there? A. Mr. McKinney, Detective Hagarty, Detective Marrinan, Detective --Mr. Dempsey, Mr. Trivisone--did I say Detective Hagarty? And Joe McKinney, and Marrinan.

Q. And during all that time, that consumed almost two days, he was in a cell continuously, was be not? A. He was in a cell from Sunday, the 15th, about one o'clock until Monday morning when we went to New York.

Q. And he slept in a cell? A. I don't know whether he slept or not.

Q. Was he fed in the cell? A. He got his meals.

Q. And his meals were brought to him down

there? A. They were brought in to him.

Q. And then after all that, came this statement, is that right? A. When we returned to the District Attorney's office, this statement he made in the office.

Q. And at the time that he signed that statement, which is about to be offered in evidence, he wasn't told that it would go easy with him if he would sign a longer statement, was he? A. Why, no, he was warned, he was told of his constitutional rights.

Q. And, what were those, officer? A. He was told that any statement he would make would be used against him, he was promised--they made no promise to him, promised him no immunity.

Q. Did he say to you anything about the fact that he had already signed a statement, so what is the necessity of signing another one? A. No, he was very anxious to tell his story in this one too.

Q. And, when you say that he was anxious to tell you a story, when, for the first time, did he become anxious? A. Why, after he told that first story, and when he came into the District Attorney's office, he was very talkative in this one.

Q. I see. And everything he said was jotted down by the stenographer. Right? A. As he went along and told the story, it was taken down in shorthand.

Q. Was he anxious before the 14th day of August, 1937, when you first saw him to talk? A. He was talkative, yes.

Q. Yes. And he was talkative concerning what his wife told him to do on that day, such as, going crabbing, isn't that right? A. Yes, he spoke of that.

Q. And he was talkative about the fact that he had been working the day before, wasn't he? A. He said that.

Q. And, he was talkative about the fact that he had been at Seaview Hospital the day before, isn't that right? A. That is right.

Q. And, did he tell you that on August 12th, before he signed this statement, that he had seen various people in Staten Island that day? A. Before August 12th?

Q. Yes. Before August 14th, did he tell you on the 13th, when you first saw him that on the 12th day of August, after having told you that his wife had told him to go crabbing, after having told you that he was at Seaview Hospital, did he tell you that he met many friends that he knew about Staten Island? A. He said he met nobody that he knew only when he went shopping.

Q. Nobody? And did he tell you when he went shopping? A. He did tell me, yes.

Q. Did he tell you the time when he went shopping? A. He told us various times, yes.

Q. Well, what times, for instance, did he tell you that he went shopping? A. Well, ten o'clock in the morning.

Q. Yes. Did he tell you how long that took him? A. Just entered the store and placed his order and left.

Q. He didn't take anything out of the store with him, did he? A. Not,-- I don't know what store you are speaking of.

Q. What store are you speaking of? A. Which one are you asking about?

Q. The A and P store? A. Yes.

Q. He did say A and P store? A. He did, yes.

Q. Did he tell you where he went after that? A. He did.

Q. Yes, where did he tell you he went after that? A. He went on a bus.

Q. On a bus, and did he tell you where he went on the bus, too? A. He did.

Q. To what place? A. He did.

Q. To what place did he tell you? A. He went to Tipperary Corners.

Q. And did you know where Tipperary Corners is? A. I think so.

Q. Where is it? A. At the junction of Richmond Road and--

Q. Rockland Avenue? A. Rockland Avenue.

Q. Yes. He didn't tell you he went to South Beach, did he? A. Not at that time, no.

Q. No? It was after he had been in the station for a period of time that he then became talkative about his confession, but he was talkative before that only as to, as regarding his whereabouts on that day, is that right officer? A. That is all he said, he went shopping.

Q. Yes. A. And, returned from getting his pay?

Q. And, after having obtained this statement, he signed that one and you were present when he signed it, is that right? A. On Monday, he gave the statement.

Q. And I understand you to say before his arraignment or arrest, he had been in a cell prior to signing that, is that correct? A. After he was booked at the precinct he was placed in a cell as the rules call, and kept there until Monday morning.

Mr. Gulotta: That concludes my preliminary examination, if your Honor please.

The Court: Is that all?

Mr. Innes: I offer this statement in evidence, if the Court please.

The Court: All right.

Mr. Gulotta: The defendant respectfully objects upon the ground that it appears from the examination of the witness, that the statement offered in evidence was obtained under duress, and that it does not represent the voluntary act of this defendant.

The Court: Overruled.

Mr. Gulotta: I respectfully except.

( Statement referred to was received in evidence and marked People's Exhibit No. 5 in evidence. )

Mr. Innes: Now, I am going to ask Mr. McKinney to read this. He prepared it.

Mr. McKinney: "County Court, Richmond County, People of the State of New York against Simon Elmore also known as Samuel Elmore, Defendant, State of New York, City of New York, County of Richmond, ss. Samuel Elmore, being duly sworn, deposes and says: I, reside at No. 37 Metcalfe Street, Stapleton, Richmond County. That on Thursday, August 12th, 1937, I left my house at about ten o'clock in the morning. I went up Metcalfe Street, to Targee Street, walked along Vanderbilt Avenue to Richmond Road. I stopped in the A and P at the corner of Mary Street and Richmond Road and left an order. I walked along Richmond Road to the bus terminal at the corner of Clove Road and Richmond Road. I there boarded a bus and got off at Tipperary Corners. I waited for a shuttle bus, got on that and went to Sea View Hospital. I got off at the circle and walked to the field house where the pay-master pays off. I don't know the name of the pay-master but he was a stout fellow. At that time it was about eleven A. M. I waited in line for about five or ten minutes and I was paid off at the tool shed and received a check for $31.70 for three days pay. While I was waiting in the line, one Barney Sieger of Great Kills was there. He got his check before me and said he would take me in his car back to Tipperary Corners and Richmond Road at Rockland Avenue. There I got on a bus that brought me to Concord where I got off. When I got off the bus I walked to the A & P store on Mary Street and Richmond Road. I picked up my order at the A & P which consisted of one dozen clams, carrots and peas and soup greens for chowder and other groceries. The bill came to $1.41. The clams were nineteen cents extra, making a total of $1. 60. I left the A & P store with my bundles, went down Richmond Road, along Vanderbilt Avenue to my home. I put the groceries on the wash tub and unpacked them. I then put the groceries in the closet where they belong and put the clams and the greens on the tub. By that time, my wife had dinner ready and I had dinner with my wife and daughter Sybil. After dinner I got out a pan, washed the greens and cut them up. There was parsley, celery, onions and carrots and peas. After they were washed I put them in a pot and left the pot on the tubs. I then opened up the clams, there were thirteen in all. I then put them in a glass bowl and put them in the ice-box. At that time, my wife said to me, "Are you going crabbing. "

And I said, "Tomorrow. " She also asked me if I was going to Stapleton and I asked if there was anything that she wanted. She said, "Yes", and wrote on a piece of paper, one tube of Ben-Gay; Oysterettes, Catsup and three cakes of Camay Toilet Soap and she also told me to get my pants while I was there. She also ordered a loaf of Vienna bread and a fifteen cent piece of huckleberry pie. I then left the house and went to the shed in my rear yard. There I got some bags and paper which I had in a bundle and took them along with me. I locked the shed door, walked through the lot to Roff Street, went to Vanderbilt Avenue, walked on the shady side of Vanderbilt Avenue to the white posts of Fox Hills Golf Club. There I took a path which brought me to Tompkins Avenue and came out near Norwood Avenue. From there I walked to Bay Street. I then cut through the B & 0 Yards and on my way there I saw John Carney. I then went to Tony's fishing boat near the bulkhead between Pier 17 and Pier 18. I gave the papers to Tony and asked him for butterfish. That I wanted enough for four pots and he gave me ten butterfish. He wrapped the fish in a newspaper and I then left the boat. I walked along Front Street to Canal Street up Canal Street, cross Bay Street to Stapleton Park, cross Water Street to the Staten Island Savings Bank, where I cashed my check, at a window on the left hand side as you walk in. I then left the bank, went up Water Street to Hardy's drug store and there I bought one tube of Ben-Gay which was $0.59 and one cent tax making a total of $0. 60. From there I went up Canal Street, and crossed over at Joe Kenny's store to Harris' Dry Goods store where I bought a pair of blue trousers which I am now wearing for the sum of $2.70. Young Harris waited on me and he told me he would take off $.25 to pay the tailor to have the pants shortened as I need a leg length of only 29 inches. I then went to the tailor store next to Mackauer's on Broad Street where I had the pants shortened. I waited until the tailor had them finished which took about twenty or twenty-five minutes. Then I went up Broad Street crossed Cedar Street to Phelps Bakery on Broad Street.

There I bought a loaf of Vienna bread and a huckleberry pie for fifteen cents. I went up Broad Street to the A & P. store located opposite General Custer St. and Broad St. There I bought two packages of oysterettes, one bottle of Anna Page Catsup and three cakes of Camay toilet soap. I left there and went down General Custer Street, crossed the lots to Meadow Street and stopped in Alex Aleski's at the corner of Warren Street and Meadow Street and had three beers. I left there and went down Warren Street to Gordon Street and there I saw an Italian who lives on Gordon Street and who was fixing his porch with some two by fours. I stood a minute or two talking to him. I then proceeded along Gordon Street to Osgood Avenue, through a lot to Targee Street, which is in back of the Laundry, up Targee Street, to Roff Street, through another lot to Metcalfe Street and then to my home where I arrived at about **1:30 P. M.**

    I left the groceries on the tubs and came out again and walked up Metcalfe Street, along Targee Street up Vanderbilt Avenue right straight up across Richmond Road, over to Steuben Street to Hanover Avenue and went down Clove Road, after having crossed over the side of the hills at Moselle Avenue, across the boulevard to in back of St. Mary's cemetery and walked down to Old Town Road, across to Olympia Boulevard, went through the meadows to a wagon path and walked that path down and went across the creek out on the beach. On the way down I passed this bungalow. I came out to the beach at Crane's on Seaview Boulevard. I went across out on the beach. I had no crabbing equipment or anything else with me. I stood around for about ten minutes near an old boat. People were in bathing there and some children were digging in the sand, and this little tot was there, near where there were some **flat bottomed boats and a man painting them**. The tot was alone when I first saw her. I kept looking at her for about three minutes. She was taking up the sand in her little hands. She had a red bathing suit and a pair of white shoes on. I was about six feet away from her. She came over towards me and I said, "Hello

Blondie". She said, "Hello". I said, "Do you want to take a walk", and we walked along the beach and came out the path the other side of Seaview Boulevard in back of bungalows near Bessi's. I walked with her up Sand Lane to Old Town Road. I held her little hand while walking to Sand Lane. During the period that we walked through Bessi's to Sand Lane the only conversation I recall was "going to take a walk". We walked up Sand Lane to Old Town Road. **Near the corner of Old Town Road and Sand Lane I went into a candy store and bought her five cents worth of candy. The store was located on Sand Lane. The youngster waited outside while I bought the candy.** She ate the candy on the way then, when **we got to Old Town Road I picked up a milk bottle and caught two big grass-hoppers. She said, "I like those grasshoppers. " I found the milk bottle near a fence. She chased some grasshoppers too but couldn't catch any. This was near Scott's Studio on Old Town Road.** We continued walking and walked along Old Town Road. We continued walking to Olympia Boulevard to the old wagon path. We crossed over to the house, I commenced to put my hands on her back and sides and she accidently hit me in the privates. Then I took her down in the cellar and I commenced to rape her. I took her bathing suit off before I raped her and she hollered. I took out my private and I put it in her front. She started to holler. She hollered, "Oh, Mama. " **I discharged in her**. I held her to me. After I finished with her in the front, I bung-holed her. She was still hollering and groaning. I didn't come in her bung-hole. I took a piece of cord and put it around her little neck. **I had it in my pocket. It was a fish cord.** Her bathing suit was on the knob of the door where I put it. I took the bathing suit off ; **I cut the straps off with a pen-knife I had in my pocket so as to get the bathing suit off her.** After I bung-holed her I laid her down. She went to get up and **I pulled a string out of my pocket and put it around her neck and then I tied it.** I held her down with my right hand while I was getting the string out of my pocket. I put the string around her neck and tied a **black knot and tied the other end of the string to the door knob.** She was still crying and hollering. I then got the brick and put it on her back. She groaned, but stopped crying and choking. It is the sorriest thing I ever did. I just laid the column on her back. I stayed there awhile looking at her but she didn't move, so I walked away. **I took her shoes off right there after I had her tied up.** I took the shoes with me one in **each pants pocket.** I left the bungalow and walked out on the path and came over the bridge, out back of Crane's, and I left the shoes out there on the beach. **There was a lot of people there and I put the shoes in the same place where I picked her up first. I took them out of my pocket and leaned over and stooped down and placed them on the sand facing the water and chucked a little sand with my hand over them. I stayed there about five or ten minutes looking around to see if anyone was looking at me.** When I raped her she bled quite a little and the blood from her got on my trunks. I had my pants open but I didn't take them off. I had my trunks open just enough to get my penis out. The blood from her got on the front of my trunks. **She bled when I bung-holed her but more when I raped her.** I came across the way I left after I put the shoes on the beach, passed the bungalow but didn't look in at her, and up the path to Old Town Road, over Mallory Avenue, back of the cemetery, passed the circle of Hyland Boulevard to Clove Road; to the Railroad crossing at Grassmere. Down Moselle Avenue, across up DeKalb Street; went down past the flagstone house; cut through the lots; came out near Hanover Avenue, crossed Britten Avenue along to Targee Street. Went down Targee Street, all the way to Metcalfe Street and home. **I got home about 3:30 P. M. I didn't see anybody I knew on the way home.** I wore a white shirt with short sleeves, a panama hat, blue socks and white stripes. I didn't get any blood on my pants. **I had on a pair of striped slacks.** I wore blue striped trunks. When I got home, I went to my room and took my slacks off and shorts and chucked the shorts in the tub. My little daughter was home but I didn't speak to her. The tub is in the kitchen near the sink. I hung my pants in the back of the living room door. **The pants and underwear that were exhibited to me in the precinct were the ones that I wore that day.** I changed clothes and then went down and sat on the stoop for about ten or fifteen minutes. I spoke to a Mrs. Smith who lives next door. The paper boy came and I got the Advance. His name is Topsy. He chucked my paper upstairs. I waited until my daughter got finished with the paper before I got up and I read the newspaper for about ten minutes and the wife came in and made supper. She was sleeping in the front room. I was reading the paper on the lounge. I had my supper with the wife and little Sybil. I finished supper about 5:15 P. M. Then I went downstairs and sat in the yard on the beach stool and little Sybil came down and said, "Get some pears and plums", and I shook the tree and gave them to her. Then I remembered that I had to report to Mrs. Wardell, so I got my report book and went to her office. That was about 6 :10 P. M. I reported to her and she said, "You will have to make one more report and that will be the last." I got back to my house about fifteen minutes to seven. I took the report book out and put it in my wife's bedroom. I didn't go out after that. I went to bed around nine o'clock. The next morning I got up about six o'clock and made the coffee and put the dishes on the table and had my breakfast of four slices of bread, two cups of coffee and butter on the bread. I finished about 6:45 A. M. Then I cleaned the bird cage and put fresh gravel in it. Then I fetched him in the front room and hung the cage on the stand. Then I went into the garden and picked some tomatoes. My wife came out and said, "Pop, go and get the News. " I got the News at Index's at the foot of Pleasant Valley Avenue and Van Duser Street. I came home with the News. Then I started to clean the fish and after I got everything ready I started out for South Beach. That was about 10 :15 A. M. I walked along from Metcalfe Street to Targee Street from Targee Street I went up Vanderbilt Avenue to Van Duser Street, across over on the other side, walked up to the A. & P. store at the corner of Mary Street and Richmond Road, went in and bought a package of cigarettes. I had the crab bag and the three pots and the fish in it and was all ready to go crabbing. After leaving the A. & P. I walked up Richmond Road to Steuben Street went down Steuben Street to Britton Avenue out through the lots over Hanover Avenue, out where there is a lot of concrete stones that has been taken out of the road, then I continued over to Moselle Avenue, up Moselle Avenue, to Glove Road, down to the Circle, across Hylan Boulevard down along the road in back of St. Mary's Cemetery, to Old Town Road, kept going down Old Town Road till I hit Olympia Boulevard, crossed over Olympia Boulevard and went down the path leading to the bungalow. I looked in the cellar window on the right hand side as you face the front of the bungalow. There are two windows, the one in the front wasn't boarded up. The one in the rear is boarded up. I looked through the front window. I seen her feet. The little feet were showing. I saw her heels. I walked around the back and looked at her. I didn't go in. As I looked at her I thought I had better report it. I got panicky. I went across the creek where I used to go crabbing. The tide was going out. I saw it was no good for crabbing so I went over to a bungalow up near the creek and had to go up a plank to get out to the street and there were two fellows sitting on the corner on the porch of a bungalow. I said, **"There is a girl up at that bungalow murdered. " Then the lady said, "That is the child who is missing since yesterday morning.** "The two fellows went down and telephoned and came back with Detective Cosgrove. They came back in about five minutes in an automobile with Det. Cosgrove. We waited there and the two men and Det. Cosgrove got out of the car. Det. Cosgrove and three men went to the bungalow with me. The third man was not seen by me before. I later found out his name to be Hann. **He led the way back to the bungalow.** All of us arrived back at the bungalow at about the same time. I pointed out the body to Detective

Cosgrove and Hann took out his watch and said it was 11:15 A. M. I was informed of my constitutional rights before making this statement, and same is made by me voluntarily, without any force, fear or promise on the part of anyone. (Signed) Samuel Elmore Sworn to before me this 16th day of August, 1937, Joseph A. McKinney, Notary Public, Richmond County. Witnessed by Thomas S. Cosgrove, William A. Hagarty, Detective John F. Marrinan, William J. Dempsey, Sheriff of Richmond County."

Examination By Mr. Innes :

Q. Officer, did you at the bungalow see a bottle containing-- A. I did.
Q. --a grasshopper? A. I did.
Q. And was that taken to the station house? A. It was.
Q. And, were the bricks? A. They were.
Q. That were on the body, also taken to the station house? A. They were.
Q. And, have they been in the custody of the Property Clerk ever since? A. They have.
Q. They are produced here today by you? A. They are.
Mr. Innes : All right, I think while we are waiting for that, this may be marked for identification also, this string.

**(Whereupon a piece of cord, referred to, was marked People's Exhibit No. 6 for Identification.)**

The Court : All these exhibits have been marked for identification at this time?
Mr. Innes : Yes, except the statements.
By Mr. Innes :
Q. Is that the milk bottle? A. It is, yes.
Q. And, do you know who brought that to the station house? A. I do.

Q. Who did? A. Patrolman Paolo and Martin of the Technical Research Laboratory of the Police Department.

Q. Now, then, I show you that, do you recognize that, officer? (Referring to the bricks. ) A. I do.

Q. Did you mark it at any time? A. I did.

Q. And are the marks that you made on it still there? A. Yes, they are still there, "T. C. " here and over here.

Q. I see, and was that marked, where was that marked by you? A. Down in the basement of the bungalow in South Beach.

Mr. Innes: I offer that in evidence, if the Court please as evidence.

Mr. Gulotta : That is objected to, if your Honor please, on the ground that there is no, it is incompetent, irrelevant and immaterial, that it appears that it is no part of the original scheme as the testimony shows that the crime was committed by strangulation; on the further ground it is calculated to inflame the minds of the jury.

The Court : I will mark it for identification at this time. There may be some purpose later on, as to whether it is or not--

Mr. Gulotta : The same objection, I think--

Mr. Innes : I do not offer the bottle now because another officer brought that in, and he will be able to testify with respect to that.

The Court : Just repeat the question with reference to that.

(Whereupon the stenographer repeated questions and answers as follows :

"Q. Now, then, I show you that do you recognize that, officer? (Referring to the bricks). A. I do. .

Q. Did you mark it at any time? A. I did.

Q. And are the marks that you made on it still there? A. Yes, they are still there, "T. C. ", here and over here.

Q. I see, and was that marked, where was that marked by you? A. Down in the basement of the bungalow in South Beach. ")

The Court : You merely testified that you showed it to him and that he marked it and it was marked in the bungalow at South Beach, there is nothing to show where it was found.

Mr. Innes : All right, just a question or two more.

By Mr. Innes :

Q. Where was this brick when you first saw it, officer? A. It was lying on the deceased's body, of Joan Kuleba, in the cellar of the bungalow.

Q. And you marked it while it was still on her body, did you? A. I marked it, one side of it there, and I marked it later in the station house.

Q. Do you know by whom it was taken to the station house? A. By patrolman Johnson.

Q. And, it has been in the property clerk's office since? A. Yes.

Q. Produced to you by the Clerk's office today? A. That is right.

Mr. Gulotta : I make my objection that it is not properly connected with the defendant.

The Court : Where did you mark it, where did you put your marks on it?

The Witness : Down in the bungalow that afternoon.

The Court : All right, mark it in evidence.

Mr. Gulotta : I respectfully except, your Honor.

(Whereupon the bricks referred to were received in evidence and marked People's Exhibit No. 7 in evidence.)

By Mr. Innes:

Q. By the way, officer, where did you first see that bottle? A. **That was lying on a shelf in the cellar of the bungalow on the left hand side as you enter the cellar, on a cement shelf.**

Q. I see. And the grasshopper? A. Was in it.

Q. Was in it at the time? A. It was.

72

Mr. Innes : I offer this for identification, if the Court please.

The Court : All right, mark it for identification.

Mr. Innes : I want the other officer to identify it.

The Court : Are you through with this witness?

(Whereupon the bottle referred to was marked People's Exhibit No. 8 for Identification.)

By the Court:

Q. Officer, what did you do with the bathing suit, People's Exhibit 1 for identification, and the cord when you found it? A. What did I do with it?

Q. Yes. A. The bathing suit was not touched or the cord was not touched by anybody until the Medical Examiner, Assistant Chief Lyons, inspected the scene of the crime and it was ordered cut down, by Patrolman Paolo and Martin of the Technical Research Department, Police Department.

Q. You didn't remove it? A. They cut it.

Q. You didn't? A. No, I did not.

The Court : All right.

Mr. Innes : All right, that will be taken care of later.

The Court : All right, we will recess until two o'clock. Are you through with this witness?

Mr. Gulotta : No, we are not through, may we cross-examine at two o'clock?

The Court : Come back at two o'clock. Gentlemen, we will recess until two o'clock. Do not discuss this case, or come to any conclusion in the matter until the case is finally submitted to you and until you retire to your Jury Room.

(Whereupon at 12:58 P. M. , Court recessed until 2:00 P.M. )

Wednesday, November 17, 1937. 2:00 P. M. AFTERNOON SESSION.

Before: HON. THOMAS F. COSGROVE,

County Judge.

APPEARANCES :Same as before. Court Clerk Kosman :

People against Samuel Elmore. (Both sides are ready. )

Motion for Withdrawal of a Juror.

MOTION FOR WITHDRAWAL OF JUROR

(Whereupon the jury was polled and all jurors answered present. )(Detective Thomas F. Cosgrove resumes the witness stand for further questioning. )

Mr. Gulotta: Is Mr. Innes finished with the direct examination?

Mr. Innes : Yes I am.

Mr. Gulotta: Now, may it please the Court, before embarking upon the duty of cross-examination of this witness, I want to address a motion to your Honor. As your Honor knows, after the Grand Jury handed down this indictment, your Honor appointed me and Mr. William Casey as attorneys for the defendant. I think it is common knowledge between yourself and the office of the District Attorney, that we have done everything to speed up this trial and that we want to be fair. In a like manner, we want everything to be fair with us and to be fair to the defendant because he must have a fair trial. It comes to my attention in this afternoon's issue of the Staten Island Advance, the City Edition, in large letters and I now hand it up to your Honor for your consideration, the Head Line which says that Innes rejects a plea. So far as I know, as one of the defense counsel in this case, I know of no such offer ever having been made and because of that report and because this paper is circulating throughout the Island, and perhaps in the hands of the Jurors and other persons, I feel at this time that a motion should be made, and I now address to your Honor a motion to withdraw a juror on the authority of the case of People against Montlase, reported in 184 Appellate Division at page 578.

The Court : Get that case please.

Mr. Gulotta : Where anything occurs during the course of a trial rendering it unfair to the defendant, to continue with the trial before the same jury, the remedy is to move for the withdrawal of a juror. And now, I so move for the withdrawal of a juror on the ground that the circulation of this newspaper is highly prejudicial to this defendant.

The Court : Get me the citation please. ( The Court reads the citation. )

The Court : Gentlemen, I have instructed you during every recess and during and before you were empaneled not to read any newspapers, not to consider any matters in evidence unless the matters were testified to by witnesses before you. My attention has just been called by counsel to the issue of the Advance of today. Needless to say, you are not to take that into consideration in coming to a conclusion. You are to take no newspaper's comment upon the case, in coming to a conclusion in the matter.

As you know, newspapers sometimes not only report matters untrue but they manufacture things which never happen, and unless any matter is submitted to you and in evidence before you, you are to absolutely disregard anything and everything, whether newspaper articles or other wise and come to a conclusion only from the testimony before you. Inasmuch as I have repeatedly warned you of this situation and repeatedly instructed you that you are not to consider matters unless they were before you, I feel that you will obey that instruction. This defendant, the same as the People, is entitled to a fair trial upon the evidence, no outside influences must or should sway you. Your oath requires that you give this defendant a fair trial, based solely upon the testimony. This matter just called to my attention is not only unfair but it is not evidence and no such thing ever took place. I merely point this out as calling your attention to the fact of the danger of being guided by newspaper comments in the case.

Now, if this sort of thing continues to excite and will be published in the future, it will be necessary for me to in every case, at least every capital case, to confine the Jury and to prohibit their reading newspapers. Now, that would be a regrettable course for me to take, because it would mean inconvenience to you, it would mean that you wouldn't be allowed to go home to your families and to take care of such business as you may have during the time you are not actually considering the case. No other course will be open to me or to any other judge, where this course of practice persists, particularly in a county such as this, where the people read the local newspapers. Now, Gentlemen, I am going to ask you individually whether or not you can disregard anything you see in the newspapers and you can be guided solely by the evidence in this case and I want you to tell me whether you honestly can or whether this newspaper article has made any impression upon you. I am going to ask each juror individually to tell me whether or not he can disregard anything he has seen in the newspapers and consider this case upon the testimony alone.

Juror No. 1, how do you answer? A. I will just consider it on the testimony alone.
Juror No. 2? A. Only on testimony I hear in this Court room.
Juror No. 3? A. Same.
Juror No. 4? A. Same.
Juror No. 5? A. Same.
Juror No. 6? A. Same.
Juror No. 7? A. Same.
Juror No. 8? A. Same.
Juror No. 9? A. Same.
Juror No. 10? A. Same thing.
Juror No. 11? A. Same.
Juror No. 12? A. Same.
Alternate Juror : Same.
The Court : I will deny your motion, Mr. Gulotta.
Mr. Gulotta : Respectfully, I except.

The Court : And I will instruct the jury you are not to consider anything but the testimony received before you. Now, Gentlemen, don't read any more newspapers until the conclusion of this case. It seems to be a necessary instruction.

Mr. Gulotta: May we have an exception, your Honor?

The Court : You may.

Cross-examination by Mr. Gulotta:

Q. Now Officer Cosgrove, I believe you testified that you visited the whereabouts of this bungalow on the 13th day of August, 1937, is that right? A. I did.

Q. And what time did you get there? A. About 11:00 or 11:15.

Q. And your getting there was occasioned because of a telephone call by someone, is that right? A. That is not right.

Q. How is it? A. I received no phone call.

Q. How did you learn of the situation? A. I learned it from a man by the name of Mr. Haff.

Q. Haff. And was Haff the man that came to call you? A. He was.

Q. And where did he come to call for you? A. I was standing in front of Crane's Hotel at South Beach.

Q. After Mr. Haff said something to you, you went somewhere, is that right? A. I did.

Q. And where did you go? A. I proceeded to the-- in an automobile so far as the creek at South Beach at the foot of Berger Avenue, where we seen Elmore and followed Haff and Elmore to the bungalow in the swamp.

Q. And how much of a walk was it from the place where you parked your automobile to the bungalow? A. Oh, I guess it is about 2, 000, maybe 2,500 feet.

Q. And all of that is very bad walking, is it not? A. It is.

Q. And there are ditches drawn in the ground? A. There are.

Q. At various places, is that right? A. That is true.

Q. Now, the first person then, that you saw in

connection with that matter is Mr. Haff, is that right? A. The first person that spoke to me about the bungalow, yes.

Q. Now, did you go into the cellar of the bungalow immediately upon reaching there? A. I did.

Q. Did Elmore go with you? A. He didn't.

Q. How long did you stay in the cellar of the bungalow? A. I went down and looked around, was satisfied that it was the girl that--

Q. No, now, how long did you stay? A. Well, a minute and a half, two minutes.

Q. And did you come out of the cellar then? A. I did.

Q. And where did you go? A. I stood along side of the bungalow, talking to Elmore, to Haff, and to Murphy.

Q. And when you talked to Elmore, did you ask him whether or not he knew anything about it? A. Not at that time, no.

Q. Did you ask Mr. Haff whether he knew anything about it? A. No.

Q. How long a time expired from that time that Elmore got into an automobile and was taken to the police station? A. How long afterwards?

Q. How long after you got there? A. Well, I made a phone call after that.

Q. Yes. A. The time it took me to walk to a phone through the swamp and return, it would be 40 minutes.

Q. About 40 minutes. A. 40.

Q. Now, up to this time and during that time, you hadn't asked Elmore whether he knew anything about it? A. I didn't.

Q. Nor had you asked Mr. Haff if he knew anything about it? A. I did not.

Q. Did you take Mr. Haff in the automobile? A. Not at that time, no.

Q. No, but you did take Mr. Elmore in the automobile? A. I did.

Q. And from the time you took Elmore to the station house until the 14th day of August, 1937, when the first paper was signed, he remained at the station house, did he not? A. We didn't take Elmore to the station house.

Q. Where did you take him? A. He was seated in the car along side of the bungalow.

Q. Yes, now what time did you reach the station house that day? A. I returned there about 4:00 o'clock.

Q. And Elmore with you? A. No sir, Elmore was there.

Q. I see. Did you leave Elmore with anyone, any police officer? A. Well, Detective Brennan and Detective Murphy.

Q. And did you give Detectives Brennan and Murphy any instructions about looking after Elmore? A. They were told to place him in the car **and keep him there until we could conduct an investigation.**

**Q. Keep him there. Did you give them any instructions to place him under arrest? A. No, sir.**

Q. When you came back was Elmore still in the car? A. When I came back, Elmore was not placed in the car until after I returned.

Q. I see. And then there came a time when Elmore reached the station house at about 4:00 o'clock that day, is that right? A. That is right.

Q. Now, it is a fact that from 4:00 o'clock, August 13th until August 14th, when the confession was signed, Elmore remained at the station house. A. That is true.

Q. And it is a further fact that he was never, during this period of time, placed under arrest? A. No he was not.

Q. All right. Now, then, it is also a fact, is it not, that from the time Elmore signed the first statement until such a time as he signed the second statement, on August 16th, Elmore remained in the station house, didn't he? A. No.

Q. Where did he go? A. He, on the morning of the 16th, he was brought to Police Headquarters.

Q. New York? A. He was photographed, he was at the lineup and returned here that morning to the District Attorney's office.

Q. All right. Now, he was brought to New York,

wasn't he? A. That is right.

Q. And he was photographed, wasn't he? A. Yes.

Q. And he was finger printed, wasn't he? A. Yes.

Q. And he was in the lineup wasn't he? A. Yes.

Q. And still, he was not under arrest? A. He was under arrest then.

Q. When did you place him under arrest? A. On the morning of the 15th about 12:30 P. M.

Q. So that it was after you placed him under arrest that this second statement was signed, is that right? A. That is right.

Q. Now, you told us before about a talk that you had with Mr. Elmore, that is the first talk you had with him, is that right? Is that right, Officer? A. I had a first talk with him.

Q. And did you ask him anything about what time he got up that morning? A. I didn't.

Q. Did you ask him where he was about 10:30 that morning? A. I didn't.

Q. Did it come to your knowledge that at the time that he was at the Sea View Hospital collecting his pay, did he say that to you? A. During the first conversation he told me that he was a painter in Sea View.

Q. Yes. A. And had worked there the day before, that this day was his day off.

Q. But, did he tell you that he had called at Sea View Hospital for the purpose of collecting his pay? A. He did, yes.

Q. He did. And as a matter of fact, that was embodied in this long statement, wasn't it? A. That is right.

Q. All right. Now, this morning you said something about Rockland Avenue and Richmond Road. Did he tell you that he was there about 11:30? A. No, before that.

Q. What time did he tell you he was there? A. He told me he received his pay about 11:00 o'clock that morning.

Q. Yes. A. At Sea View.

Q. At Sea View. But, did he tell you that right

after he collected his pay he was at Richmond Road and Rockland Avenue? A. Yes, he later on said that he met Barney Siegar.

Q. Right. A. At Sea View Hospital.

Q. And did he tell you that Barney Siegar was the one that drove him down to Richmond Avenue and Rockland Road. A. That is true.

Q. All right. Now, did he tell you about meeting a woman by the name of Emma Keel or something? At about 12:00 o'clock at No. 600 Richmond Road. A. He didn't.

Q. He didn't. Did he tell you that about the same time, 12:00 noon of that day, he went into a store known as an A. & P. at 568 Richmond Road. Did he tell you that? A. He told me he was there, before noon.

Q. What time? A. About 11:30.

Q. All right. Did he tell you that a person by the name of August Bacarezza waited on him, did he tell you that? A. He did.

Q. He did. And after that, did he tell you that after coming out of the A. & P. store, he went to the bank, to the Staten Island Savings Bank. A. From there he returned home.

Q. He returned home. And did he tell you what time he left home? A. He said about shortly before 1:00 o'clock.

Q. He didn't say exactly 12:50, did he, those words? A. He may have.

Q. Yes. Now, did he tell you that a Miss McKittrick saw him leave the house at 12:50 that day? A. He didn't.

Q. Did he tell you that Mrs. Elmore saw him leave the house at that time on that day? **A. Mrs. Elmore knows what time he left.**

Q. Yes. And is that time 12:50? A. About that.

Q. Yes. Now then, after that, did he tell you that he had gotten some paper bags? Brown bags? A. That is right.

Q. Yes, and did he tell you that the purpose was

to go down there and get some bait for crabbing the following morning? A. That is right.

Q. Yes. And did he tell you that he met a man by the name of John Peroni while he had these bags? A. He did not.

Q. He did not. Did he tell you that about 1:30 to 2:00 P. M. he went in the Hardy's Drug store? A. He told me he went to Hardy's.

Q. Yes. A. But, it was later on than that.

Q. Don't you remember him saying that he particularly went there to purchase a tube of Ben-gay? A. He said that.

Q. And that statement is embodied in this long statement is it not? A. It is.

Q. Now, did he tell you that he went to the B. & O. yard at Clifton about 2:15 to 2:30? A. He walked through the passage way there yes.

Q. Right. And did he tell you that at or about that time he met a man by the name of John Carney? A. He seen a man by the name of John Carney,

Q. Yes. A. --he said.

Q. Yes. And did he then tell you that about three o'clock he went in to a store located at No. 152 Broad Street, which store is owned by Edward Harris? A. He went to a store by the name of Harris.

Q. And did he tell you that the purpose in going into that store was to purchase a pair of pants? A. That is right.

Q. Right. Now, did he tell you that after he got these pants that they were too long for him and that he was obliged, or did go to 116 Broad Street in the shop of a tailor? A. He did.

Q. And did he tell you the name of that tailor? A. He did.

Q. And was it Louis De Lacy? A. That is right.

Q. Yes. And did he tell you that he did, as a matter of fact, have these trousers shortened? A. He did.

Q. Yes. Now then, did he tell you that after he had these trousers shortened and at about three to half past three, he was walking through Gordon Street, did he tell you that Officer? A. He did.

Q. And did he tell you that he saw anyone when he got to No. 256 Gordon Street? A. He did.

Q. And did he tell you that man's name? A. I think he did.

Q. And was that name Enrico Boggieni? A. That is right.

Q. And did he tell you that he had a conversation with this man about painting a house? A. He said he spoke to him.

Q. That is right. Now then, after that, did he tell you that he went back to, or went to another A. & P. store for the purpose of making certain purchases that his wife had asked him to make? A. I think he said he went to a beer garden from there.

Q. Well, this is, I am not there yet. Did he tell you about the A. & P. store? A. He told me about an A. & P. store in Stapleton, yes.

Q. Did he tell you about meeting a man in there who waited on him by the name of Al Miller? A. He spoke of Al Miller.

Q. Yes. And did he tell you that later on he went in to buy a huckleberry pie? A. He did.

Q. And did he tell you who waited on him there? A. He did.

Q. Did he say that the name of that person was Ellen Feldrap? A. He did.

Q. Now then, you mentioned Alex's saloon, did you not? A. Yes, he said he went there.

Q. And you know who owns that saloon, don't you? A. I do not.

Q. Did you ever hear the name of John Techky? A. I have heard of it since.

Q. What is your answer, please? A. I don't know whether that is his name or not.

Q. And did he say he went in there to have a beer? A. Yes, he had a couple of beers there.

Q. Did he tell you that after having a couple of

beers he reached home about the hour of four P. M. ? A. Before that.

Q. Before that? What time did he tell you? A. He told me he returned about, in the statement, I think, about 1:30.

Q. I am not talking about his statement I am talking about what he told you, Officer. A. Yes, he said about two o'clock, 1:30, to 2 o'clock.

Q. Two o'clock? A. 1:30, 2 o'clock.

Q. Two o'clock. Did he tell you he stayed home the balance of the afternoon? A. No, he said he went out later on.

Q. Well, didn't he say something about cooking clam chowder with thirteen clams? A. He didn't say whether he cooked it or not, but he said he opened thirteen clams.

Q. I see. And that was after he got home from Alex's saloon, was it not? A. No, that was after he come home from the A. & P. store, after he got paid.

Q. Now, did he say anything about making a visit to the office of Mrs. Wardell? A. He said he went to the office of Mrs. Wardell after six o'clock.

Q. Did he tell you what time he made that visit? A. After supper, after six o'clock.

Q. All right. Now, you know where Metcalf Street is, don't you, Officer? A. Yes.

Q. And you are acquainted with that part of the town, aren't you? A. Well, I know some of the streets there.

Q. Yes. And you know where the location of this bungalow is, don't you? A. Yes.

Q. Have you ever gone from a point near Metcalf Street to a point near the place where this bungalow is located, by bus? A. By bus, no.

Q. Have you ever gone there by automobile? A. I have.

Q. How long did it take you? A. Ten minutes.

Q. Ten minutes? A. Between ten and fifteen minutes.

Q. Did Elmore tell you that he drives an automobile? A. No.

Q. Did he tell you that he never drove an automobile? A. I never mentioned it to him, about driving an automobile.

Q. Have you ever walked that distance, Officer? A. No, I haven't.

Q. What in your opinion would it take to walk it? A. Well, it is, there are a lot of short cuts, I believe, you can take to that bungalow from his home.

Q. Now, what short cuts have you in mind when you talk about short cuts, Officer? A. Well, if you went down through Clove Road, you could cut through the back of St. Mary's cemetery, there is maybe another field around Moselle Avenue where you take a short cut.

Q. Yes. A. Then, there may be another one or two that I just can't recall.

Q. Well, now, having in mind the short cuts that you are now visualizing, how long would it take to walk it from his home? A. Gee, I don't know, I have never walked it.

Q. It would take some time, wouldn't it, Officer? A. I don't know what kind of, how fast a walker he is.

Q. All right. Now, you said before that you kept Elmore there from four o'clock, August 13th, in the station house, until certainly until the 14th when he signed the first statement, is that correct? A. He was there, yes.

Q. Now, between four o'clock on August 13th and the time, August 14th, when he signed the Statement, did you talk to him at all? A. Occasionally I spoke to him, yes.

Q. And occasionally, did you ask him whether or not he committed this crime? A. I did not ask him anything of the kind.

Q. Did anybody else so far as you know ask him? A. Oh, yes.

Q. How many people asked him? A. Well, I don't think more than Inspector Lyons, Inspector McGrath.

Q. Yes. A. There may have been one or two other

detectives, but--

Q. Four or five? A. Yes, four or five.

Q. Or six or seven? A. No, no six or seven.

Q. Four or five. And how often would they ask him whether or not he committed the crime? A. **Well, they went on and had him relate from the time he got up that morning, what he did and checked on it, through that method.**

Q. Now, these police officers were continually there during this period, were they not? A. They were in and out.

Q. And there would always be some one police officer with the defendant, would there not? A. Inspector Lyons was there all the time.

Q. All the time? So that Inspector knows just exactly what took place during that time, doesn't he? A. He will know.

Q. Now, he never before he signed this statement, said to you anything about having committed this crime, did he? A. No, he never said it to me.

Q. Had Mr. Innes, the District Attorney of the County, been there before the occasion upon which the, on which the statement was signed? A. **He was there just about five or ten minutes before he spoke of committing the crime.**

Q. I mean, on a separate occasion before this statement was signed was he there? A. When do you mean, what date?

Q. On any, any time before August 14th at the time that the statement was signed. A. I think he was there the evening of the 13th.

Q. Yes. Now, on the evening of the 13th, did Mr. Innes go in there and say, "Well now, did you do it?" A. No, he did not.

Q. He did not? He didn't ask him a thing about whether or not he had committed this crime? A. The police were conducting the investigation and he just looked on.

Q. But,, we do find that before this statement was

signed he did ask him on August 14th, is that right? A. He spoke to him on the 14th.

Q. And may I ask you now, is 5:45 P. M. on August 14th, the correct time the statement was signed? A. It is, yes.

Q. And Elmore that morning woke up in the station house, did he not? A. Well, he was laying on the couch there.

**Q. And Inspector Lyons was there until 5:45 P. M. continually, was he not? A. No, he left early in the morning of the 13th, I mean of, yes, the 14th.**

Q. Was Elmore taken to the Morgue at any time? A. Not by me.

Q. Do you know that he was taken to the morgue of your own knowledge? A. I have heard it.

Q. Do you know that while the dead body of this girl was stretched out there he was asked, "Did you commit this crime? " Do you know that as a fact? A. I don't know anything about it.

Q. You don't know. At any rate, you do not know of anything that Elmore said when he was taken to the morgue, do you? A. I do not.

Q. No. Now, you didn't think of Haff at all, did you, about taking him to the police station? A. Yes, we brought him in later on.

Q. And how long did you keep Haff? A. We took a statement from him.

Q. And after, --is that a signed statement? A. No.

Q. A verbal statement? A. Yes.

Q. And right after he made this statement, Haff was dismissed, is that correct? A. He was, yes.

Q. Now, while Elmore was in the station house, you approached another man, didn't you, by the name of Nolan, I believe? A. No.

Q. Wasn't somebody else taken in and questioned? A. Oh yes, I brought a fellow in.

Q. Well, now, what is his name? A. His name is, it was an Italian name.

The Court : Was it Terrinova? A. His name was

Terrinova.

Q. Terrinova? And did you have a talk with somebody before you went after Terrinova? A. What do you mean, before I went after him?

Q. Well, where did you go after Terrinova? A. I found him on the beach at--

Q. All right? A. --Seaside Boulevard.

Q. When you say--pardon me. When you say that you found him, does that mean that you were looking for him? A. No, sir, not in particular.

Q. Did you find him accidentally? A. **Anybody I didn't know and was a stranger on the beach, that I didn't know, I spoke to them about what he was doing.**

Q. Is Terrinova a stranger in town? A. He is.

Q. You know that Elmore is not a stranger in town, don't you? A. I don't know, I never met the man before.

Q. You didn't? Now, what time did you meet Terrinova? A. Oh, it must have been around a little after three o'clock, maybe half past three.

Q. That is August 14th? A. August 13th.

Q. Thirteenth? Now, that was while Elmore was at the station house, is that right? A. He may have been there, yes.

Q. Now, the reason for taking Terrinova, or asking him to the station house, the reason is in connection with an alleged crime, is that right? A. We were investigating a homicide.

Q. Well, you didn't come after me or didn't ask me, did you, Officer? A. Well, if I met you, I would know who I was talking to.

Q. Well, did you know who you were talking to when you took Terrinova to the station house? A. I did not.

Q. You didn't know him at all? A. I did not.

Q. So that you brought to the station house a man with whom you were unacquainted, is that correct? A. That is right.

Q. And this man with whom you were unacquainted, you questioned at the station house, didn't you? A. I did.

Q. And concerning a murder? A. I didn't mention to him about a murder, I questioned his movements.

Q. All right. And after he made answers to your questions, he left the station house? A. That is right.

Q. And this is a man who was a total stranger to you, being a detective on the New York City Police Department, is that right? A. I never seen him before.

Q. All right. Now, how long did you question Terrinova? A. Well, he was there, I should judge, two hours, possibly three.

Q. Two hours? And did he leave immediately after you questioned him? A. After we were satisfied about him we let him go home.

Q. On the other hand, up to that time, Elmore had not been questioned, according to your answers, had he? A. He was questioned.

Q. By whom? A. Inspector Lyons, Inspector McGrath.

Q. And did he say at any time that he committed a crime? A. Not at that particular time.

Q. On the other hand, he was held, wasn't he, he was held? A. He was held for investigation.

Q. Held for investigation. Not under arrest, of course? A. No.

Q. Is that correct? A. That is right.

**Q. Now, Officer, when you went down to the cellar, did you notice that there was a piece of cord tied to a door knob? A. The bathing suit was tied to the door knob.**

**Q. And what door knob is that? A. It is not a knob, it is where the door has been broken,** the panelling.

Q. All right. And the other end was tied to the little girl's neck, is that right? A. That is right.

Q. Now, did Haff say anything to you concerning the fact that Elmore had reported something to him? A.

Yes.

**Q. Yes. And did he say that there was a child or a little girl in the bungalow? A. He did.**

Q. You never found out whether or not Elmore had spoken to anyone before he addressed these remarks to Haff, did you? A. Where do you mean, at the beach?

Q. Yes. A. The only men he seen was Haff.

Q. The only man he seen, and so far as you know, this conversation, or the advisement that something wrong had happened, that was a voluntary proposition, insofar as you knew, on the part of Elmore, is that correct? A. **Well, Mr. Haff had seen Elmore walking from the bungalow and had him under observation.**

Q. But,, the statement, so far as you know, was it a voluntary proposition? A. Oh, yes.

Q. That is the question. A. So far as I know.

Q. And you say that it was? A. So far as I know, yes.

Q. So that, you have the picture of Elmore advising Haff of a situation and after having done so, he was brought to the police station, is that right? A. After a while, yes.

Q. Now, what was Elmore fed while he was in the station house? A. He got coffee, he got sandwiches, he got cigarettes, he smoked some cigarettes there.

Q. And there were not hot meals there, were there? A. No, he got what we ate, sandwiches and coffee.

Q. Well, sandwiches and coffee are good fare. A. Well, good enough for me.

Q. Do you eat sandwiches all the time, Officer? A. No.

Q. Now, Officer, the question that I have asked you concerning a conversation that Elmore had with you, that is the verbal conversations, most of them are embodied in this written statement, this second statement, is that right, which is dated August 16th, I believe, is that right? A. Those are the conversations he had with Mr. McKinney in the District Attorney's office.

Q. I see. Now, how was Elmore dressed that day,

do you remember? A. Yes, he had a--what day do you mean?

Q. On the 13th. A. Yes.

Q. How was he dressed? A. **He had on a dark gray pair of pants, he had a dark blue or dark gray hat.**

Q. Yes. A. White shirt, and brown or black shoes, I just can't recall. I think he had black shoes on.

Q. **Now, did he have a coat such as I am wearing now? A. I don't think he did.**

Q. If so, you say you don't think. Are you sure about that, Officer, or you just don't know? A. I am not sure whether he had a coat or not.

Q. All right, now, you are now telling us, Officer, that you are not sure whether Elmore had a coat such as I am wearing now? A. No, I am not quite sure.

Q. And you were in his company for quite some time, that day, is that right? A. Well, he, at least a half an hour.

Q. Yes. You were in close proximity to him for a half an hour? A. I was.

Q. But,, you can't tell us whether or not he had a coat, is that right ? A. I just can't recall. I think he had a coat I am not sure.

Q. Just one moment, please. Now, Officer, did Elmore at the time that he was about to sign a statement, tell you anything about where it was that he met this little girl? A. Before?

Q. Yes. A. He made the statement?

Q. Yes. A. He made a statement before it was typewritten.

Q. Did he tell you where, is the question? A. Yes, he said he met her on the beach front, in front of Crane's.

Q. Now, Crane's is on the ocean front, is that right? A. It faces the new board walk.

Q. And it is some distance away from, a close distance away from Bessi's hotel, is that right? A. Yes, it is.

Q. Now, the street on this side of the ocean front is Seaside Boulevard, is it not? A. That is right.

Q. Now, you know that there is a bus line that runs there, don't you? A. I do.

Q. And that bus line comes up Sand Lane, is that correct? A. Yes, there is a bus line goes up Sand Lane.

Q. And then it turns into McClean Avenue, is that right? A. Right or left?

Q. To the left. A. Well, I believe there are three routes go up that street.

Q. McClean Avenue, there is a bus route is that right? A. There is a bus line crossing it.

Q. And McClean Avenue runs into Norway Avenue, is that right? A. That is right, yes.

Q. Now, at right angles to Norway Avenue is a street known as Scott Avenue, is that right? A. Yes, I recall a Scott Avenue, yes.

Q. And there is another street known as Appleby Avenue, is that correct? A. I don't recall that.

Q. All right. Well now, the bungalow in reference to Scott Avenue, and Norway Avenue, is some distance away, is that correct? A. It is, yes, from Norway.

Q. Did you say that in his statement which, was finally reduced to writing, Elmore was seen by anyone at Norway Avenue? A. He was seen by somebody.

Q. Yes. And did that somebody; in your impression now, is it the bus driver? A. He is, yes.

Q. Whose name is Flick? A. That is right.

Q. Right. Now, can you give us the approximate distance if you went around Seaside Boulevard, up Sand Lane and down McClean Avenue to Norway, what that approximate distance is, can you give us that? A. Well, I can give you the approximate distance from Crane's along Seaside Boulevard.

Q. Right. A. Up Sand Lane.

Q. Right. A. And over Olympia Boulevard.

Q. That is Old Town Road. A. Yes, it was.

Q. Well, give us that please, give us that, please. A. Through that bungalow?

Q. Yes. A. It is about a mile and a half.

Q. A mile and a half. Now, will you kindly give us

the distance and in doing so, please visualize the shortest distance between two points, Peter Crane's Hotel and the bungalow in the marsh land? A. A short straight direct route?

Q. That is right. A. Instead of the roadway?

Q. That is right. A. Well, I think you would have to go up Seaside Boulevard to Burgher Avenue.

Q. Right. A. And across the creek there and walk through the swamps--the road I took that morning.

Q. Right. Now, what is that distance, about, in your opinion? A. Well, that is a good half mile, I believe.

Q. Half mile? A. Almost a half mile.

Q. **So that it is in any event, less than half the distance going down Seaside Boulevard, Sand Lane, Old Town Road, is that correct? A. I would say about half that distance, along that route, yes.**

Q. **The latter distance having been designated by you as about a mile and a half, and the former about half a mile? A. The first a mile and a half.**

Q. **Yes, so that would be about one third, is that correct? A. About one third, yes.**

Q. One third. And now, you said something about the way, that is the way you went to the bungalow. Did you do it on foot? A. No, I got in the car at the rear of Crane's and I drove the car to, as far as the creek, and I walked the rest of the distance.

Q. Yes, that is the short way, is it? A. Well, there may be some shorter routes through the back of some of those bungalows.

Q. So far as you know, it is shorter even than the other route, isn't it? A. Much shorter.

Q. In fact, one-third shorter? A. Yes.

Q. Now, you had no trouble getting in there with your car, did you, up to a certain point? A. Well, it is an ash road off the main street there.

Q. Yes, and the way you went, it is very sparcely situated, isn't it? A. Not at that time of the year, it is well populated, that bungalow section.

Q. I see. Well populated right there, you say, in

the meadow? A. Well, a lot of children--no, not in the meadows, there is nothing in the meadows but the house.

Q. **Nothing in the meadows. Now, Seaside Boulevard, taking the longer route, is quite a populated street at that time of the year, is it not? A. It is a summer colony.**

Q. There is no question in your mind that Sand Lane is a populated street? A. In the summer time it is.

Q. There is no question in your mind that Old Town Road is a populated street in the summer time? A. People going back and forth to the beach.

Q. And there are stores in there, are there not? A. There are stores when you come to Olympia Boulevard.

Q. And now, as you have told me, you remember that in the statement Elmore had said something about being seen at Norway Avenue by Flick, the bus driver? A. I do remember it.

Q. And he told you that preparatory to signing the statement? A. He did, yes.

Mr. Gulotta : That concludes my cross-examination.

Redirect examination by Mr. Innes :

Q. Just a question or two, officer. Do you know whether or not at the time I came to the station house on the thirteenth, I saw Elmore? A. When I seen you, you were in the back room of the Station house, where the, at the water pump, with Mr. McKinney.

Q. And where was Elmore at that time? A. Elmore was in the middle room in the Detective Office.

Q. Do you know whether or not I spoke to him on that occasion? A. I don't know.

Mr. Innes : All right, I think that is all. Now, Mr. Haff.

The Court : Mr. Innes, we will take a recess for a few minutes. Gentlemen, we will take a recess for about ten minutes. Do not discuss this case or come to any conclusion in the case until the case is finally submitted to you. You may go upstairs.

(Whereupon, at 3 P. M. Court recessed until 3:28 P. M.)

PROCEEDINGS AT SCENE OF CRIME

Court Clerk Kosman : People against Samuel Elmore.

(All parties were ready. Whereupon, the jury was polled and all jurors answered present.)
The Court : Have the officers been sworn?
Court Clerk Kosman : Not yet.
The Court : Swear the officers.
(Thereupon, three officers were sworn to take the jury to the scene of the crime and keep them together and allow no one to speak to them concerning the case.)
The Court : Gentlemen, you are going to be taken in a bus down to the scene of this crime. You will be in the custody of the officers and the officers have been sworn and you will be instructed not to speak to any one concerning this case in any manner whatever. You will be taken there and conveyed back to the Court House. You will be kept together.
A Juror : May I ask something, your Honor? May I make a telephone call before we go?
The Court : Yes, I will send one of the officers, who will take you to the telephone before you leave. The bus is waiting whenever you are ready, Mr. Innes.
Mr. Innes : All right.
(Whereupon, at 3:29 P. M. the Court and Jury visited the scene of the crime, first going to Fifth Place and Burgher Avenue, South Beach, S. I., where the following occurred.)
The Court : That is the bungalow, over there. You may make any inspection you wish of the bungalow or of the surroundings.

A Juror : Is there any road leading out there?

The Court : You will have to observe that, but I will see if counsel can point it out. Mr. Innes, Mr. Casey and Mr. Gulotta, one of the jurors asked whether there is any road leading into the house.

Mr. Innes : Around from the other side, from the Boulevard, there is a wagon road leading there.

The Court : We will have to go around.

Mr. Innes : This is the only way you can go into that.

The Court : That is, if you approach from this point, you would have to go through the marsh.

Mr. Innes : Yes.

The Court : But, there is another road around the other way.

Mr. Innes : This is the place where Cosgrove said he found him.

The Court : Gentlemen, you cannot ask me any questions. You are here merely to view the premises and to observe. I am merely pointing out the location to you of the premises. You may stay here, gentlemen, as long as you deem it advisable and make such inspection as you deem advisable. When you get through, then we will proceed to the other point, so you can get the view from the other side. Gentlemen, when you have completed your examination, will you walk up this way, please? You will observe, gentlemen, these two houses and the passageway between the houses. (Referring to Nos. 85 and 86 Fifth Place. ) When you have completed your inspection and examination, you may return to the bus.

A Juror : Is there any significance to this, Judge?

The Court : You are not here to ask me any questions. You will just observe what you see and ask no questions. When you have finished here, return to the bus.

(Whereupon, the Court and Jury went around the roadway to the site of the bungalow where the crime was committed and the following took place) :

The Court : These are the premises here. The point from which you just came is located over there, where you can see the boats, and the place where you stood when you were on the road is between the two houses there. (Indicating. )You can make any inspection you want of the house, or the surrounding territory. Go into the house, if you wish, make any inspection you wish.

A Juror : All right, your Honor.

(Whereupon, the Jury visited the site of the bungalow and inspected it, then returned to the bus and all parties assembled in the Court room at 4 :36 P. M. , where the following occurred)

Court Clerk Kosman : People against Samuel Elmore.

(Both sides were ready. Whereupon, the jury was polled and all jurors answered present. )

The Court : Gentlemen, we will recess until tomorrow morning at 10 o'clock. The instructions which I have given you at previous recesses apply to this one, do not discuss this case or come to any conclusion in the matter until the case is finally submitted to you and until you retire to your jury room.

I have previously instructed you with reference to reading newspapers or forming any conclusion from anything you do read in the newspapers. Keep your minds open. When the time comes for the case to be submitted to you, I will instruct you that you can consider this case only upon evidence produced before you and upon nothing else. Tomorrow morning at ten o'clock.

(Whereupon, at 4:38 P. M. Court recessed until the following morning at 10 :00 A. M. )

## COUNTY COURT,
### RICHMOND COUNTY.

PEOPLE OF THE STATE OF
NEW YORK,

against

SAMUEL ELMORE,

Defendant.

Indictment No. 55/1937.
Murder 1st Degree.

Before Hon.
Thomas F. Cosgrove, County
Judge, and a
Petit Jury.

At the Court House, St. George, S. I., N. Y.,
Thursday, November 18, 1937, 10:00 A. M.

APPEARANCES:

HON. FRANK H. INNES, District Attorney.

JOSEPH A. MCKINNEY, ESQ., Assistant District
Attorney, For the People.

PETER GULOTTA, ESQ.,

WILLIAM C. CASEY, ESQ., Attorneys for Defendant.

Court Clerk Kosman: All manner of persons having any business to do with this term of County Court, held in and for the County of Richmond, draw near, give your

(Whereupon the Jury was polled and all Jurors answered present.)

Mr. Innes : I call Mr. Kuleba for just a few

98

questions.

WILLIAM KULEBA, recalled as a witness on behalf of the People, resumed the witness stand, and testified further as follows:

Direct Examination by Mr. Innes :

Q. Mr. Kuleba, what--I show you this pair of sandals and ask you if you recognize those? A. That is right.

Q. And, did you buy them? A. No, my wife did.

Q. She bought them. But, were they worn by your daughter, Joan? A. Yes.

Q. And were they--you recognize those as the same sandals as she wore during the summer while she was with her aunt, Mrs. Lesandi? A. Yes.

Q. Now, they were delivered to you by a police officer, were they not? A. That is right.

Q. And you have had them in your possession since, and you have delivered them to me or to my office for the purpose of this, trial? A. Yes.

Mr. Innes : That is all. I now offer these in evidence if the Court pleases.

The Court : All right, mark them in evidence.

(Whereupon People's Exhibit No. 2 for Identification was received in evidence.)

Mr. Innes : Now, Mr. Haff.

Mr. Gulotta : If your Honor pleases, I wish to desire, in order to keep the testimony straight to recall detective Cosgrove this morning.

The Court : Do you wish to call him at this time?

Mr. Gulotta : Yes.

The Court : Call him.

Mr. Gulotta : Detective Cosgrove.

DETECTIVE THOMAS S. COSGROVE, recalled for further examination, having been previously sworn, resumed the stand and testified further as follows :

Cross-examination by Mr. Gulotta:

Mr. Innes : You told me, Mr. Gulotta, that that was produced from the typographical bureau.

Mr. Gulotta : Yes, it was.

Mr. Innes : And I have no objection to it being marked in evidence.

Mr. Gulotta : I so offer it in evidence, if your Honor pleases.

The Court : No objection. Mark it in evidence.

( The map referred to was received in evidence and marked Defendant's Exhibit A in evidence. )

By Mr. Gulotta:

Q. Now, Officer Cosgrove, yesterday you told me that you had had a conversation with the defendant prior to his signing the statement, dated August 16, 1937, is that right? A. That is right.

Q. And in that conversation did he tell you that he lived on Metcalfe Street? A. He did.

Q. Now, you know where Metcalfe Street is, don't you, Officer? A. I do.

Q. And he told you how he walked from Metcalfe Street to South Beach, is that right? A. He did.

Q. Yes. And as I understand it, he told you that from Metcalfe Street he walked down to Targee Street, is that right? A. Targee Street, yes.

Q. Targee Street. And then he walked down on Targee Street as far as Steuben Street, is that right? A. That is right.

Q. And that then he proceeded down Steuben Street until he came over to Hanover Street, is that right? A. Hanover Avenue, I believe.

Q. Yes. Hanover Avenue is correct. That then he cut across and walked across to Moselle Avenue, is that right? A. I think he said he cut through a lot or a field.

Q. That is right into Moselle Avenue? A. Moselle Avenue.

Q. That when he got to Moselle Avenue he went in to Clove Road, is that right? A. He might have said

Clove Road, I was under the impression he went--yes, he went to Clove Road.

Q. Clove Road. And then he proceeded through Clove Road and down through Hylan Boulevard, where the Circle is, is that right? A. He crossed--he went down Clove Road and across Hylan Boulevard.

Q. Right, to the rear of St. Mary's Cemetery. A. Yes.

Q. That then he picked up Norway Avenue and walked down Norway Avenue into Olympia Boulevard, is that right? A. He went down Norway Avenue to Olympia Boulevard to the path leading to the house.

Q. Then he took that path leading to the house, as you have testified and walked as far as Evergreen Avenue, is that right? A. That is Evergreen Avenue, yes.

Q. And then from Evergreen Avenue he walked directly to the beach, is that right? A. Yes, that is right.

Q. All right, now, he told you that he walked this distance, is that right? A. He did.

**Q. Now, Officer, in your talk with the defendant, did he tell you anything about how long he was in that bungalow from the time he entered there with this little girl until the time that lie left the bungalow on August 12th? A. He didn't specify any time.**

**Q. He didn't. Did you ask him? A. No, we didn't.**

Q. And you have testified that you practically went over the entire sum and substance of this written statement before it was reduced to writing, is that right? A. I read it, yes.

Q. Yes, but you didn't ask him how long he stayed at this bungalow? A. Not that I can recall, no.

Q. All right, now, when you were called by Mr. Haff, down to this bungalow, did you see any fishing nets in the possession of the defendant? A. He had some.

Q. Or crab pots? A. He had some crab pots, those collapsible crab pots.

Q. And where were those crab pots? A. He had

them in his arms, in his hands.

Q. And how many of them were there? A. I think three or four.

Q. Three or four?

Mr. Innes : We have them here, Mr. Gulotta, if you want them.

Mr. Gulotta : That is all right.

By Mr. Gulotta:

Q. Now, I think I asked you this, Officer and it is not my desire to repeat, but I want to make sure. You picked up a man by the name of Teranova, did you not, on August 13th? A. I did.

Q. Teranova was released before this confession or the first confession was signed? A. That is right.

Mr. Gulotta : I think that is all.

Redirect examination by Mr. Innes :

Q. Is this the bundle that he had the crab pots in? A. That is the bundle of crab pots that Elmore had that day.

Q. And he was carrying it, was he? A. He was.

Q. Now, I notice that there is a hat inside the bundle. A. That is Elmore's hat.

Q. Was he wearing that? A. He had that hat that day.

Q. And it was put in here for convenience? A. I placed it in that bag.

Mr. Innes : For any purpose?

Mr. Gulotta: We have no objection, do you want to offer them in evidence?

Mr. Innes : I do.

The Court : All right, mark them. Set forth on the record just what they are please, a bag and a hat and crab pots, and offer them as one exhibit.

Mr. Innes : Yes.

The Court : How many crab nets are there?

Mr. Innes : I am not enough familiar with them to know how many there would be if they were unfurled.

The Court : For the purpose of the record, we have to have it.

The Witness : I think it would make four crab pots.

The Court : Four crab pots? Four crab pots, a hat and a bag?

The Witness : Yes, a bag with red stripes.

The Court : Mark them as one exhibit.

(Whereupon the crab pots, bag and hat were marked People's Exhibit No. 9 in evidence. )

Recross-examination by Mr. Gulotta:

Q. Now, Officer, you saw these crab pots, you said--People's Exhibit No. 9 in the possession of the defendant on that day? A. That is right.

Q. And did you inspect them minutely? A. I did.

Q. Now, did you notice that along with these crab pots, these crab nets, there is attached the necessary cord used in the operation of these nets. Just take a look at them? A. Yes.

Q. Now, feel of that twine please, will you? A. Yes, it is fishing tackle, it is fishing line.

Q. Do you know what fishing line is? A. Yes.

Q. Is fishing line noted in your opinion for its strength? A. It is. There are various sizes, all indicating the strength of the line.

Q. And in your opinion this variety is a strong variety of line, isn't it? A. That is usually used for a drop line but that is painted with aluminum.

Q. Right. It is painted with aluminum for the purpose of giving the cord strength? A. No, these pots here have been freshly painted with aluminum paint.

Q. Yes. A. And there are brush marks along this line. They are not painted for the strength in the cord.

Q. So that they were used in connection, the string was used in connection with these pots, is that right? A. I believe so, yes.

Q. Now, did you notice attached to these crabbing pots any fish? A. There were no fish attached to those crab pots.

Q. Did you look? A. I did.

Q. And did you take those in your possession when you first saw them? A. I did, yes.

Q. Immediately? A. No. When I returned after making a phone call.

Q. And how soon after you saw these pots is it that you took these fishing pots in your possession? A. I opened them up at the top and I seen they were crabbing pots, there was no fish in them.

Q. You misunderstood my question. How soon after you saw these pots did you take them in your possession? A. After I made the phone call and came back I looked at those pots.

Q. How soon after is that, Officer? A. Well, 40 minutes about.

Q. 40 minutes.

Mr. Gulotta : That is all.

Mr. Innes: Now, that is all, Officer. Mr. Haff.

WILLIAM JOSEPH HAFF, 31 Oceanside Avenue, South Beach, Staten Island, New York, called as a witness on behalf of the People, being first duly sworn, testified as follows :

Direct examination by Mr. Innes :

Q. Mr. Haff, what is your business? A. My business?

Q. Yes. A. I am not doing anything, sir.

Q. What is that? A. I am not working at all.

Q. Well, did you, in the summer time, what did you do? A. Well, I--down around my boat, I go out fishing and catch some shrimps and some killies like that, people come around and want bait.

Q. You have a boat, do you? A. Yes.

Q. Where is that boat kept? A. Kept down by Mr. Mahr's, New Creek. Burgher Avenue and Fifth Place.

Q. At the bottom of those two streets, Burgher Avenue and Fifth Place? A. Yes.

Q. And I think you were there yesterday

afternoon? A. You were there all right, because my boat was right in front of where you were standing.

Q. I see, now, do you remember the 13th day of August last? A. Yes.

Q. Were you at or near your boat at the corner of Fifth Place and Burgher Avenue? A. I had been to my boat, yes.

Q. And was your attention attracted, --I withdraw that. From the position where your boat is located, is this bungalow in sight, this abandoned bungalow that stands out in the meadows? A. Yes.

Q. Did you see anyone at or near that bungalow that morning? A. I saw him when I came out on Fifth Place and Burgher Avenue.

Q. And what did you see?

Mr. Gulotta : I object to it and move to strike it out as not responsive.

The Court : Yes. The question is, did you see anyone. That calls for a yes or no, and if you can fix the time, Mr. Innes, of the day.

By Mr. Innes :

Q. Yes. A. I can tell you when I saw the man.

The Court : You weren't asked that. Don't volunteer anything unless you are asked, please.

By Mr. Innes :

Q. Did you see anyone at or near that bungalow that morning? A. Not until they came out on the street, Fifth Place.

Q. I see. You came out on the street on Fifth Place, is that right? A. Yes.

Q. And then did you see someone at or near the bungalow? A. I saw one man coming toward the bungalow.

Q. Coming toward the bungalow? A. Yes.

Q. From what direction, Mr. Haff? A. We called it--we used to call it Old Town Road from the west side, comes in from—

[Ed. Note: Old Town Road is going to become Norway Ave. and Olympia Blvd (top). Burgher Ave. is center and the proposed streets right center were not developed it seems. The abandoned bungalow appears it was about in the center of today's Ocean Breeze Park. This map was not in evidence and is only for the purposes of orientation.]

Q. And about how far was that man from the bungalow when you first saw him? A. Well, that is pretty hard to tell, come directly at me that way it would be a couple hundred feet, something like that.

Q. And did you notice what that man did? A. I did.

Q. And what did he do as he approached the--? A. He came along, come up to the front of the bungalow, went on the west side of it, detained there about a minute or so, then came out; on the cellar side of it was a little house, has been moved since, was standing there about 20 feet from the house or 25 feet, stood there about two minutes looking down towards the cellar, all to once, he looked over towards where I was standing and started down across the meadows.

Q. Now then, did he come towards you? A. Not until after he went down on the meadows a ways, then he stopped and looked over towards me, and then came direct towards me.

Q. And did he come in the direction, the direct way towards you? A. The best he could, jumping across the ditches.

Q. I see. And he approached you there, did he? A. He come along over and he came between the bungalow and the house there where the gate is there.

Q. Yes. Now then, did you recognize--do you now recognize the man that you saw there? A. Why, certainly.

Q. Who is he? A. He is sitting right here in the Court Room, Elmore.

Q. You know him as Elmore, do you? A. That is all I know him now.

Q. You didn't know him before that time? A. No, I never knew him before.

Q. Now then, when you he came near you, did he say anything? A. No, I said to him first,--

Q. All right, tell us what you said. A. I will just tell you the way I addressed him because we don't allow anybody to go through the bungalow, see, it is Mr. Mahr's order, it is only our way of going up home. I forgot to lock the back gate. There is a back door in the end of that alley, he comes up to the gate and I just went up to him and I said, "What the hell do you want coming through here? " That is just the way I addressed him.

Q. I see. A. He said, "I want to telephone. " I said, "What do you want to telephone for? " He said, "I want to get a policeman. " I said, "What? " He said, "I found a little girl in that house. " He said, "She has got a lot of rocks and cement on top of her. " I said, "You stay right here and I will get a policeman for you", and I went out on the beach by Mr. Crane's, Mr. Murphy was there, "Mr. Murphy", I said, "Hello. " He said, "What is the trouble? "

I said, "I want a policeman. " He said there is one right there.

Q. Who was that policeman? A. Mr. Cosgrove.

Q. Was there--did you know him before that time? A. No, I didn't.

Q. And he was in plainclothes at that time? A. Plainclothes, yes.

Q. All right. A. So he said, "What is the trouble? " I told him, so he said, "All right, come along with me." So we went in. Mr. Elmore was standing there where I left him. I said, **"Where is she?"** So we went through that gate of Mahr's and across to the house.

Q. After you got through the gate, across the creek, you had to walk a plank, did you not? A. We had to walk across that creek on the plank and right over across the meadows.

Q. Now then, you went over across the meadows with Cosgrove, and Elmore, and did somebody else go? A. Yes, Mr. Murphy and two other gentlemen.

Q. And who were they, if you know? A. I think their names is Crave.

Q. You came along the ditch that runs down toward New Creek? A. It is pretty difficult place to get into from there--**if you don't know the way.**

Q. I appreciate that. A. See, because you have to go across the ditches until you get, then there is a road that runs within about a hundred feet or so, goes right on out to Old Town Road, so we went right along the ditch, leading pretty near direct to the house.

Q. I see, and when you got to the house what-- was anything said at the time that you were walking? **A. The only thing was said when we went around the front of the house on the west side, we come to the first window on that side and Elmore said, "There she is. " Pointed into the window.**

Q. Yes. A. Because you could just distinguish something in the distance, you couldn't tell what it was, so then we went right around to the back of the house.

Mr. Gulotta: I object to that as not responsive,

and I move to strike it out.

The Court : Strike it out. Don't volunteer any statement, just say exactly his words.

The Witness: That is what I am just telling the words what he said to me.

By Mr. Innes :

Q. All right. Now then, then where did you go, Mr.-- A. I went right around on the south side of the house by the cellar.

Q. Yes. A. He said, "There she is. "

Q. You saw the body of this little girl. Did you go in the cellar? A. No, sir.

Q. Did you remain there? A. The detective left us there until he went over to telephone over to the beach for something.

Q. He went down the same path that you came along? A. Yes.

Q. And across the creek? A. Yes.

Q. And went out of your sight? A. Yes.

Q. And about how long was the officer gone, if you recollect? A. Oh, I guess maybe about fifteen minutes.

Q. I see. That is your best recollection? A. Best recollection, yes.

Q. Then he came back? A. Came back.

Q. Did Elmore remain there? A. Yes.

Q. Did he have anything with him at the time? A. He had a package under his arm.

Q. And I show you this package, Exhibit No. 9, and ask you if that looks like it? A. One just like it.

Q. I see. You are not able to state whether that is the package or not? A. No, I can't, but it was a package looking just like that.

Q. Just like this. Crab pots? A. Well, it was crab pots after it was opened up. I couldn't tell what was in it until it was opened up.

Q. And who opened it up? A. Elmore opened it up.

Q. I see. Now then, after that time where did Elmore go, if you know? A. What? After this, he went away.

Q. After the officer came back? A. Well, there were some officers; he went away in an automobile, I think with some officers.

Q. And you remained there, did you? A. I remained there until I was told to go home.

Q. Other officers came? A. Oh, I can't tell you how many, yes.

Q. Did you see me there? A. I--maybe I did, I can't say.

Mr. Innes : I think that is all. Oh, yes.

Q. I show you Exhibit, People's Exhibit No. 4 for identification. Do you recognize that, the object that is shown there, Mr. Haff? A. Yes, quite well.

Q. **And can you point out the window through which you say Elmore looked and said "There she is"? A. Yes.**

Q. And is it shown on that picture? A. Right there.

Q. Will you mark that with a pen? A. Yes.

Q. Will you mark that with an "X" mark there, Mr. Haff, and put your initials under it?

(Whereupon witness marks picture. )

A. It is so slippery I can't write on it.

Q. Was that window towards the front of the house or the rear? A. It is on the west side of the house.

Q. And toward the front? A. Yes, front window.

Q. **And there is a little building shown in the rear of that? A. Yes.**

Q. **That is an outhouse? A. An outhouse, yes.**

Mr. Innes : I think that is all, if the Court pleases.

The Court : Just a minute.

Examination by the Court:

Q. You live down there, don't you, Mr. Haff? A. Yes.

Q. You see this building every day? A. Most every one.

Q. You saw the building yesterday or the day before? A. I did.

Q. Did you notice that the windows are out now?

A. Yes.

Q. Do you notice in this the windows are in? A. Yes.

Q. Were the windows in or out at that time? A. Well, they were smashed up at that time, some of them.

Q. Now, I am talking about the 13th day of August? A. The windows was out.

Q. The windows were out. Which windows were out? A. That front window was out, this one here was out, this--

Q. Where it is shown boarded up on the photograph? A. They were boarded up afterwards.

Q. The window was boarded up, the other window was there? A. No, I think that was boarded up since too.

Q. And the building you describe, that isn't there? A. That has gone since, there is more gone, the porch is gone since too.

Q. Just one question. Does that fairly represent the situation as you saw it there the 13th day of August? A. The house?

Q. The house. Is that a fair representation? A. Yes, that is a fair picture of it.

Mr. Innes : I offer it in evidence now, if the Court please.

Mr. Gulotta : No, I think it is in evidence.

Mr. Innes : No, it is for identification only.

The Court : Mark it in evidence.

(People's Exhibit No. 4 for Identification was received in Evidence. )

Cross-examination by Mr. Gulotta:

Q. Now, Mr. Haff, how long have you lived down there at South Beach and Fifth Place? A. I don't live on Fifth Place.

Q. Well, wherever you said you lived? A. I guess I have been living steady there around fifteen years.

Q. And, you lived there both winter and summer? A. Yes.

Q. Now, surrounding this bungalow, there are a

lot of ditches, aren't there? A. Yes, sir.

Q. And they run every which way, don't they? A. yes.

Q. And, are those ditches there, if you know, for the purpose of drainage? A. The Board of Health put them there.

Q. Yes. And there are so many of them that if you happen to be walking in one direction and you meet with a ditch you have to perhaps walk to the right or to the left? A. Well, there is only one wide one, goes into to the west, but the others you can step right across.

Q. Yes, you would have to jump over them? A. Jump over them.

Q. And, it is a pretty good size jump, if you do jump over, isn't it? A. Not much of a jump.

Q. For a young fellow like yourself, we will say? A. Oh, I can jump over them all right.

Q. Now, what time is it that you addressed the defendant for the first time on August 13th? A. I couldn't tell you, it was around eleven o'clock, I couldn't tell you whether it was before or after.

Q. Well, when you say eleven o'clock, I take it you mean eleven o'clock in the morning? A. Eleven o'clock in the morning, yes, I couldn't tell you exactly whether it was eleven o'clock or afterwards because I had no time with me.

Q. **Now, what approximately is the distance, if you know, between your house and the bungalow**, assuming that you walk a straight line? A. Oh, I couldn't, it is pretty hard to tell, it is three thousand feet, more or less.

Q. 3, 000 feet? A. From my house.

Q. And, of course, even with these ditches that you yourself could jump over, it is possible, is it not, to walk from your house to this bungalow, isn't it? A. Well, you can't walk direct to it.

Q. Well, you can walk it, can't you? A. Yes, you can walk it.

Q. How many more feet do you think you would have to add to it because you can't walk a straight line, how many more feet to 3,000 feet? A. Well, you might add a couple hundred feet.

Q. A couple of hundred feet? All right. Now, as I understand it you were the first one to address a remark to the defendant, is that right? A. Yes.

Q. And your remark was, "What the hell do you want?" A. That was my remark.

Q. Is that correct? There aren't so many people that go around that bungalow, are there, Mr. Haff? A. Well, there are very few people go around it, there are people pass now and then going down for crabs, you know.

**Q. Well, how many people would you say you would see around this bungalow in that marsh land, between, we will say, June, July and August, those three months? A. How many people?**

Q. Yes. A. Well, that would be hard for anyone to say.

Q. Would there be hundreds? A. Yes, sometimes there may be 30, 40 children in there.

Q. Yes. So that, before you addressed your remark, this interrogation, "What the hell do you want?" I take it you didn't know what Elmore wanted, did you? A. I did not.

Q. When there is a child in the field, do you also make it your business to inquire of that child in the same manner? A. I do not.

Q. No. And, do you inquire in any manner? A. I don't inquire of anybody over there.

**Q. Yes. But, it just happens that on this day, August 13th, 1937, you did inquire and inquired in that fashion that you have described? A. Described?**

**Q. Right. A. To Elmore, yes.**

Q. All right. You were--you heard what Elmore had to say? A. I did.

Q. And, I take it, that you heard what Elmore had to say to Detective Cosgrove at the time? A. I heard--

Q. Didn't you? A. --heard some part of it, yes, I didn't hear it all.

113

Q. Well, you didn't hear it all, is that right? A. No.

Q. And, do you remember exactly what conversation was exchanged between you and the defendant while you and he were waiting and standing there together? A. I do.

Q. Minutely? A. I remember it.

Q. Now, didn't he say to you, Mr. Haff, "There is a little child murdered in that bungalow"? A. He said--

Q. Did he, or did he not? A. **He didn't say, murdered, no, he said he found a little child over there.**

Q. Child? You have repeated two or three times to this court and to this jury that Elmore said, "There is a little girl over there. " A. That is what he said.

Q. Now, you tell me that when he addressed you for the first time, he said, "There is a little child," is that correct? A. Well, a little girl, he said.

Q. Is that correct or is it not correct? A. A girl, that is what he said.

Q. **Did he say child? A. He said, "A little girl, a child," that is the way he come out with it.**

Q. Did he say both? A. He said both, yes.

Q. **You didn't tell that to the District Attorney when he interrogated you that he said both, did you? A. He didn't ask me.**

Q. I see. Well, when I asked you about a minute ago what he said, didn't you tell me just simply, "There is a little child, " but not murdered? A. He didn't mention about murdered. He found it over in a bungalow, he said, "A little girl," that is what he said.

Q. **And then you testified that he said "Child, " didn't you? A. After he said "A little--" I says, "A girl"? "The little girl child, " he says, that is what he said.**

Q. Did you just say, add, "girl"? A. I did not.

Q. Meaning that you asked Elmore whether it was a boy or a girl? A. I asked him nothing, he told the whole thing himself.

Q. Now, I am just paying attention to the remark

you just made. A. Well--

Q. When you said, "I asked him 'girl' " what do you mean by that? A. I asked him, he said he found a little girl over there. **I says, "A child? " and he says "Yes. "**

Q. Will you say, Mr. Haff, definitely now, whether he said to you, "There is a little girl? " A. That is just what he said, yes.

Q. And will you say definitely now that that is the only thing he said and didn't use the word "child"? A. He did use the word child.

Q. Yes. All right. Now, his response to you. when you said, "What the hell do you want? " was, "I want a policeman, " wasn't it? A. No. "I want to telephone, " he said.

Q. Didn't you testify on direct examination when Mr. Innes interrogated you that the first thing he said, was, "I want a policeman"? A. No, I didn't.

Q. And you are sure about that? A. I am sure about that.

Q. So, you now say that what he told you is, "I want to telephone"? A. Yes.

Q. You hadn't said anything else to him in addition, to, "What the hell do you want?"

A. No, didn't.

Q. Prior to his answer to the effect that he wanted to telephone, had you? A. No.

Q. No. And what did you say, if anything, about a telephone? A. I asked him what he wanted to telephone for.

Q. Yes. And then he told you about his observations, is that right? A. He said, "I want a policeman. "

Q. Yes. So that he said both. Now, as I understand, first, "I want to telephone, " and immediately thereafter, "I want a policeman. " A. Yes.

Q. Yes. Now, when you found out what the trouble was you went for a policeman? A. I did.

Q. And how far did you have to travel to get a

policeman? A. Well, I can't tell you the distance, it was out in front of Mr. Crane's place.

Q. Approximately, Mr. Haff, you will help us out if you can? A. Approximately, that is a pretty hard thing for anyone to say the distance because the way you have to walk around to get out there.

Q. Well, is it the same distance from your house to the bungalow? A. Not so far.

Q. Is it half the distance? A. Well, about half the distance.

Q. About half. So that we have that it is about half the distance between your house and the bungalow about 3,000 feet? A. More or less, I am not sure.

Q. More or less. So that, I beg your pardon--I withdraw that, I mean 300 feet wasn't that your answer?

Mr. Innes : No.

Mr. Gulotta : 3,000 feet, 3,000 feet, so then I am right.

By Mr. Gulotta:

Q. So that you went approximately 1,500 feet for a policeman, is that right? A. No, not 1,500 feet from where I met Elmore, it is not 1,500 feet.

Q. Well, you said the distance you went for a policeman was about half the distance between your house and the bungalow. The distance between your house and the bungalow, you said, is approximately-- A. You mean the bungalow over on the meadows? Or the one where he came through.

Q. On the meadows. A. He was on Fifth Place when I went for a policeman and Burgher Avenue.

Q. Can you help us out as to the distance you had to go for a policeman? A. I guess I could figure that out.

Q. If you can't you don't have to. A. I can't tell you, but four or five blocks you could make it anyhow.

Q. And you found a policeman, didn't you? A. I did.

Q. And you went back to the bungalow? A. I did.

Q. Now, when you went back to the bungalow, did you find Elmore there? A. He was standing where I left him.

Q. And was anybody there with him? A. Well, they was not right by him, there was plenty of people there all around, summer visitors all over there, any amount of them.

Q. So that so far as being incumbent, you will say, will you not, that Elmore was alone? A. He was alone.

Q. Waiting for you and the officer to return? A. Yes.

Q. And you were gone about how long, Mr. Haff? A. Well, I wasn't gone very long. I can't say. Maybe--

Q. Would you say fifteen minutes? A. Well, around that.

Q. Around 15 minutes. And there was no police officer there who remained with Elmore while you had gone for Officer Cosgrove, was there? A. Nobody there.

Q. Now, your home, I would say, is about the nearest one to this bungalow, Mr. Haff, and I say that when I say bungalow without qualifying it in any way I mean the bungalow in the marshland. A. The nearest one?

Q. Yes. A. Oh, no.

Q. Whose is the nearest bungalow to this bungalow in the marshland? A. Well, there is quite a few of them right along the creek, there is quite a few.

Q. And there on Seaside Boulevard, on the side of the Seaside Boulevard, is that right? A. Yes.

Q. Is that right? A. Sure, there on Warren Manor.

Q. And that is the general direction that Elmore was walking at the time you saw him? A. No, it is not.

Q. Is it the opposite direction? A. He come from, well, I could explain it to you if you would let me, just if you want it, just the way he went and I can take you over there and show you just where he went, and where he stopped and turned around and the way he come across.

Q. Well, of course, I can't now--well, all right, Elmore appeared to you calm, when he told you what was wrong, did he? A. He did.

Q. And he had these crab nets in his possession? A. I can't say, he had a package, I didn't know at the time what they were.

Q. He, at any rate, had a package under his arm, is that right? A. Yes.

Q. Now, you were never taken to the station house, were you? A. I was taken up with the detective in a car.

Q. Yes. You said before that you remained there and when you were asked about what happened to Elmore, you told the Court and the Jury he went off in an automobile, that is correct, of course? A. Well, that is--

Q. Well up to that time you hadn't gone to the station house, had you? A. No.

Q. How soon after that did you go to the station house? A. Well, I can't tell you how soon after.

Q. Would you say it was half an hour after? A. Oh, maybe more.

Q. More. Did any police officer remain with you after Elmore left in this automobile? A. Oh, there was a bunch of policemen after I left there.

Q. Yes. And who asked you to go to the station house? A. The detective.

Q. And what detective is that? A. Cosgrove, I believe he said his name was.

Q. I see. So it wasn't Cosgrove who went with Elmore in the car, was it? A. Not that I know of.

Q. Well, do you know Detective Murphy? A. I do not.

Q. Do you know anybody by the name of Murphy? A. I do.

Q. Who? A. I know a man by the name of Murphy who was with me when I was over to the--we went over to the bungalow.

Q. Yes. And is that the same Murphy whose name you mentioned on direct examination here? A. Yes, Murphy.

Q. Right. All right. Now, you finally got to the station house and you had a talk with some one, didn't you? A. I did.

Q. And who did you talk with? A. I don't know

who it was.

Q. Was it a detective? A. I couldn't tell you because I couldn't tell if he was a detective or what he was.

Q. Well, it was someone in authority, wasn't it? A. It was, yes.

Q. Did he question you? How long did he question you? A. Oh, maybe about five minutes, ten minutes, something like that.

Q. And after he had questioned you, you went about your business, is that right? A. Yes.

Q. Now, can you help us out on what kind of a day August 12th was, was it a sunny, bright day? A. Well, it was a pretty fair day.

Q. Was the sun shining? A. It was shining off and on.

Mr. Innes : May I say, Mr. Gulotta, that this all occurred on the 13th, as far as this is concerned.

Mr. Gulotta: I beg your pardon. Thank you very much, Mr. Innes. That is the 13th I have reference to.

By Mr. Gulotta:

Q. And you said that it was--the sun was shining off and on? A. That is right.

Q. Do you remember whether there had been any rains shortly prior to the 13th of August? A. Why, I can't state, there are rains pretty near every day down there, but I won't--

Q. Now, you spend your time fishing down there in the summer? A. I go fishing, yes. I spend--

Q. There is considerable crabbing by different people around that neighborhood, isn't there? A. Oh, plenty of it.

**Q. Plenty of crabbing. And would you say that on that day the marshlands were dry or reasonably dry, or wet? A. Well, they are not reasonably dry, hardly at any time.**

Q. At any time? A. Yes.

**Q. They are always wet, aren't they? A. They are always wet and damp.**

Q. Yes. Somebody from my office came to see

you, is that right, Mr. Haff? A. I don't know--there was a man came to see me, I don't know whether--

Q. Did a man by the name of McKittrick come to see you? A. He did.

Q. And did he repeat to you that he was an investigator sent there from the attorney for the defense in this case? A. He came and saw me, and he come again and give me a summons.

Q. Yes. That is a subpoena. A. Subpoena.

Q. To be here? A. Yes.

Q. Now, you had, before you were served with that subpoena, talked with this Mr. McKittrick. did you not? A. We had a very few words, yes.

Q. And did you have these few words to say to Mr. McKittrick? That Elmore--that you asked Elmore, "What the hell do you want? " And he said, "There is a little child over there. " Did you have that few words to say? A. I didn't say child at all.

Q. I see. You didn't say child at all to Mr. McKittrick? A. Not to Mr. McKittrick, no.

Q. And you are sure about that? A. I am.

Q. Well, now, you were earnest in trying to tell everything you knew to Mr. McKittrick, weren't you? A. I told him very little of anything.

Q. I see. So that investigation, so far as you are concerned, was more or less fruitless, because you told him little or nothing? A. He didn't ask me very much of anything.

Q. Had anybody told you not to tell anybody anything? A. Nobody told me not to tell anybody.

Q. Had anybody from the District Attorney's Office said to you if anybody comes to you who is not from the District Attorney's Office not to tell them anything? A. No, they didn't tell me that.

Q. All right. Now, you had a talk with the District Attorney in this case, did you not?

A. I had a talk with a man in his office.

Q. Yes, and you told him what you knew about it? A. I told him just the same.

Q. And you told him honestly what you knew about it, didn't you? A. Yes.

Q. But, at the same time you didn't tell McKittrick much of anything, did you? A. Much of anything, no.

Mr. Gulotta : All right, that is all.

Mr. Innes : That is all, Mr. Haff. Is Miss Goller here?

SELMA GOLLER, 1559 Clinton Place, Hillside, 565 New Jersey, called as a witness in behalf of the People, first being duly sworn, testified as follows :

Direct examination

By Mr. Innes :

Q. Now, Miss Goller, during the month of August last, were you employed at or near South Beach in this County? A. Yes. My father had a hotel there.

Q. And what hotel is that? A. **The Silver Wave**.

Q. And you were attending a booth or something there, were you, on August 12th? A. Yes, he has a concession at the Hotel.

Q. And you were attending that concession? A. Yes.

Q. And that is on the boardwalk near the stores, isn't it? A. Well, that--not directly in front of the boardwalk. You see there are no concessions right up next to it.

Q. Yes. A. But, right as far back--

Q. Well, as far back as the old line? A. Yes.

Q. The old line of buildings on the beach? A. Yes.

Q. Now, did you know this little girl, Joan Kuleba ? A. Yes, I did.

Q. Did you see her on the 12th of August last? A. Yes, I did.

Q. Where did you see her? A. She was running past, she ran past rather.

Q. I see. You had known her at that time, had you? A. Yes.

Q. You had seen her on previous summers there, had you? A. Yes, her people had one of our bungalows two years before.

Q. And at about what time was it you saw her? **A. Well, it must have been shortly after lunch because I usually have my lunch about twelve-thirty, and she ran past about five minutes after I had come out.**

Q. I see. And how was she dressed at the time? A. I don't remember.

Q. You don't remember. But, you do recognize-- A. Yes, because she called me--

Q. What is that? A. She called me, that is how I remember seeing her.

Q. She spoke to you? A. No, she just said, "Hello." Called me, my name, and said, "Hello."

Q. She said, "Hello." She had light curly hair, did she not? A. Yes.

Q. And quite a profuse lot of hair? A. Yes, she had a lot of hair, very curly.

Q. You don't remember how she was dressed? A. No, I don't.

Mr. Innes : All right, that is all.

Cross-examination by Mr. Gulotta:

Q. Now, Miss Goller, your place or your father's place down near the beach is known as the Silver Wave Hotel, is it? A. Yes.

Q. And that is a licensed restaurant and bar, isn't it? A. Yes.

Q. For the consumption of liquor and wines on the premises, as I understand it? A. Yes.

Q. Now, you, on this 12th day of August, 1937, had had your lunch? A. Yes.

Q. And how long before that day and that time had you known this little girl? A. Well, I believe it was either two or three years before this day that her people had had a bungalow, one of our bungalows.

Q. Yes. Of course, at that time, the girl was about a year old, wasn't she? A. Yes.

Q. Now, is that the only time you saw her on this day? A. On August 12th, you mean?

Q. Yes. A. Yes.

Q. And there are people down at the beach, especially the month of August, are there not, that go around in bathing suits? A. Yes.

Q. And, of course, as you stand near your place, some one goes by, fully dressed, you might say, well, if you were asked later on, you don't know how they were dressed, is that right because so many people go up and down, is that right? A. Yes.

Q. Now, in like manner, if you saw someone wearing a bathing suit, at least you would know that person was wearing a bathing suit from where you would be looking, wouldn't you? A. Well, if I--if I knew the person, if I notice anything outstanding about them.

Q. I think you would, wouldn't you, Miss Goller? A. Yes.

Q. Now, you had known this little girl for about three years, hadn't you? A. Yes.

Q. And, as I understand it, at the present time, you can't tell us how she was dressed?

A. No.

Mr. Gulotta : That is all.

Mr. Innes : That is all.

[Ed. Note: Did Mr. Gulotta bungle this? It is because of this testimony that the police concentrated on the crime happening after 12:25, and that is why Selma Goller's testimony conflicts with Mrs. Lesandi's. This was a most vital point that Mr. Gulotta should have pursued. Instead he is trying to link the good memory of Goller as compared to "superhuman" memory in testimony below, which is a minor point in comparison. What if instead of not being able to remember the red bathing suit, she could not remember what Joan Kuleba was wearing on the day she actually saw her? It is frustrating that this point is not fleshed out. What was the conversation between Aunt Lesandi and Selma Goller and why did Aunt Lesandi doubt the time frame?]

Lieutenant HOWARD W. GIFFORD, New York

City Police Department, Shield Number 223, 9th Detective District, called as a witness in behalf of the People, first being duly sworn, testified as follows :

Direct examination by Mr. Innes :

Q. Officer, how long have you been connected with the Detective Division in this County? A. Since 1927.

Q. Were you at the 120th Precinct Station House on the afternoon of August 13th? A. Yes.

Q. And were you present at the time when I was there? A. Yes.

Q. And were you present at the time when this paper, People's Exhibit No. 3, was prepared and submitted to the defendant? A. That was on the 14th.

Q. 14th? A. 14th, yes.

Q. That is right. Now, did you see the defendant sign this paper? A. I did.

Q. And did you sign it as a witness? A. I did.

Q. Will you tell the Court and Jury under what circumstances that paper was presented to the defendant, Elmore?

Mr. Gulotta : I object to that, if your Honor pleases, it is too vague. I believe there is too much latitude in that question. Under what circumstances?

The Court : Tell us first who was present when the paper was signed. A. How is that?

The Court : Tell us first who was present when the paper was signed?

The Witness: Detective Cosgrove, Detective Hagarty, Detective Marrinan, the defendant and myself.

By Mr. Innes :

Q. And where was that paper signed? A. On the second floor of the 120th Precinct Station House.

Q. Do you know by whom it was prepared? A. I do.

Q. And who prepared it? A. Detective Marrinan.

Q. And after it was prepared, was it handed to the defendant? A. I handed it to the defendant, yes.

Q. And what, if anything, did he say when you

handed it to him? A. I asked the defendant to read it and he said he couldn't read it, he didn't have his glasses.

Q. Yes. A. So I gave him my glasses and he read the paper to me, to us.

Q. Read it aloud? A. He did.

Q. And after it was read, what did he say? A. I asked him, I said, "is that the truth, the whole truth and nothing but the truth? " And he said it is. And I asked him to sign it. I lent him my pen and he signed it.

Q. Yes. Now, after this paper was signed, did you say something about it? A. I did.

Q. Tell us what you said to him and what he said to you? A. I went over and sat on the sofa along side of him and asked him to have a cigarette, which he had. I had one myself. Now, I says, "Mr. Elmore, " I says, "there are certain things that I am not quite clear on. Will you enlighten me? " And he says he would. I said to him, I says, "How is it that you walked this little girl so far as you say you did and her feet were clean? "

Q. Yes. A. Her feet were **perfectly clean** and well, he says, **"After I got her in the cellar I took her shoes off, put one in each pocket and took them down and put them on the beach front.**

Q. Yes. Did he tell you where he put them? A. He did.

Q. Tell us what he said? A. He said he was asked if there was any big object around where he placed the shoes? He says, "Yes, along side a flat bottom boat, turned upside down. "

Q. Nothing was said by him before that time as to the flat bottom boat? A. Nothing.

Q. He volunteered that himself? A. He did.

Mr. Innes : That is all.

Cross-examination by Mr. Gulotta:

Q. Now, officer, you didn't know before you talked to the defendant where those shoes were, did you? A. That is right.

Q. Do you know any members of the police department that did? A. I do.

Q. Who? A. Pagana, and Detective Bohan.

Q. They knew exactly where those shoes were before you asked Elmore? A. They knew where they found them, yes.

Q. Who found them? A. Detective Pagana and Detective Bohan.

Q. And you had knowledge of that fact when you were interrogating Elmore about, it didn't you? A. Yes, I did.

Q. Yes. How many officers, detectives, were present when Elmore signed that statement? A. There were Detective Cosgrove, Hagarty, Marrinan and myself, there was, might have been one more, but I am not sure.

Q. And you were all in close proximity to him, were you? A. We were, yes.

Q. Now, you knew about the fact that your brother officers knew about those shoes before Elmore signed the statement? A. I knew that they found them, yes.

Q. But, you didn't incorporate that in your statement, did you? A. In my statement?

Q. In the statement obtained from the defendant? A. The confession?

Q. Yes. A. I had nothing to do with that.

Q. I see. Well, since you had nothing to do with it, you did ask the defendant--"There is one thing that is on my mind, " you said? A. Yes.

Q. "How is it that the little girl's feet were clean whereas you tell us that you walked this long circuitous route? " You did say that, didn't you? A. I did.

Q. And wasn't that on your mind, immediately before this statement was signed? A. I had nothing to do with the statement.

Q. Yes. You were right there when it was being prepared, weren't you? A. In and out, yes.

Q. Yes, in and out. Was the knowledge of the fact that you knew your brother officers had found the shoes, was it with that knowledge in mind that you asked Elmore the question that you did? A. It was.

Q. It was, wasn't it? A. It was.

126

Mr. Gulotta : That is all.

By Mr. Gulotta:

Q. Officer, you were there from the time, August 13th, until that statement, that first statement was signed, weren't you? A. Not all the time.

Q. Well, how much of the time? A. Well, part of the time.

Q. Did you go down to the morgue with Elmore? A. I didn't.

Q. Was Inspector Lyons with you at any of the time? A. Not with me, no. He was in the building.

Q. Were you with Pagana at any time? A. Yes.

Q. Were you with Pagana when he was making a search for the shoes? A. I was not.

Q. You learned about the shoes from Pagana as a statement he made to you, not as the result of any investigation you made, is that right? A. Yes.

Q. And you are in charge of the detectives at the 120th Precinct, aren't you? A. I was at that time.

Q. Yes. At that time, I mean. A. Yes.

Q. And did you have anything to do with the directions which were given to Officer Pagano? A. I didn't quite understand the question.

Q. Did you have anything to do with the directions given to Officer Pagano concerning the investigation of this case? A. Part of the time.

Q. Part of the time? A. Yes.

Q. Well, you were in charge, weren't you? A. Yes, but the inspector was there.

Q. Did you give instructions as to the matter of locating those shoes? A. I did not.

Q. Did it occur to you at all, until you were told? A. I wasn't there at the time.

Mr. Gulotta : I think that is all.

Redirect examination

By Mr. Innes :

Q. Officer, you had in mind that the shoes had been found on the beach? A. I knew it.

Q. Near Crane's Hotel? A. Yes.

Q. At the time when you interrogated the defendant? A. Yes.

Q. And you didn't know how they got there at that time, did you? A. I didn't.

Q. And the purpose of your interrogation--was to ask the defendant? A. Right.

Q. And he told you that he put them in his pocket, one in each pocket and placed them near this flat bottom boat?

Mr. Gulotta : I object to that as leading.

Mr. Innes : I was simply restating--

The Court : This officer didn't testify to that, that he put these in his pocket. Objection sustained.

Mr. Innes : Yes, he did.

The Court : Did you testify to that, officer?

The Witness : I did.

The Court : On your direct examination?

The Witness : I think so.

By Mr. Innes:

Q. **What did the defendant say to you with reference to the shoes? A. I asked him about the shoes and he said that--he took her shoes off, put one in each pocket and took them down and placed them on the beach.**

The Court : All right.

Mr. Innes: Yes, that is my recollection. That is all, Officer. Now, Officer Bohan.

JAMES A. BOHAN, Shield No. 1231, 120th Squad Detective, New York City Police Department, called as a witness in behalf of the People, first being duly sworn, testified as follows :

Direct examination by Mr. Innes :

Q. Officer, was the fact of finding the body of this little girl in this bungalow brought to your attention at some time on the afternoon of August 13th? A. Yes, it was.

Q. And did you go to the bungalow that afternoon? A. Yes, I did.

Q. And did you go any other place? A. Yes, I did.

Q. And where did you go? A. On the afternoon of August 13th?

Q. Yes. A. I went to the Station House at St. George.

Q. Yes, on the 12th of August, was the matter of the disappearance of this little girl brought to your attention? A. Yes, it was about 6:00 P. M. I was notified that there was a little girl missing from down at South Beach, Bungalow No. 8, I believe. Detective Cosgrove was assigned to the case and he told me that if I hadn't heard anything from the family, would I go down and look around, so Detective Pagana and I went down about, about a quarter to seven we arrived at the bungalow, I asked the aunt of the child who had reported her, Mrs. Lesandi, I believe her name is, if she had heard anything from the child. "No, " she said, "We haven't heard a word."

Mr. Gulotta : I am going to object to it.

Mr. Innes : If that is objected to, I consent to its being stricken out.

The Court : Strike it out.

By Mr. Innes :

Q. And you had a talk with the aunt, Mrs. Lesandi? A. I did.

Q. And then after that time what did you do? A. In company of Detective Pagana I went along the beach, the waterfront of the beach, in front of Crane's Hotel, I was walking along looking at the waterfront there. I observed a little pair of sandals on the beach. I picked them up and I said to Detective Pagana, I said, "Here. "

Q. No, you can't tell us that. A. So I walked across the street to the bungalow, to the aunt of the child, and I said, "Are these the child's shoes? " And she said, "Yes. "

Mr. Gulotta : I object to that, if your Honor pleases, as not binding on this defendant.

The Court : Objection sustained.

Mr. Innes : All right.

Mr. Gulotta : I move to strike out the answer.

The Court : Strike it out.

By Mr. Innes :

Q. You had a talk with the aunt? A. I did.

Q. And showed her the shoes? A. Yes.

Q. And she said something to you at the time? A. Yes.

Q. Now, then, I show you these little shoes and ask you if those are the ones that you picked up in front of Crane's Hotel? A. Yes, they are the shoes.

Q. Were they near any object on the beach? A. Yes, they were about 2 1/2 foot to the left of the flat bottom boat turned upside down on the beach, about 10 or 12 feet from the high water line on the sand.

Q. Yes. And, were you there at the time when the police were dredging in the waters?

A. Yes, I notified the marine Division.

Mr. Gulotta : I object to that as not binding on the defendant.

The Court : Objection overruled.

A. I was there when the Marine boat arrived, and I was there when they were grappling around, trying to locate the body.

Mr. Innes : All right, that is all.

Cross-examination by Mr. Gulotta:

Q. Now, Officer Bohan, you, of course, are acquainted with your superior officer Gifford, aren't you? A. Yes, I am.

Q. And know that he has just been testifying in this case? A. That's right.

Q. Now, did he give you any instructions regarding an investigation in this case? A. Yes, he instructed me.

Q. All right, now, he did, did he? A. Yes.

Q. Now, when did he give you those instructions? A. In the night of the 14th.

Q. August 14th, is that right? A. That is right.

Q. Did you talk to him about this case before the night of August 14th? A. Well, yes, I spoke to all of them over there about it.

Q. I have particular regard for the proposition as to whether or not you reported to him the finding of the girl's shoes? A. No, I didn't report to Lieutenant Gifford of finding the girl's shoes.

Q. Who did you report it to? A. I reported it to Inspector McGrath and Detective Cosgrove.

Q. And Inspector Lyons--I see. And was a report to be made to Detective Gifford? A. Lieutenant Gifford.

Q. All right, Lieutenant Gifford. A. Yes, Lieutenant Gifford was squad commander that night.

Q. Yes. And he knew about the finding of those shoes before August 14th, didn't he? A. Well, I don't--I can't answer that.

Q. No, but did you report it to him? A. No, I didn't report it to him.

Q. Did anyone else that you know report it to him? A. I can't answer that.

Q. Do I understand you to say that you made a find of a pair of shoes? A. That is right.

Q. Under a situation where a little girl was reported missing, and you didn't report the finding to your superior officer? A. Yes, I did report it to my superior officer. I reported it to Inspector McGrath and to Detective Cosgrove, who was assigned to the case.

Q. Yes. And you reported the finding of those shoes on the night of August 12th, didn't you? A. That is right.

Q. Now, do you know how long this little girl had been missing on August 12th? A. I believe around one o'clock or something. I am not sure, I don't know the exact time.

Q. One o'clock? A. It was six o'clock when I was first notified of it.

Q. Who first gave you any directions or orders concerning the disappearance of this child? A. Well, at six o'clock I reported for night duty at the 120th Squad Office and Detective Cosgrove told me that there was a little girl missing.

Q. All right. You learned it about six o'clock? A.

About six o'clock.

Q. Do you know whether or not any of your brother officers were already out on the case? I believe Detective Cosgrove and Hagarty were out.

Q. Were already out on the case. Now, what kind of a report did you make to Inspector McGrath about the finding of the shoes? A. I didn't have, just a verbal conversation with him.

Q. I see. And the Inspector is a superior officer to Lieutenant Gifford, isn't he? A. That is right, yes.

Q. Were you there on the night of August 14th, at about a quarter of six, at the station house? A. Yes, I was.

Q. And was Elmore there? A. He was.

Q. And was Inspector Lyons there? A. Yes.

Q. Yes. And was Inspector McGrath there? A. Yes.

Q. And was Lieutenant Gifford there? A. Yes.

Q. And was Officer Hagarty there? A. Yes.

Q. And was Officer Hagarty there? A. Yes.

Q. And, of course, you were there? A. Yes.

Q. And was Detective Thomas Cosgrove there? A. Yes.

Q. Were there any other detectives? A. Yes, there were quite a few other detectives.

Q. How many in all, about, were there? A. Well, I don't--I would say around twelve.

Q. Twelve. And it was during the time ; the twelve officers of the law were there, in close proximity to this defendant, I take it? A. No, sir.

Q. In the same room? A. No, sir.

Q. Well, where? A. We were downstairs in the Squad Room, Inspector Lyons, Inspector McGrath, Lieutenant Gifford, and I believe Detective Cosgrove and Hagarty and one or two others were upstairs with the defendant.

Q. Were you present when Elmore signed the statement? A. No, sir, I wasn't.

Q. Do you know who was? A. No, sir, I don't.

Mr. Gulotta : That is all.

Mr. Innes : That is all. Officer Pagana.

Detective ROMOLO PAGANA, Shield No. 43, 9th Detective District, New York City, Police Dept., called as a witness in behalf of the People, being first duly sworn, testified as follows :

Direct examination by Mr. Innes :
Q. Now, Officer, was your attention called to the so-called disappearance of the little girl at South Beach at some time during the evening of August 12th? A. Yes.
Q. Yes. And did you accompany Officer Bohan to South Beach? A. I did, yes.
Q. And were you there during all the time that he was there? A. I was.
Q. Were you with him when he picked up a pair of shoes near an overturned boat in front of Crane's Hotel, or near the Crane's Hotel? A. I was.
Q. And I show you the shoes and ask you if you recognize them, as the ones that you found? A. I do, those are the shoes.
Q. Found, Officer Bohan picked up? A. Yes.
Q. You were with him at the time, were you? A. Yes.
Mr. Innes : I think that is all. Will the Court excuse me just a moment?
The Court : Yes.
Mr. Gulotta : May I continue?
Mr. Innes : Yes.

Cross-examination by Mr. Gulotta:
Q. Officer Pagana, these shoes look to you about the same as when you found them, is that right? Will you take them up and inspect them? **A. Well, they are much dryer now than they were then.**
**Q. They were wet at the time? A. They were much more wet than they are just now.**
Q. I see. Save for that difference, they are the same? A. Yes.

Q. As when you found them? A. Yes.

Q. And there is no doubt about that in your mind? A. No, there isn't.

**Q. And when you say they were wet, were they soggy? A. Well, they had been under water and they had been used and they are much more wet than they are now.**

**Q. Yes. Visibly damp, were they? A. Yes, they were, yes.**

**Q. To sight and to touch? A. That is right.**

**Q. You didn't see any mud on those shoes, did you? A. Well, there was some sand around it, yes.**

**Q. Around where? A. Well, covering the front part of the shoe and I believe, if I remember right, there was some on the inside of the shoes, not much sand.**

**Q. Such sand as you pick up when you play on the beach? A. That is right.**

**Q. But,, outside of that, nothing else? A. No.**

Q. Now, you were with Officer Bohan about six o'clock on the night of August 12th?

A. I was.

Q. And a disappearance of a little girl had been reported to you? A. No, sir.

Q. How did you--how were you notified? A. The disappearance of the child had been reported some time during that afternoon.

Q. Yes. What time did you learn about it? A. Well, it was about six o'clock.

Q. About six o'clock, that is what I mean? And you proceeded down towards the beach, didn't you? A. At about seven o'clock, yes, sir, I did.

Q. And then there came a time when you and Officer Bohan found these shoes? A. That is right.

Q. Did you go back to the station house? A. That night?

Q. Yes. A. Yes, we did.

Q. Yes, and took these shoes with you? A. No, sir.

**Q. And where did you--what did you do with**

the shoes? A. We left the shoes with the child's aunt.

Q. The child's aunt? You knew about this time that the disappearance of a little girl had been reported, is that right? A. Yes, sir, I did.

Q. And you found these shoes, didn't you? A. I did.

Q. And, after finding them, was that significant to you? A. Yes, sir.

Q. So significant, was it not, that they were dredging the bay for the body? A. Well, as a result of finding those shoes on the beach, Detective Bohan notified the Harbor Police and they were grappling for the child, we assumed she was drowned.

Q. But,, nevertheless, the shoes were left with the mother? A. With the aunt.

Q. With the aunt, I mean? A. Yes.

[Ed. Note: Now it is obvious why Aunt Lesandi made a point of pointing out the shoes were dry. How did she know Det. Pagana or someone was going to testify they were wet? She must have heard a strategy session of sorts. The strategy may have been to counter any claim that Lieutenant Gifford fed the fact of the shoes being found near the boat to Elmore, and at the same time wet shoes would connect Elmore with the crime, the only physical evidence to do so. It would have worked perfectly if Aunt Lesandi had not blurted out that the shoes were dry. It worked anyway, but not perfectly, because everyone ignored that contradiction.]

Q. And they were not brought to the station house? A. Not by me.

Q. Now, do you know when anybody went back to the aunt's house to get these shoes? A. I do not.

Q. Do you know when they came into the possession of the police department? A. I do not.

Q. You haven't seen them since that day? A. I have not.

Q. Now, who was on duty on the date of August

12th, 1937, after six o'clock? A. At the police station?

Q. Yes. A. You mean detectives?

Q. Yes. A. I was, Detective Bohan and myself.

Q. Yes, and was Lieutenant Gifford on duty? A. That night?

Q. Yes, sir. A. I don't remember.

Q. I see. A superior officer was on duty, wasn't he? A. There was.

Q. Who was that? A. Well, we left the office shortly before seven o'clock and we went down to South Beach and there we remained until about ten o'clock.

Q. Yes. A. And we were ordered from there to go to this collapse, over in Jersey Street, where those people were killed.

Q. Yes. A. To cover that job, and Detectives Cosgrove and Hagarty were left down to the beach.

Q. Right. A. We went to the scene of this thing over in Jersey Street.

**Q. You misunderstand me, officer, I don't like to break in on your narrative, but the question is who was the superior officer, if you know, that was on duty after six o'clock at the station house? A. I didn't see anybody after the time we went to Jersey Street.**

Q. All right. That answers my question. Thank you. Now, did you make a report about the finding of the shoes that evening? A. Yes, sir.

Q. And, to whom did you report it? A. To Detective Cosgrove, that was handling the case, when he came down there, we told him we found the shoes and gave them to the aunt.

Q. Did you or Detective Bohan say anything to Inspector Lyons about it? A. Not that night. I didn't see Inspector Lyons that night.

Q. Did you or Detective Bohan say anything to Inspector McGrath about it? A. I believe Detective Bohan spoke to Inspector McGrath over the phone and he told him that he found the shoes.

Q. All right.

Mr. Gulotta : All right, that is all.

Mr. Innes : That is all, officer, thank you. William Flick.

Mr. Gulotta : I wonder if I could have a five minute recess before this witness is sworn?

The Court : All right. Gentlemen, we will take a recess for five or ten minutes. You can go upstairs. Do not discuss this case or come to any conclusion until the case is finally submitted to you and you retire to your jury room.

(Whereupon at 11:21 A. M. , the Court recessed until 11:45 A. M. )

209 William A. Flick--For People--Direct. 625

Court Clerk Kosman : People against Samuel Elmore.

(Both sides were ready. )

(Whereupon the Jury was polled and all Jurors answered present. )

The Court : Notify all witnesses on the part of the defense to come here tomorrow morning.

Court Clerk Kosman : All witnesses inside the Court Room.

The Court : You can notify them out in the hall, have the Sheriff notify them.

Court Clerk Kosman : All witnesses on behalf of the defendant will appear here tomorrow morning without further notice or subpoena.

WILLIAM A. FLICK, 17 Barry Street, Rossville, Staten Island, New York, called as a witness in behalf of the People, first being duly sworn, testified as follows :

Direct examination by Mr. Innes :

Q. Mr. Flick, what is your business at the present? A. I am a coach operator for the Staten Island Coach Company.

Q. And how long have you been such an operator? A. Up till today.

Q. Now, how long? A. Nine months.

Q. And, do you operate different routes as such operator? A. Why, we have it picked, three or four times a year, we are on different routes, sometimes four months, that is at a stretch, sometimes five months at a stretch. We have what we call Fall, Summer and Mid-Winter picks.

Q. I see. Now, on August 12th last, what was your run as such operator? A. I was working on **route No. 2,** South Beach, Villa-McClean Avenue.

Q. And where did that--will you describe the route from the time that you started until you finished? A. I left St. George ferry, proceeded along Bay Street, to--

Q. I mean, do you start at the ferry? A. That is right.

Q. I see. All right, all right. A. Start at St. George ferry, proceed along Bay Street, Wadsworth Avenue, turn left on Wadsworth Avenue, into Tompkins Avenue, turn right on Tompkins Avenue into McClean Avenue, continue on along McClean Avenue until you come to Norway, you turn left into Norway, you continue about four blocks on Norway, you make a left turn into Olympia Boulevard, you proceed along Olympia Boulevard to Sand Lane, then make a right turn to South Beach, which is our terminal there, and turn around.

Q. And, do you run on schedule? A. Absolutely, as near as possible, as we possibly can.

Q. Now, then, were you an operator on that route on the 12th day of August, this year? A. I was.

Q. And, at about 1:00 o'clock or after one, in that afternoon, was your bus run towards South Beach on Norway Avenue and Olympia Boulevard? A. I was on Norway Avenue at that time.

Q. Was your attention attracted to something that you saw at that time? A. It was.

Mr. Gulotta : Just a moment. I object to that on the ground that the time is not definitely stated.

The Court : He said about one o'clock.

Mr. Gulotta: After one, he said.

Mr. Innes : I am going to fix the time later on.

Mr. Gulotta: All right.

The Court : All right.

By Mr. Innes :

Q. What attracted your attention at that time, Mr. Flick? A. Why, I seen a man walking on the sidewalk on my right with a little girl ahead of him in a red bathing suit, and it looked very peculiar, the way they were walking.

Mr. Gulotta : I object to that, and I move to strike it out.

The Court : Strike it out.

Mr. Innes : That is consented to.

By Mr. Innes :

Q. Well, your attention was attracted to him for some reason, is that right? A. That is right.

Q. Now, without telling what it was, on what part of your route, did you see this man and the little girl in the red bathing suit? A. **Between Cameron and Scott Avenue, on Norway Avenue.**

Q. And in which direction were they walking? A. They were walking toward the beach.

Q. On which side of the--of your bus were they walking? A. On the right hand side of the street, on the right hand side of my bus.

Q. Did you have them under observation for any length of time? A. For a period of about a, minute, a minute and a half.

Q. Were you on time? A. I was within minute.

Q. And would you fix the time that you saw this man and the little girl? A. Between 1:00 and 1:01, one minute after one that afternoon.

Q. I see. And what was your time at your terminal? A. At 1:15--at the terminal.

Q. Yes. A. I was due at the terminal at 1:15.

Q. And you say it was shortly after 1:00 o'clock? A. Beg pardon. I made a mistake. It was between 1:10 and 1:11 and I was due at the terminal at 1:15.

Q. I see, about how large was the child? A. Why the child looked like she was about six years old to me, a girl would be about six years old, I can't say just how tall or anything she was.

Q. Did you, did you see her face? A. No, I didn't.

Q. Could you tell us why you didn't? A. Why, as I passed--

Mr. Gulotta : I object to that as incompetent, irrelevant and immaterial.

The Court : Objection sustained. Could you or could you not?

The Witness : No, I couldn't see her face.

By Mr. Innes :

Q. Did you see the face of the man? A. I did that.

Q. And did you stop, cause your bus to decrease its speed? A. Why, I didn't exactly come to a complete stop, but I did slow down to almost a stop.

Q. And while you were observing this man? A. That is right.

Q. And you say they were walking in a direction toward the beach? A. That is right.

Q. Do you see that man in the court room? A. Yes, I do.

Q. And who is he? A. That gentleman right there, seated right there.

Q. And he is the defendant in this case, Samuel Elmore? A. He is the man that I seen walking on the sidewalk that day.

Q. How was he dressed at that time, Mr. Flick? A. Well, as near as I can explain, he had what I would call a pair of **dirty gray trousers** on and a white shirt.

Q. Yes. A. He didn't have any hat and he had something in his left hand which I can't say what it was, but he was carrying something in his hand.

Q. What did it appear to you to be? A. It appeared like something--

Mr. Gulotta: I object to that as already answered.

The Court : Objection sustained.

Mr. Innes : All right.

By Mr. Innes :

Q. Will you describe as near as you can what you saw?

Mr. Gulotta : Same objection, if your Honor pleases, on the ground the witness has already answered.

The Court : I will let him describe what he had in his hand. A. Well, it appeared to me, it looked like a glass.

Mr. Gulotta: I am going to object what it looked like.

The Court : Describe the package, whatever it was, the size of the package, whether it was wrapped, or unwrapped, or anything, in that connection. A. Well, it wasn't wrapped, it was a thing, an object I will say, about 10 or 12 inches in length, and it was glass, whatever it was I can't say, whether it was a pitcher or what it was.

By Mr. Innes :

Q. It was something glass? A. That is true.

Q. And you say that the defendant was under your observation for about a minute? A. That is right.

Q. He was walking along, was he? A. Yes.

Q. Now, is there anything that attracted you so far as the little girl was concerned? A. Why, yes, she was walking ahead of him, she was about, I would say, two or three feet ahead and she kept turning around as if she looked like she was--

Mr. Gulotta : I object to that and move to strike that out.

The Court : All right, strike it out.

Q. Her face was--

Mr. Gulotta: I object to this as leading.

Mr. Innes: All right.

By Mr. Innes :

**Q. Could you see her face? A. No, sir. I couldn't see her face.**

Q. Could you describe her hair that you saw? A. Yes. She had light curly hair, it was hanging down.

Q. Could you--you say it was a red bathing suit she had on? A. That is right.

Q. And do you know whether or not she had anything on her feet? A. Well, she didn't walk as if she was barefooted on those cinders that were on the sidewalk.

Mr. Gulotta. : That is objected to and I move to

strike it out.

The Court : Objection sustained. Strike it out.

By Mr. Innes :

**Q. You didn't notice anything on her feet then? A. No, I couldn't get a view of her feet because of the grass.**

Mr. Gulotta: I object to it because--

The Court : Strike it out, the answer is "No. "

By Mr. Innes :

Q. Now, then, was the bathing suit that you saw something on that color?

Mr. Gulotta : I object to that as too speculative, something like this.

The Court : He said it was a red bathing suit, I will permit him to describe whether it was a bathing suit of that particular color of red.

Mr. Innes : All right.

By Mr. Innes :

**A. It was a red bathing suit something on that style, I couldn't exactly say it was that color.**

Mr. Innes : All right, that is all.

Cross-examination by Mr. Gulotta:

Q. Now, Mr. Flick, how long have you been an operator for the bus company? A. Nine months up till the present month.

Q. And, that length of time for the Richmond Bus Company? A. Staten Island Coach.

Q. Staten Island Coach Company, and how long have you been on the route that you have described as route #2, Villa-McClean Avenue? A. Well, I couldn't exactly tell you how long, but it is within a period of four, to four and one-half months, I was on that route, I was practically there all summer.

Q. And you have, I take it, become familiar with that route, have you not? A. Very much so.

Q. Now, is Norway Avenue a stop street? A. Is Norway?

Q. For the bus? A. No, not to my knowledge.

Q. In other words, ordinarily speaking, there is nothing to stop for unless there is a passenger? A. That is true.

Q. To stop for, is that right. ? A. That is true.

Q. Now, when you first found this little girl, your bus was in motion, was it not? A. Yes, sir.

Q. Were there any passengers aboard the bus? A. Yes, I had a few. I can't just recall, I don't think I had over five at the most on that day.

**Q. And, were these five people men, women or children? A. Why, that I couldn't very well explain.**

Q. Now, that is very hard for you to tell us whether or not these five passengers were men, women or children, isn't it? A. Yes, sir.

Q. Where would you have picked these five passengers up? A. I pick up all along the route.

Q. From what point? A. St. George in.

Q. I see. Well, your route is from St. George to South Beach, isn't it? A. Yes, sir.

Q. When you got to South Beach, did every one get off the bus? A. What was left got off.

Q. Yes. So that there was a time while you were at South Beach, when your bus was empty of passengers, that is true? A. Yes.

Q. So that you must have picked up these passengers from a point where you last stopped at South Beach and Norway Avenue, is that right? A. Counsellor, you are a kind of a little off. I was inbound to South Beach, you are thinking about outbound, from South Beach, are you not?

Q. You were bound to South Beach? A. That is true.

Q. I see. All right. So that you had five passengers on there, is that right? A. I say about five passengers.

Q. And these five passengers had paid their fare, had they not? A. That is right.

Q. They had paid their fare at that point before getting off? Not upon getting off, is that right? A. That is right.

Q. And, I understood you to say definitely that as you could state now, you don't know whether they were men, women or children, is that right? A. Yes.

Q. Now, you have a mirror in front of you as you drive along, haven't you? A. That is right.

Q. Is that mirror adjusted that you are able to see passengers seated in the bus? A. A certain portion of them, yes.

Q. And, were any of these five people seated along any portion that you could see through that mirror? A. Why, I couldn't answer that question now, that is quite awhile ago.

Q. Yes. In other words, you weren't looking out for that feature of the thing at all? A. At my passengers?

Q. Yes. A. Just explain that again, I didn't quite understand it.

Q. Well, I am asking you to explain why you can't explain where these people were seated, because you couldn't see them through the glass, is that right? A. Yes, that is right.

Q. And you will now testify that you didn't see any of them through this glass in front of you, is that correct? A. At that time, no, I wasn't looking in it.

Q. Now, as you were proceeding along at or about the time that you first saw the little girl walking, and as you have said, you saw the defendant, Elmore, walking on the side walk, how many miles an hour would you say your bus was traveling? A. Why, I wasn't traveling very fast, because when we make--

Q. I didn't say that you were, I asked you. A. I would say about five miles an hour.

Q. Five miles an hour, and I understood you to say that when you saw what you described as having seen, you slowed down your bus? A. That is true.

Q. But,, you did not come to a complete stop? A. Right.

Q. Now, how many miles an hour would you say you cut your speed down to when you say you slowed down? A. Possibly two miles an hour.

Q. Two miles an hour? And was your bus in high gear at the time? A. No, sir.

Q. What gear was it in? A. Second speed.

Q. Second speed. And you, I take it, were looking in the direction in which the bus was traveling at the time? A. That is true.

Q. And, your superiors instruct you to the effect that when the bus is in motion, you must look ahead of you, is that correct? A. That is right.

Q. And they do that because of safety to pedestrians, is that right? A. Yes.

Q. Now, on this occasion when you saw something on the sidewalk, you were looking in front of you, weren't you? A. That is right.

Q. And you always do, don't you? A. Right.

Q. Now, when you said that you saw something on the sidewalk, was that to the left of you or to the right of you? A. To the right.

Q. To the right? So that for the moment that you saw what you said you did, you weren't looking in the direction in which the bus was traveling, were you? A. Why, I just took my eyes off for the moment, yes.

Q. All right. Well, now, did you see the defendant Elmore as you said you did at several different times, or at one continuous time? **A. No, I was proceeding towards the beach and he was ahead of me, and as I came up, I had him in my view while I came abreast of him.**

Q. I see. And you had the defendant in your view while you were in back of him, is that right? A. In back of the defendant, yes.

Q. In back of the defendant. So that you could see, I venture to say, the defendant's back of his head. Is that right? A. That is right, yes.

Q. And, for how long a time did you make that observation about seeing the defendant's back of his head? A. Why, the distance of a half a block.

Q. Well, could you tell us, you being a bus driver, and having been thus employed for about ten months, how long a time that consumed, going at the rate of speed that you were going? A. I would say about half a minute.

Q. Half a minute, so, by the time a half a minute passed, I would say you were abreast of the defendant, is that right? A. That is true.

Q. And then, did you look to the right? A. I did.

Q. And for how long a period of time did you look to the right? A. Well, as I came abreast of him, I slowed my bus down and I glanced over like that (indicating).

Q. Yes. A. I will say about half a minute.

[Ed. Note: What about the other passengers? If you were riding in a bus and the driver slowed down to glare at something that intently, would you notice? Was there any attempt to find these passengers? Were they found but not supportive?

Q. A half a minute, and for the first half a minute that you have described, when you saw the defendant and the little girl in front of you, had you made an observation about the little girl? A. Why, for the first half a minute?

Q. Yes. A. For the first half a minute, I did for the simple reason she came--

Q. No, now wait a minute. Did you or did you not? A. I did.

Q. All right. And you also made the observation in that first half a minute, that this little girl was wearing a red bathing suit, is that right? A. That is right.

Q. And, you further made the observation that this little girl was two or three feet in front of this man that was walking along? A. That is right.

Q. And, you made the observation, did you, that the defendant was wearing a dirty pair of gray trousers? A. Yes.

Q. During that half a minute? A. No, I noticed them when I came abreast of him.

Q. You hadn't noticed the trousers at the time? A. No.

Q. But,, you had noticed the color of the girl's bathing suit? A. That is right.

Q. Had you made the observation in that half a moment that the defendant was wearing a white shirt? A. No, I seen that, I seen that when I was--

Q. When you-- A. The first half a minute.

Q. All right. So that for the first half a minute the only thing you saw was the back of a man's head, is that right? A. And his whole form of the back of him.

Q. I see. And his whole body? A. That is right.

Q. Including the legs? A. That is right.

Q. Below the knees? A. I couldn't say that, just a vision of the man walking ahead of me, that is all.

Q. Just a vision of a man walking, that is all you saw, is that right? A. For half a minute.

Q. That was for the first half a minute. Now, when you came abreast of the man, your bus was still in motion, was it? A. Just about.

Q. So that the observation about the gray pants was made in the next half a minute, is that right? A. Why, I took everything in.

Q. Yes, you took everything in and this, I take it is during the time that you are driving a bus? A. That is right.

Q. After having been instructed by your superiors to look in the direction in which the bus is going? A. Right.

Q. All right. You also made the observation about the color of the shirt he was wearing, didn't you? A. Yes, sir.

Q. And what color was it? A. A white shirt.

Q. And was it dirty or clean? A. That I couldn't say.

Q. Was the shirt buttoned up? A. That, I couldn't say.

Q. I see. Well, now, you say positively, however, that the shirt was white? A. Yes, so far as I-- what my eyes seen was a white shirt.

Q. Well, now, aren't we listening to your testimony now? A. Yes, sir.

Q. And we are paying attention to what you say, aren't we? A. Yes, sir.

Q. So now, can you tell us with any degree of

certainty as to whether the shirt was dirty or clean? A. No, I couldn't say whether it was dirty or clean.

Q. Yes, and will you say whether or not the defendant was wearing a necktie at the time? A. I didn't notice that.

Q. Will you tell us what kind of shoes he was wearing? A. I didn't notice that either.

Q. Now, did you ever stop your bus at any time, at any time after having observed what you told us you did, did you come to a stop? A. Oh, I must have, I must have left some people off after that.

Q. Well, that was after that? A. Yes, sir.

**Q. When you made the stop, the man that you saw and the girl that you saw was not in the line of your vision any more, were they? A. No.**

**Q. No. So it was just while that bus was passing by, is that right? A. That is right.**

Q. All right. Now, at the same time that you made these observations that you told us about, you noticed that the little girl was wearing a red bathing suit? A. That is right.

Q. And, I take it the color attracted your attention? A. Yes, sir.

Q. And, the bathing suit was red in its entirety, was it not? A. That I don't know. I just seen a red bathing suit.

Q. Well, what part of it did you see that was red? A. I couldn't say what part I seen, I seen the bathing suit.

Q. Well, you know the parts to a bathing suit, don't you? A. I do.

Q. Today, they are very--there are very little parts to them? A. Very little of them, right.

Q. Now, what part of it did you see that was red, if you can tell us? A. That I couldn't say what part I seen, I just didn't pick out any particular part, I just happened to see--

Q. Well, would you say there was any part that was not red? A. No, I wouldn't say as to that either.

Q. In other words, you saw a bathing suit which might have been partly red and partly some other color, is that right? A. It could be that, I couldn't say that.

Q. You couldn't say. Could it be a bathing suit that was partly red and partly blue? A. No, I don't think it was partly blue.

Q. Well, could it be one that is partly red and partly gray? A. That, I don't think so.

Q. I see. What makes you say that it couldn't be blue? A. That part--why I think if it had been blue, I would have noticed it.

Q. Oh, is that the reason why you tell us that--A. That is right.

Q. And, if it had been any other color, which is outstanding as colors go, you would have noted that too, wouldn't you? A. Possibly.

Q. Can you now tell us of a certainty whether or not the entire part of this bathing suit was red? A. No, I couldn't say that.

Q. Now, you expressed an opinion, did you not, that this girl appeared to be about seven or eight years of age? A. No, I didn't, I said six years old.

Q. You said six years of age, didn't you, Mr. Flick? A. Yes, I did.

Q. **And when did you first form that opinion that the girl might have been about six years of age? A. Why, after I heard, after I read in the paper about this little girl that was murdered.**

Q. Now, you saw only half of the man's face whom you claim to have seen on that day, is that right? A. I didn't say I saw half of his face.

Q. What did you say you saw, his entire face? A. I didn't say that either. I wasn't asked that question, I don't think.

Q. I see. Did you see his face at any time? A. I did see his face.

Q. And what part of his face did you see? A. I seen his whole face.

Q. You seen his whole face? A. That is right.

Q. Now, as you were passing with your bus a man was on the right of your bus? A. That is right

Q. Is that right? And he was on the sidewalk? A. He was on the right of me.

Q. There came a time when you passed that man? A. That is right.

**Q. Traveling about two miles an hour? A. Right.**

**Q. Did you turn around to look? A. I did.**

**Q. I see. And did you turn around--how long a time did you turn around for? A. Oh, I couldn't exactly--I didn't take my watch out and time myself, just how long it was, I said about half a minute.**

Q. Now, you have seen men walking in the street and particularly on sidewalks before, haven't you? A. Oh, yes.

Q. And, you have noted them, during the time that you are driving a bus, haven't you? A. Yes.

Q. Now, it is not considered singular by you that you see a man walking on the sidewalk now, is it? A. No.

Q. But, I suppose you do regard it as singular when you see a little girl walking in front of a man on the sidewalk with a bathing suit on? A. Well, that all depends.

Q. All depends? Did it seem singular to you in this instance? A. It did, very much.

[Ed. Note: By various accounts, the three murdered children in the Albert Dyer case were either walking a few feet ahead of him or he walked a block ahead of them. This was nation wide news at the time. See *Colder Case.*]

Q. It did? But, nevertheless, as you turned back-- with this little girl walking two or three feet in front of this man, you didn't see the little girl's face, did you? A. No.

Q. You only saw the back of her head? A. I seen the left side of her body.

Q. The left side of her body? Didn't you testify

that you saw the back of her head? A. If I did, I don't think I did.

Q. I see. Did you testify that she had curly--A. Yes.

Q. --blonde hair? A. That is right.

Q. And, you made that observation as your bus was passing along? A. Right.

Q. And, I believe you just said that seemed singular to you, didn't you? A. I think I did.

Q. And, Norway Avenue is somewheres near the beach, is it not? A. Quite a ways from the beach.

**Q. It is somewheres near the beach, isn't it? A. Well, I would say it is quite a ways away from the beach.**

**Q. Did you ever see anybody in a bathing suit before? A. Oh, I have seen plenty of them.**

**Q. At or near Norway Avenue? A. Yes, I guess I have. . Yes.**

Q. But, in this sense, however, it did seem singular to you, is that correct? A

Q. Well, after having seen something that seemed so singular to you, you didn't stop your bus? A. No, not quite.

**Q. You kept on going about your business, didn't you? A. That is right.**

**Q. And you kept on working as if nothing whatsoever had occurred? A. That is right.**

Q. Is that right? A. That is right.

Q. Now, did you notice whether or not on that day the defendant wore glasses? A. No, I didn't.

Q. Did you notice it? A. Did I notice whether or not he did?

Q. Yes. A. No, he didn't have no glasses on that day.

Q. Did you notice whether he did that day? A. I noticed whether he did, and he didn't have no glasses on that day.

Q. And, you are positive about that? A. Yes, sir.

Q. Did you notice whether or not he had a

mustache? A. Yes, I noticed that.

Q. Did you notice the color of his mustache? A. No, I didn't take that particular notice, the color of his mustache.

Q. And what type of mustache did you observe on that day? A. Well, he just had an ordinary mustache like a person will wear. It wasn't one of those long ones that curled, I know that.

Q. Well, you know a mustache, it is not one like with handle bars? A. No.

Q. Was it a very sharp one? A. No, it was kind of a heavy set mustache.

Q. Heavy set mustache, and you noticed that as you were passing going two miles an hour, is that right. ? A. As I looked at him.

Q. And, was that at or about the time that you noticed the girl was wearing a red bathing suit? A. Well, I had her in my observation there even after I got by, I could notice that in my glass, I was watching them out of the glass as I passed them.

Q. Now, did you see anything through your glass after you passed these two individuals walking along the sidewalk? A. Yes, I was watching in my looking glass.

Q. And, is it then through your looking glass that you saw a man who you now say is the defendant? A. No sir, no sir.

Q. Well, did you see the little girl through the looking glass? A. After I had passed, after I had noticed them, I kept watching them in my looking glass.

Q. How soon after, or how many feet past the individuals who are now two or three feet apart, did you look back through your mirror? A. Well, I watched them there for practically, I could see them back maybe 40 or 50 feet in my mirror.

Q. 40 or 50 feet? A. Yes.

Q. And how long would you say it took you to travel this 40 or 50 feet? A. Possibly two minutes.

Q. How many? A. Possibly a minute and a half, two minutes.

Q. A minute and a half. In other words, it was a longer period of time than the time it took you to make the observation that you have testified to? A. About the same.

Q. All right. Now, this mirror permits you to see what is coming from the rear, is that right? A. Yes, sir.

Q. And, that, of course, is the purpose of the mirror, is it not? A. That is right.

Q. And, did you have such a mirror as permitted you to see things, objects in back of the bus? A. Yes.

Q. And, does that mirror permit you to see anything on the sidewalk to the right? A. Well, we have a mirror on the bus for that.

Q. Do you have--did you have it on that day? A. I imagine it was on that bus, I don't just remember.

Q. Then, you don't know? A. I don't remember what was on that day.

Q. You don't remember looking on the mirror, if you had it? A. I don't remember looking at the side mirror. It was the mirror in the bus I was looking at.

Q. You, Mr. Flick, testified that you saw something which impressed you as being singular, is that right? A. That is right.

Q. And if you had a mirror that would have permitted you to see objects on the sidewalk to your right, you could have seen those objects? A. Well, my mirror in the bus permits me to see things on the sidewalk also.

Q. Did you see anything through that mirror? A. Through what mirror?

Q. Through the mirror that was in the side of the bus. What did you see? A. I was watching this man and this little girl I had passed.

Q. And, did you see the face of the man then? A. I could see the face, but I couldn't recognize him in the mirror.

Q. I notice you are smiling? A. I am not smiling.

Q. I want the answer, did you see his face? A. In the mirror?

Q. Yes. A. No, I couldn't exactly say I seen his

face.

Q. Did you say that you had a mirror that would have permitted you to see his face? A. Yes, but you can't see a man's face that is to identify it in a mirror after you pass a man, you can't see his face.

Q. After--in your opinion then, after you have passed a man and you have gone up to a distance of more than 40 feet, if you looked through the mirror, even though that mirror permits you to see the full face of a man, in your opinion, you couldn't identify him? A. I didn't say that.

Q. Well, what did you say? A. Well, I said I didn't identify his face by looking through the mirror.

Q. Did you see his face is the question. A. Well, you could see the man, you could see the little girl.

Q. Well, could you see his face? A. Yes, you could see his face.

Q. And, did you see his face? A. I must have, I was watching him in the mirror.

Q. Now, that is not the answer you must have. Do you identify this defendant because you were looking through that mirror? A. No sir, I didn't say that.

Q. No. You identify this defendant because you saw him some distance in front of you, you saw the back of his head and then you passed him, is that correct? A. I seen him when I passed him by.

Q. When you passed him. When you looked through that mirror the little girl was in front, wasn't she? A. That is right.

Q. Could you see her face? A. No, I didn't see her face.

Q. Could you see any part of her? A. I could see her body.

**Q. Could you see her bathing suit? A. Yes, I could see her bathing suit.**

**Q. Was it still all red? A. That, I couldn't say.**

Q. Now, Mr. Flick, you went to the police station, didn't you? A. Yes, sir.

Q. And you spoke to somebody about this case,

didn't you? A. I spoke to somebody?

Q. Yes. A. Yes, sir.

Q. And you told that somebody the same story you told us, is that right? A. That is right.

Q. Now, let me take you, if you will--do you know where Peter Crane's Hotel is? A. No, sir.

Q. Do you know where Bessi's Hotel is? A. No, sir.

Q. Do you know where Seaside Boulevard is? A. Yes, sir.

Q. All right. Does your bus go around Seaside Boulevard? A. No, I turn around at the corner of Sand Lane and Seaside Boulevard.

Q. Right. So, you start at Seaside Boulevard, do you not? A. That is inbound to the ferry. We start there, yes.

Q. And, the course that your bus takes then is a left turn into Sand Lane, is it not? A. Yes.

Q. Yes. And then where do you make the next--A. Left turn into Sand Lane?

Q. Yes. A. No, I go straight up Sand Lane.

Q. Straight up Sand Lane? A. That is right.

Q. You come down in such a manner that you pass Norway Avenue? A. We go down Norway Avenue.

Q. Down Norway Avenue and do you then pick up McClean Avenue? A. Pardon me, are you going into the ferry or out from the ferry? I would like--are you starting from South Beach?

Q. From St. George. A. Oh, you are starting from St. George?

Q. Right. A. We go down McClean Avenue and turn into Norway Avenue.

Q. All right. You come down **McClean Avenue**, turn into Norway and then what street do you pick up? A. Olympia Boulevard.

Q. That is the street that is known as Old Town Road? A. Formerly.

Q. I guess it is known as Olympia Boulevard now. A. Yes.

Q. And then you turn into where? A. Sand Lane, down into the beach.

Q. And then, it is Seaside Boulevard? A. We turn around there, that is right.

Q. Your bus doesn't take you anywhere toward Fifth Place, does it? A. I don't know where it is.

Q. You don't know where it is? Does your bus take you past Scott Avenue? A. Scott, yes.

Q. Yes. And, past Appleby Avenue? A. Yes.

Q. And it is then, after having passed those streets that you hit McClean Avenue? A. No.

Q. Or, I should say, Olympia Boulevard? A. That is right.

Q. That is right. Now, you didn't make any report to anyone about having seen these singular things that you saw, did you? A. No sir, I did not.

Q. Now, you were, as you told me, at the terminal at 1:15, is that right? A. Yes sir, yes sir, that is right.

Q. And this, you referred to on direct examination, is what terminal? A. South Beach, Sand Lane, end of Sand Lane and Seaside Boulevard.

Q. Now, what is the distance in the matter of time between Norway Avenue, when you saw what you have described, and your terminal? A. I will say about three minutes.

Q. About three minutes. Would you also say that you were early? A. No, sir.

Q. That day? A. No.

Q. Weren't you due at 1:15? A. That is right.

Q. And didn't you say that you saw what you did see, or claim to have seen at 1:10? A. Between 1:10 and 1:12.

Q. Didn't you say before between 1:10 and 1:11 on direct examination? A. Yes sir, 1:11 is right.

Q. Do you mean 1:10 or 1:11? A. No, I will say 1:11.

Q. Now, you have a clock on your bus, don't you? A. No, sir, what kind of a clock?

Q. Well, one that tells time? A. No.

Q. Did you have one on your wrist? A. I have one on now.

Q. Did you look at it that day? A. No, I don't think I looked at it that day.

Q. Did you see any clocks around anywheres at the time you saw this little girl? A. No.

Q. You are able to tell us, however, the time so minutely, that it was between 1:10 and 1:11? A. Yes. The reason I do that--

Q. Did I ask you for a reason? A. No, beg your pardon.

Q. Now, tell us the reason. A. Well, the reason we do that, we have time place, we hit a certain place at a certain time and we try to run on time as near as possible, and when we hit McClean Avenue and Norway Avenue, we generally allow ourselves five minutes from there into our terminal.

Q. Now, allowing yourself five minutes as you say, you did--and having told me that it takes about three minutes, you still had a minute or two to spare, didn't you? A. Why, I was down at--between Scott and Cameron Avenue. That isn't Norway.

Q. Now, Mr. Flick, you were due at the terminal at 1:15? A. Yes, sir.

Q. Now, that is understandable? A. Yes, it is.

Q. You made this observation at 1:10 or 1:11, is that right? A. Yes.

Q. You say that you allow yourself five minutes, is that right? A. That is right

Q. On this day you didn't allow yourself five minutes, did you? A. Oh, yes.

Q. Well, then, it was 1:10, wasn't it? A. No, sir.

Q. Was it 1:11? A. I had traveled two blocks from Norway Avenue from the time, the point I set for five minutes.

Q. So, if it takes three minutes, wouldn't you still have one minute to spare? A. Wouldn't I have a minute to spare?

Q. Calculating that you give yourself five minutes?

A. It is possible I might have a minute to spare.

Q. Yes, so that you were in no particular hurry, were you? A. I was just to get in on my time, as I usually do.

Q. Just to get in on your time, and you didn't think enough of your observations to make a report to anyone, did you? A. No, I didn't, not that day.

Q. I see. Now, in addition to all the observations that you have told the Court and the Jury, you made another observation, didn't you? A. What was that?

Q. About the fact that the defendant had something in his hand? A. Well, he was carrying something, yes.

Q. And, you made that observation and described it this way, that it was something made out of glass? A. That is what it looked like to me.

Q. Was he carrying this in his left hand or his right hand? A. In his left hand.

Q. And, of course, you are equally sure about that? A. I am positive of that.

Q. Positive of that? And you couldn't be positive as to whether or not you saw anything in that glass, that glass container, are you? A. No, no.

**Q. Now, do you know whether this object was being carried upwards or downwards with the left arm? A. He had his hand like this, walking like this ( indicating ) .**

Q. Like this he had his arm? A. That is right.

Mr. Gulotta : Indicating with the left hand towards--

Mr. Innes : Left at the elbow and bent against his chest.

By Mr. Gulotta:

**Q. And, was it wrapped up? A. That, I couldn't say.**

[Ed. Note: In the confession, Elmore said he got the bottle on Old Town Road at the old movie studio. That location would come after where he said he saw

Elmore, so he wouldn't have the bottle yet. No wonder the prosecution kept trying to say he lured the little girl away from the beach with the bottle and grasshoppers despite no evidence supporting that theory. The fact of the matter was, they found a bottle with a grasshopper in on the wall of the entrance to the cellar, and they had no idea how it got there. The only thing certain is they did not find fingerprints on it that matched Elmore's.]

**Q. Well, now, I understand you even at this very moment to express some degree of doubt as to whether or not this object was wrapped up or not? A. That is right.**

Q. Since there is that degree of doubt in your mind, do you still say now that object is made out of glass? A. That is what it looked like to me, I couldn't say it was made out of glass.

Q. Well, will you answer my question? A. No, I couldn't say it was made out of glass.

Q. Didn't you tell the District Attorney on direct examination that that object was made out of glass? A. I don't think so. I think I told him that it looked like something that was glass.

Q. All right. You told him that it was something that looked like glass? A. Yes.

Q. All right, now, Mr. Flick, you have expressed an opinion that you do not know whether this object was wrapped up in paper or anything else? A. That is right.

Q. Now, I now ask you again, having made the statement that there is some doubt as to whether the object was wrapped up in anything, will you now explain to me what it is that makes you say that it was an object of glass? A. Well, it was just something that I seen him have in his hand, which looked like a glass pitcher to me.

**Q. But, you can't say whether it was wrapped up or not? A. No, I couldn't say whether it was wrapped up or not.**

Q. Are you able to see glass, Mr. Flick? A. Oh, yes.

Q. If it is wrapped up in something? A. Oh, not if it is wrapped up in something, that is, if the whole thing is wrapped up.

Q. So that you don't know--well, yes--would you say now, that any part of it was wrapped up? A. No, I couldn't say whether it was wrapped up.

Q. You couldn't say whether that object was made of glass or not, can you? A. I couldn't say whether it was.

Q. All right. So, you can say now to me, and to this Court, and to the Jury, that you saw the defendant carrying an object? A. Something in his hand.

Q. All right. Now, how long was this object that you saw? A. Well, I think I described it, it was about ten or twelve inches to my estimation.

Q. You couldn't give us any geometrical description of it, could you? A. No.

Q. Would you say whether it was round or square? A. No, I couldn't say that.

Q. Would you say whether it was long or short? A. Well, no, I couldn't say that.

Q. Do you know what a pitcher looks like? A. I think I do.

Q. Why did you express the opinion to the District Attorney, that it looked like a pitcher? A. Because, when I went by, the man was bent over this way (indicating).

Q. Did I ask you how the man was bent over? A. No, but that is why I couldn't see what he was carrying, that obstructed my view from seeing it.

Q. So, you didn't see the thing he carried, did you? A. I seen something in his hand.

Q. But, you don't know what that something is? A. It looked like glass to me.

Q. Now, Mr. Flick, naturally being in the business that you are, you see many people coming in the bus? A. That is right.

Q. And you see many people leave the bus, don't you? A. Yes.

Q. And you see all types of faces, don't you? A.

Yes.

Q. You see young ones and you see old ones, don't you? A. Yes.

Q. You see men? A. Right.

Q. And you see women? A. Yes.

Q. And you do that continually throughout the day? A. That is right.

Q. Is that right? A. That is right.

Q. And yet, you tell us in this fleeting half a minute, you observed all the things that you tell us you' observed? A. Half a minute or a minute, did you say?

Q. The other half a minute, Mr. Flick, you testified you saw nothing, didn't you? A. That I don't think I said, I didn't see anything.

**Q. Did you say that you passed these people after half a minute and that you spent a half a minute looking through the glass? A. Yes, but I had them under my observation for the half a minute that I came up upon them.**

**Q. Yes. How many times did you speak to anybody about this case? A. Oh, I don't know, I didn't try to speak to anybody very much, I was asked a lot of questions, I didn't answer any more than I really had to.**

Q. Just one moment, please? A. Yes, sir.

Q. Now, I am going to show you a map here and this map is marked defendant's exhibit A, and I am going to point out to you Scott and Appleby Avenue there and Norway Avenue. Just look at that and place a cross mark where you claim you saw this little girl. A. (Witness marks map).

Q. Is it marked? I want you to please place your initials on there so that there will be no, right on that same mark. (Witness marks his initials on map). Just hold that there a minute. And will you now mark in this fashion, if you can, the direction in which your bus was traveling? A. I am not very good at drawing maps. I will do the best I can.

Q. Well you don't have to draw, draw us a triangle

with the points in the direction in which you were going. A. Where is Olympia Boulevard? (Witness marks map.)

Q. Now, Mr. Flick, when you left St. George, you leave the ferry terminal and go over the viaduct, is that right? A. Yes, come out this way.

Q. And then from there you pick up Bay Street, don't you? A. That is right.

Q. And then do you go to what street after leaving Bay Street? A. Wadsworth Avenue.

Q. And then I take it that from Wadsworth Avenue you go into Tompkins Avenue? A. Turn left on Tompkins Avenue.

Q. And is it then that you pick up McClean Avenue? A. Turn right on McClean Avenue.

Q. And is it then that you pick up Norway Avenue? A. Yes, after you cross Sand Lane, I pick up Norway Avenue.

Q. How far from McClean Avenue had you turned your bus into Norway Avenue before you saw what you described? A. How far?

Q. Yes. A. As I turned into Norway Avenue?

Q. Yes, as you turned into Norway Avenue. A. Why, as I hit Scott Avenue, I hit it just before I hit the approach of Scott Avenue.

Q. And, about how many feet before you hit Scott Avenue on Norway Avenue? A. Well, about, I will say, 40-50 feet.

Q. 40, 50 feet? Now, there is no doubt in your mind that you saw a sidewalk? A. Yes, there is a sidewalk there.

Q. And, is that a concrete sidewalk? A. No, it is, I think it is ashes, I am pretty sure it is ashes.

Q. Anyway, you call it a sidewalk? A. Yes, we call it a sidewalk.

Q. All right, now, did you ever say to anyone, Mr. Flick, that what you saw looked funny to you? A. Well, it looked, what I seen looked funny.

Q. The question is not, how does it look to you now, the question is, Mr. Flick, did you at any time after having seen what you did see, did you ever say to anyone, "It looked funny to me"? A. I think I said it looked peculiar.

Q. Peculiar? A. To me.

Q. **Not funny. And who did you say that to?** A. Why, I think I told it to one of the inspectors up at the station house when I went up there.

Q. And was that on August 13th? A. That was on August 14th.

Q. That was two days after? A. That was on Saturday, yes.

Q. And that was when you had your first talk with the law? Is that right? A. That is right.

Q. When did you first discover about a missing girl? A. Why, I think it was Friday night when I got home from work, that night I read something in the paper about it, there was a little article, if I ain't mistaken, I didn't pay much attention to it, though.

Q. Well, now, your answer is Friday, isn't it? A. Yes, that was the first time that I--

Q. And that answers my question. Then did you express to the same person this, that you were under the impression at the time that it was father and daughter, walking along? A. Yes, I made that statement.

Q. Yes. And who did you make that statement to? A. I think I made it to the officers down in the Precinct.

Q. Now, I take it, that at the time you were impressed with all these things that you have testified to, you made an observation as to the man's age, did you? A. No, I didn't.

Q. Did it strike you as if it was an old man or a young man? A. Yes, he struck me as if he was an old man.

Q. About what age? A. Well, about, I will say, 50, 55 years of age.

Q. Well, would you say this side of 55 or the other side? A. No, I would say the other side more.

Q. The other side more? A. Yes.

Q. Would you say 60? A. No, I wouldn't say.

Q. Well, how much? A. I would say between fifty and 55.

Q. Between 50 and 55? Now, let us have no qualms or dispute about that, your answer is between 50 and 55? A. Yes, that is the age I take the man to be.

Q. And I take it that you formed that opinion at the time your bus was passing? A. Yes, that is right.

Q. And, you, with all the other things that you noticed, having noticed that he was carrying something, having noticed that he had gray trousers which were dirty, noticing the fact that he had a white shirt, noticing the fact that he had a mustache, at the same time noticing a little girl who had blond hair and curly hair, noticing that she was wearing a red bathing suit at the time that you were passing this scene, formulated the idea that this man was between 50 and 55 years of age, is that right? A. Yes, that is right.

Mr. Gulotta : That is all.

Redirect examination By Mr. Innes :

**Q. Just a few questions, Mr. Flick. At some time on Saturday or prior thereto, you read an account, did you not?** A. That is right.

Q. And, did you see a picture in connection with it? A. I did, I seen a picture of this man.

Q. I see. And did you recognize that picture? A. As soon as I seen that picture, I recognized that face, yes.

Q. And was that--did you go to the station house voluntarily? A. I went of my own accord.

Q. And, you there saw the man that you saw on Norway Avenue? A. Yes, sir.

Q. Two days before? A. He was the man that I seen walking on Norway Avenue.

Q. And he is the defendant here? A, That is the man, there.

Q. No question about that in your mind? A. There is no question in my mind about that.

Mr. Innes : That is all. Now, Officer Paolo.

DOMINICK PAOLO, Shield No. 15954, Technical 727 Research Laboratory, New York City Police Department, called as a witness in behalf of the People, first being duly sworn, testified as follows :

Direct examination by Mr. Innes :

Q. Officer, how long have you been attached to that precinct, that research bureau? A. A little over two and one half years.

Q. And do you make investigations in homicide cases? A. Yes, sir.

Q. And was your attention, or were you called to this bungalow in the meadows near South Beach? A. Some time on Friday afternoon, yes, sir.

Q. At about what time did you get there? A. Between three and three thirty.

Q. What did you see there at the time when you arrived? A. When I arrived at the scene, I saw a young--I saw a body lying face down with a brick on its back, sections of brick, and she was suspended by a string, which I will term as a halter strap, that was attached to the door and tied around the body's throat.

Q. Was the head resting on the floor or was it suspended, by this cord? A. Well, it was suspended, I will say, about half an inch, the face was.

Q. Above the floor of the cellar? A. Above the floor.

Q. Now, then, did you observe a bathing suit there? A. Yes, sir.

Q. Will you describe that? A. It was a red bathing suit usually worn by children.

Mr. Gulotta : I object to that and move to strike it out as not responsive.

The Court : I think that is descriptive. A child's bathing suit.

A. That bathing suit was wrapped around the girl and the halter strap attached to it leading down to the throat of this body.

Q. And how, did the halter strap make any indentation in the neck? A. Yes.

Q. About how deep an indentation? A. About nearly half an inch.

Q. And was that knotted in any way? A. Yes.

Q. How was it knotted? A. **Well, I don't know but it was knotted very tightly.**

Q. I show you this cord or halter strap and ask you if you recognize that as the strap that you saw there at that time? A. Yes.

Q. Did you cut it from the little girl's neck? A. Yes.

Q. And can you point out there where you cut it? A. These two points here (indicating).

Q. But, were there strands of hair matted into the knot? A. Yes, sir. It was necessary to, with difficulty, to try to get underneath so I could get the knife not to cause any more injury than possible, and some of the hair of the victim was imbedded in with the knot, in with the strands, and I took this piece of red string to tie where this cut was executed.

Q. And is that in the same condition that it was when you removed it? A. Yes.

Q. And you recognize that as the halter strap that was around that little girl's neck? A. Yes.

Q. And which you cut to release her? A. Yes.

[Ed. Note: The cords were so tight around the necks of Melba and Madeline Everett, and their friend Jeanette, it was extremely difficult to cut them free in 1937.

Mr. Innes: I offer it in evidence, if the Court pleases.

Mr. Gulotta : Objection is made on the ground that the string has not been identified, that the proper foundation has not been laid, and that there is no continuity of possession of the string in any means, nor connected with the defendant in this case.

The Court : What did you do with the string

afterwards, what did you do with the string?

The Witness : You mean this whole thing, your Honor?

The Court : Yes.

The Witness : I took that string, halter strap, with the bathing suit and I delivered it to Detective Thomas Cosgrove, where, in my presence, he marked "T. C. " on different straps for identification purposes.

By Mr. Innes :

Q. And you find those marks there now? A. Yes.

Mr. Innes: All right. I renew my offer if the Court pleases.

Mr. Gulotta : Objection is made to it on the ground that there is no foundation laid, no testimony as to what was done with it after it was turned over to Officer Cosgrove.

The Court : He says he recognizes the string as being the string taken over, he said he cut it off, I will allow it.

Mr. Gulotta : I respectfully except.

The Court : You say the condition of the string is now the same as it was at the time you took it from the body?

The Witness : Yes.

The Court : I will allow it.

(People's Exhibit No. 6 for identification, was received in evidence. )

By Mr. Innes :

Q. Now, then, officer, I show you this article and ask you if you will be good enough to look at it, and tell me if you recognize it? A. I do.

Q. What--where did you first see that? A. I saw this wrapped around the door of this house where this body was found.

Q. And about how far from the body? A. Well, about, I would say about two feet, this was wrapped right around the door and the other two pieces attached to the string were around the victim's neck.

Q. And do you recognize that as the bathing suit

you saw there? A. Absolutely.

Mr. Innes : I offer that in evidence.

Mr. Gulotta : The same objection is made by the defendant.

The Court : Same ruling.

(People's Exhibit No. 1 for identification was received in evidence. )

Mr. Gulotta: May we have an exception to that?

Mr. Innes : I think that is all.

Mr. Gulotta: No cross.

Mr. Innes : Oh, officer, just a question.

By Mr. Innes :

Q. You had a brother officer with you at the time? A. Yes.

Mr. Innes: That is all.

Call Mr. Ihnken.

JAMES H. IHNKEN, Shield No. 156, 9th Detective Squad, New York City Police Department, called as a witness in behalf of the People, first being duly sworn, testified as follows :

Direct examination by Mr. Innes :

Q. How long have you been attached to the Detective Bureau in this Borough? A. Oh, about 12 years.

Q. And are you the official photographer of the Bureau? A. One of them, yes.

Q. One of them? And do you from time to time take pictures of the scenes of crime? A. Yes.

Q. Did you go to South Beach in this County to a bungalow in the meadows and take pictures of certain things there? A. Yes.

Q. When did you do that, officer? A. That was Friday, August 13th, 1937, about 1:30 P.M.

Q. You got there about 1:30? A. About 1 :30.

Q. And you had your camera with you? A. Yes.

Q. And did you take pictures of different parts of that bungalow? A. Yes.

Q. I show you this picture and ask you if you

recognize what is shown there? A. Well, this picture here wasn't taken on that date.

Q. It was taken later? A. Yes.

Q. Yes. A. Yes, I took these other pictures later.

Mr. Gulotta : Any pictures of the bungalow, if Mr. Innes will show them to me, the possibility is that I can consent that they be marked in evidence.

Mr. Innes : There is one.

Mr. Gulotta : No objection.

The Court : No objection.

(Whereupon photographs were received in evidence, and marked People's Exhibit No. 10. )

Mr. Gulotta : There is no objection to this.

The Court : Are you marking them separately?

(People's Exhibit No. 11, a photograph, was marked in evidence and received in evidence. )

Mr. Gulotta : And similarly, I have no objection to this one.

Mr. Innes : That we all agree is looking at the house from the easterly side, I believe.

Mr. Gulotta: That I can't tell you. It is hard to know east or west on there, I can't say.

Mr. Casey : Looking from which direction, from the beach?

Mr. Innes: Yes, from the beach toward the upland. (Another photograph was received in evidence and marked People's Exhibit No. 12. )

Mr. Gulotta: No objection. (Another photograph was received in evidence and marked People's Exhibit No. 13 in evidence. )

By Mr. Innes :

Q. Now, then, taking these in the order in which they have been marked, No. 10, will you state from where you took that picture with respect to the bungalow? A. This picture was taken in the rear of it, this is the back of the bungalow, and I was taking the picture facing the east.

The Court : Show it to the Jury.

By Mr. Innes :

Q. I show you Exhibit No. 11 and ask, you say

that was taken later, but that shows what part of the bungalow? A. That shows the front of the bungalow, looking west.

By Mr. Innes :
Q. No. 12, will you look at that, officer, and tell me what that is? A. That is looking north.

Q. It shows the bungalow. And No. 13, will you look at that? A. That is looking southeast.

Q. And shows the rear and side of the bungalow. A. It shows the rear and north side.

Q. I show you another picture also and ask you if that was taken by you? A. Yes.

Q. What does that represent? A. That was taken from the back of the bungalow in the cellar, showing the front and sides.

Mr. Innes: I offer that in evidence.

The Court : No objection?

Mr. Gulotta : I haven't seen that one, Judge, I would like to look at it. May I ask a question, when this was taken? The Witness : That was taken the following Wednesday, the 18th.

Mr. Gulotta : I have no objection.

(Whereupon the photograph referred to was received in evidence and marked People's Exhibit No. 14 in evidence. )

By Mr. Innes :
Q. Now, then, officer, I show you another picture and ask you if you recognize that? A. Yes.

Q. What does that represent? A. That is a picture of the body looking in the cellar, looking towards the front of the building from the rear.

Q. Through the cellar door? A. Yes.

Q. That is shown in the other pictures?

Mr. Innes: I offer that in evidence. By the way, when was that taken, officer?

The Witness: That was taken about, right after

1:30 of the 13th, Friday, the 13th.

Mr. Gulotta: May it please the Court an objection is made to this picture on the ground that the position of the body has already been fully described, that this picture is calculated only to inflame the minds of the Jury.

(The Judge looks at the picture.)

Mr. Innes: May I ask a further question?

By Mr. Innes:

Q. Does that correctly represent what you saw there at the time before the picture was taken? A. Yes.

Q. And is it a true and correct picture of the scene that it purports to show? A. Yes.

By the Court:

Q. Who was there, officer, when you took those pictures? A. There was Inspector McGrath, Assistant Chief Inspector Lyons, oh, there was a number of detectives around, just who they were, I don't know, they were in and out going back and forth, there was Cosgrove, and Hagarty, and Brennan, and Murphy, they were in and out a number of them--they--I think Sergeant Hildebrand.

Q. Had they been there before you got there? A. Why, Cosgrove and Hagarty were there. I think they left and came back, I am not sure.

Mr. Gulotta: May I, if your Honor pleases, add to my objection the further ground that the only time when a picture of the body of the deceased is admissible in evidence in a murder trial is only on the question of identity, and that showing a picture, is only calculated and designed to inflame the minds of the Jury on that point.

The Court: I will reserve decision on this motion.

Mr. Innes: The further reason, if the Court please, that I might add that that in and of itself wouldn't indicate the section of the child.

The Court: Well, did you say you got there at 1:30?

The Witness: Yes, 1:30.

The Court: The other officers were there at the time you got there?

The Witness : Yes.

The Court : Do you know how long they had been there before you got there?

The Witness : No, I couldn't tell you that, I had just come from the cave-in. I was taking photographs over there, and I stopped in to get lunch and let them know in the office where I was going and they told me--

The Court : I didn't ask you all that, I asked you when you got there, did you know how long the other officers had been there before you--

The Witness : No, I don't.

The Court : You say there were numerous police officers there at the time? A. Yes.

The Court : I will reserve decision on this until after recess.

By Mr. Innes :

Q. I show you another picture, officer, which-- if the Court pleases, is along the same lines, and ask you if you took that picture? A. Yes.

Q. At about what time? A. Well, maybe about--

The Court : Just let me see the picture, please.

A. About five minutes difference between the pictures.

The Court : Well, all right, you just hold off on this. I will consider the one motion as to all of them.

Mr. Gulotta : May I have the same objection to this picture?

The Court : You may have the same objection.

By Mr. Innes :

Q. Now, then, I show you another picture and ask you if you took that picture and what it purports to represent? A. Why, this picture was taken along side of the cellar window, on the north side of the bungalow right from the front porch, as close to the window as I could get, showing the body, what you could see from that window.

Q. And I notice, there appears to be on the side a little concrete construction, something on it. A. There is a high shelf, a high table.

Mr. Gulotta: I object to it on the ground that there is a description being offered of the picture without it being in evidence.

The Court : Objection sustained. The question is whether that fairly represents a part of the building.

The Witness : Yes.

By Mr. Innes :

Q. And is there an object on that little shelf? A. Yes.

Q. Shown in your picture.

Mr. Gulotta : Just a moment, now, I make the same objection.

The Court : Is this what you are referring to?

(Witness points out to the Court, on the photograph. )

The Court : Well, I will reserve decision on this one.

Mr. Innes : May I ask just one question further?

The Court : Yes.

By Mr. Innes :

Q. What is that object that is shown there, officer?

Mr. Gulotta : I object to that.

The Court : Objection sustained.

By Mr. Innes :

Q. I show you another picture, and ask if you took that? A. No, that was taken by Detective Marrinan, my partner.

Mr. Innes : All right, that is out. Your Honor wants to reserve decision?

The Court : Come back at two o'clock. Gentlemen, we will recess until two o'clock. Do not discuss this case or come to any conclusion in the matter until the case is finally submitted to you and you retire to your Jury Room.

(Whereupon at 12:58 P. M. , Court recessed, until 2 :00 P. M. )

AFTERNOON SESSION. Thursday, November 18, 1937, 2 :00 P. M. Before : Hon. THOMAS F. COSGROVE, County Judge. And a Petit Jury.

Appearances : All parties as before.

Court Clerk Kosman : People against Samuel Elmore.

(Both sides were ready. Whereupon, the jury was polled and all jurors answered present. )

Detective JAMES H. IHNKEN, resumes the witness stand for further examination.

The Court : Repeat the last question.

Whereupon, the stenographer repeated as follows :

Q. And I notice there appears to be on the side a little concrete construction, something on it. A. That is a little shelf, a little table.

Mr. Gulotta I object to it on the ground that there is a description being offered of the picture without it being in evidence.

The Court : Objection sustained. The question is whether that fairly represents a part of the building. A. , Yes, sir.

Q. And is there an object on that little shelf? A. Yes.

The Court : All right, the last question is you show him certain pictures.

Mr. Innes : Yes.

The Court : You have only shown them to him, Mr. Innes, according to the last question.

Mr. Innes : I made an offer of something that is not before the Court at the present time, for instance, the Exhibit No. 8 for Identification.

The Court : As I recollect, the pictures you now hold in your hand, were offered just before recess.

Mr. Innes : They were offered, all of them.

The Court : They were offered, and I reserved decision on that. I haven't decided up to the last question. Now, the last question you asked was who took the photographs.

Mr. Innes : And he answered that he took all of these.

The Court : Did you answer all of these?

The Witness : Yes, sir, I took all of those.

The Court : All right, and you stated previously that you got there and when you got there the Police Officers were there? A. Yes.

The Court : And you stated that Officer Cosgrove was among them?

The Witness : Yes, sir.

The Court : At that time.

The Witness : And Hagerty.

The Court : All right, now, subject to connection, I will allow them.

Mr. Gulotta : May we examine before your Honor rules on that?

The Court : Yes, all right.

Mr. Innes : I have another witness.

Mr. Gulotta : I will examine on the admissibility of these photographs preliminarily before the offer is made of the pictures in evidence.

The Court : All right.

Cross-examination by Mr. Gulotta:

Q. Now, officer, when did you go down to this bungalow to take these pictures, these three pictures that were shown to you? A. I went down at 1:30 P. M. August 13th, Friday, 1937.

Q. August 13th? Now, when you got there who was there? A. Why, there was Detective Cosgrove and Hagerty, and Detective Brennan and Murphy.

Q. Is that all? A. That is all I remember.

Q. And were these four officers whose names you have just mentioned, were they moving about the cellar of these premises? A. No, they were outside.

Q. They weren't inside at all? A. No, sir.

Q. Did you learn whether or not they had been in the cellar? A. Why, I don't know that.

Q. Somebody notified you, had they not, to enable you to bring your paraphernalia down there in order to take a picture? A. Yes.

Q. And they had notified you that there was a

body of a little girl in that cellar, is that right? A. Yes.

Q. Now, when were you notified? A. Why, I came into the Station House about one o'clock.

Q. August 13th? A. Yes, I just come from another job and I was going back to take more pictures on that job, two hours, I was having a job done there, so I said I was going to lunch and would be back, and should they be looking for me up at the scene, let me know where it would be, so they said, "We have a little case where we found that little girl murdered."

Q. Now, when you say "We," how many persons talked to you about that? How many notified you? A. Why, the clerical man was there and he told me about it when I come into the station house.

Q. Yes, and you don't know who had been there, do you, before you were notified? A. No.

Q. For that matter, other police officers might have been there, is that correct? A. I don't know who was there.

Q. Do you know what time it was reported that the body of a little girl was found? A. No, sir.

Q. So that it might have been early on the morning of August 13th, is that right, so far as you are concerned? A. I don't know what time.

Q. And you have no way of telling how many people had entered the cellar of these premises? A. Well, the only thing, when I got there, there was, I don't know whether it was an old door or what, was thrown over there, over the back of that cellar door, or over the back of that partition leading into the cellar, and they said they didn't want anybody to go in, that was across the doorway.

Q. And was this cellar door down on the floor of the basement? A. No, this was outside, like a partition off the back of the building.

Q. I see. So that you cannot tell us how many persons had been in the premises, in the cellar of the premises before you got there? A. No.

Q. Nor can you tell us, officer, whether or not the condition that you found-- A. What do you mean by the condition I found?

Q. The condition as you found it and portrayed by this photograph? A. It was just like that.

Q. Existed prior to the time you went down there? A. Yes.

Q. You can tell us that? A. No, the pictures are just as they were taken.

Q. That is the condition as it existed when you took the pictures? A. Yes, sir.

Q. But, you cannot tell us whether or not the condition was the same prior to that time, can you? A. No.

Mr. Gulotta : In view of that, if your Honor please, the defendant objects to the admissibility of these photographs in evidence, first, on the ground that witnesses have repeatedly expressed their opinion, and the manner in which the body of the little girl was found, the slab of stones that were found on the body of the little girl, are now in evidence, the witnesses have minutely described the manner in which the body was found, and therefore, at this time, the pictures in my opinion, serve no other purpose than to inflame the minds of the jury. There is no question here about identification, and, therefore, in my opinion, the pictures could only be allowed upon the question of identification, since there is no denial of the fact that the body was there and the manner in which it was found.

Mr. Innes : Before your Honor rules on the question of the admissibility of this, I want to call another witness. May I ask to withdraw this witness?

The Court : Withdraw the officer. Step down, Officer.

(Witness was withdrawn. )

Mr. Innes: Detective Cosgrove.

DETECTIVE THOMAS S. COSGROVE, recalled, resumed the witness stand and testified as follows :

Direct examination by Mr. Innes :

Q. You told us you were the first officer at the scene of this crime? A. I was.

Q. I show you these three exhibits for identification and ask you to look at them carefully and tell me whether or not those pictures correctly show the situation as you saw it first, when you arrived at the scene? A. They do.

Q. Now then, who was the next officer that came here after you? A. There was a--when I returned from making a 'phone call, there was a Patrolman by the name of Dahlberg from the 122nd Precinct, in response to a radio call, walking through the meadows towards the house ahead of me.

Q. And did you see Detectives Murphy and Brennan there? A. They came about five or ten minutes after I arrived from making the 'phone call.

Q. And while you were still there at the place? A. That is right.

Mr. Innes : All right, that is all.

Mr. Gulotta: May I examine?

The Court : Yes.

Cross-examination by Mr. Gulotta:

Q. Now, Officer Cosgrove, you, I take it, made a minute investigation of this cellar, didn't you? A. At first, yes.

Q. At first. And when you say "at first," you mean when you first went into the cellar, is that right? A. That is right.

Q. And as I understand it, you were the first police officer down there? A. That is right.

Q. Now, having told me that you made a minute inspection of the premises, that is the cellar of the premises, in what connection did you do so? A. Well, I had this little girl reported to me as a missing person.

Q. No, I don't mean that. A. I wanted to --

Q. Excuse me. Did you see pieces of rock around the cellar? A. I seen a number of--

Q. Did you see a number of slabs of brick, mortared together, such as this exhibit? A. I did, yes.

Q. Did you see other debris in the cellar? A. I did.

Q. Did you see any old newspapers? A. Yes..

Q. How many old newspapers did you see? A. Well, I can't say how many.

Q. Will you tell me? A. There were newspapers and other articles scattered about the floor of the basement.

Q. Now, how many newspapers would you say, about, you saw in the cellar of the premises? A. I couldn't exactly say.

Q. And were these newspapers all strewn about, as if used and crumpled up? A. Yes, they were thrown there, as though they were discarded.

Q. As having been discarded? A. And throwaway, but not--

Q. But, not discarded in the manner you might read the evening paper and carefully folded up, is that correct? A. I can't recall, I don't know that.

Q. You were the person who made this inspection, officer, did you see any newspapers all crumpled up in the cellar? A. I didn't see many, no.

Q. I see. Did you see many newspapers that were nicely laid on the floor of the cellar, or near the wall, we will say. A. There may have been a paper here and a paper there.

Q. A paper here and a paper there.

Mr. Gulotta. : May I have that glass, your Honor?

Q. Now, these papers that you saw, were they Staten Island newspapers? A. I didn't pick any papers up.

Q. Did you read any headline that might have appeared on any of the papers? A. I did not.

[Ed. Note: Once again, Mr. Gulotta concentrates of the observations here as compared to the "superhuman" observations of the bus driver, Flick. He knows the identification can be suspect but he has no way of proving that. Today we know the eyewitness identification is the number one cause of wrongful convictions even with the common use of lineups. The

Innocence Project found that, "Eyewitness misidentification is the greatest contributing factor to wrongful convictions proven by DNA testing, playing a role in more than 70% of convictions overturned through DNA testing nationwide."]

Q. All right. Now, I take it that in a serious crime of this kind that you look about for various articles, is that right? A. I did.

Q. In the hopes of perhaps you would find something? A. That is right.

Q. And you now say that you saw no newspaper out of which you might have read a headline, or anything? A. I read no newspapers at that particular time.

Q. No, or out of which you might have read the date of a newspaper? A. No.

Q. Now, I am going to ask you to look at this photograph and ask you whether you saw that newspaper which is on that photograph? A. That paper was there.

Q. Was there? A. That was there.

The Court Do you want a glass?

Mr. Gulotta: Here is a better one, Judge.

(Witness, examines photograph with magnifying glass.)

Q. Thank you. Now, you are positively sure now that that paper was there at the time. A. There was a paper there.

Q. Yes. Now, what is there about the paper that you have looked at through this glass, what is there about that paper that you recall since you are now positive that that paper was there? A. It was a very dirty paper, as I remember it.

Q. Yes. A. There were, it looked like fragments of bottles, or dishes, or saucers--

Q. Don't talk about anything but the newspaper now, please. A. That is about all I can recall.

Q. And you say that it was a very dirty paper? A. I say, parts of it were stained like blots of--

Q. And this paper that you now recall wasn't torn

up? A. No, it was not.

Q. And it wasn't crumpled, was it? A. What do you mean, crumpled in a ball, or--?

Q. That is, crumpled up in a sort of ball? A. No.

Q. Where was that paper that you told us before that was crumpled up? A. I believe there were some papers around the stand where the bottle stood with the grasshopper.

Q. Yes. Now, you saw the bottle down there, did you? A. I did.

**Q. Did you take that bottle? A. I did not.**

**Q. You didn't believe it significant enough to take it, did you? A. I knew it was significant.**

**Q. But, you didn't take it? A. No, nobody is supposed to touch that but a fingerprint expert.**

**Q. And when you went to the station house, you left that bottle there, didn't you? A. I did not.**

**Q. What did you do? A. That bottle was left there 'till Detective Paola and Detective Martin from the Technical Research Bureau arrived.**

**Q. And Detective Paola is the same gentleman who has already taken the stand in this case? A. This morning, yes.**

**Q. Is that right? Now, officer, you don't remember what that paper said, the paper that you now recall that was there at the time, do you? A. I do not, no.**

Q. You didn't look at it enough to read, did you? A. Not at that time, no.

[Ed. Note: So the conclusion is with normal observation and memory not observing or remembering the newspaper and the fact there was no testimony about fingerprints on the bottle. Why didn't the defense call Detective Paola and ask?]

Mr. Gulotta. : All right, same objection is pressed as to this witness on the admissibility of the pictures.

The Court : There is no objection to this witness's

testimony?

Mr. Gulotta : No, not to the testimony, same objection to the admission of evidence of the pictures.

The Court : Make it at the proper time when the other witness is recalled.

Mr. Innes : All right; Officer Brennan. Oh, may I ask one question?

Q. Did Officer Brennan come there while you were there? A. He did, with Detective Murphy.

Examination by the Court:

Q. Just one more question. Were you there continuously until the time Officer Ihnken got there? A. I was there when Detective Ihnken arrived with his camera.

Q. That is from what time of the--what time did you get there? A. Why, I 'phoned about 20 after 12, or 12 :30 and then in response, then I returned about ten minutes to one or one o'clock.

Q. And you were there at 1:30? A. I was there when Detective Ihnken arrived.

By Mr. Innes :

Q. And, officer, one question more. Was anything disturbed in that cellar before Ihnken took those pictures? A. There was nothing disturbed in that cellar whatsoever.

Mr. Innes : All right.

DETECTIVE JOHN M. BRENNAN, Shield No. 1251, 122nd Squad Detectives, New York City Police Department, called as a witness in behalf of the People, first being duly sworn, testified as follows :

Direct examination by Mr. Innes :

Q. Officer, was your attention attracted to this bungalow at some time during the morning of the 13th of August? A. It was.

Q. And did you go to that bungalow? A. I did.

Q. About what time did you get there? A. I arrived there about 12:25 P. M.

Q. And who was there when you arrived? A. Detective Cosgrove and Patrolman Dahlberg, and about four other Cops from Radio cars, the father of the girl.

Q. Were you there continuously from the time, from the time you arrived until Officer Ihnken came and took the pictures? A. I was.

Q. And was anything moved or disturbed in that basement prior to the time he took the pictures? A. There was not.

Q. In fact, was there anything disturbed in that basement until after the Medical Examiner had viewed the scene? A. No, sir, there was not.

Cross-examination by Mr. Gulotta:

Q. Well, officer, when you got there at 12:25, there were Detective Cosgrove and Mr. Dahlberg and you said four cops in radio cars? A. There was about four cops from radio cars.

Q. Did you ask them whether they had gone down to the cellar? A. There was nobody in, near the cellar, because--

Q. The point is right now, did you ask these other officers whether they had gone down to the cellar? A. Yes, I did.

Q. What was the answer? A. No.

Q. Were you appraised of the fact Detective Ihnken had already been directed to take certain photographs at 12:25? A. He, they had called up for him and they were waiting for him to arrive.

Q. Yes, so somebody had been in the cellar, isn't that right? A. Not in the cellar; from the outside, you can look down from the back door and the body was laying about three foot from where you would be standing on the ground in the rear of the house.

Q. And no one had gone into this cellar at all, is that right? A. No, sir.

Q. And you are sure about that? A. Positive.

Q. Of course you can't say who had been in there during the middle of the night can you? A. No, but--

Q. The first you were there was 12:25? A. That is true.

Q. And you have heard by now that this crime was committed on the 12th day of August, 1937, is that right? A. That is true.

Q. Some time, as the indictment says, between 11:00 and 4:00, is that right? You know that to be a fact? A. That is right.

Q. Now, did Detective Cosgrove make his inspection after you got there or before? A. I imagine previous to the time I got there.

Q. Previous to the time you got there? And did you just hear Detective Cosgrove say something about the fact that he made a minute investigation? A. No, sir, I did not.

Q. Would it surprise you if I told you that Detective Cosgrove did testify that he made a minute investigation?

Mr. Innes : Oh, I object to that, if the Court please.

The Court : Objection sustained.

Mr. Gulotta : All right, that is all.

Mr. Innes : Now, I again offer these photographs in evidence.

The Court : Same objection, same ruling, mark them in evidence.

Mr. Gulotta: May we have an exception?

The Court : Yes.

(Three photographs referred to were received in evidence and marked People's Exhibits Nos. 15, 16 and 17, in evidence. )

The Court : Gentlemen, you just look at them and pass them, please.

(At this point the jury examined the three exhibits which had just been received in evidence. )

Mr. Innes: Now, may I recall Officer Cosgrove for one question?

THOMAS S. COSGROVE, recalled as a witness, resumes the witness stand.

Direct examination By Mr. Innes :

Q. Officer, I show you Exhibit No. 16 and ask you if you will look at that and tell me if you see in that picture a concrete shelf in the cellar of that building? A. I do.

Q. And there is something standing on that shelf, is there not? A. There is.

Q. And what was it?

Mr. Gulotta : Just a moment, I object to, it on the ground that the photograph speaks for itself.

The Court : Oh, I think he may call his attention to that in reference to that.

Mr. Gulotta : I respectfully except.

A. There is a bottle containing a grasshopper there, a milk bottle, a Sheffield milk bottle.

Q. Yes. Did you see that milk bottle there prior to the time that Ihnken took that picture? A. I did.

Q. Did you disturb it or touch it at all? A. Nobody handled that bottle.

Q. And you say, Officers Paola and Martin were sent for from the laboratory, research laboratory? A. They answered

Q. For the purpose of determining whether or not there were any prints on the bottle? A. That is right.

Q. I show you this bottle, Exhibit No. 8, for identification and ask you whether or not you recognize that as the bottle that you saw standing on that shelf? A. I do.

Q. Did you mark it in any way? A. I did.

Q. And are your marks there still? A. Part of them, yes, yes, you can see both of them.

Q. "T. C. "? A. That is right.

Q. And was the grasshopper in it? A. It was, it is still in there now.

Q. It is still in there now.

Mr. Innes : I offer the bottle in evidence, if the Court please as evidence.

Mr. Gulotta: I object to it upon the ground that that has not been connected with the defendant in this case. It is irrelevant, and immaterial.

**The Court : I will allow this bottle as part of the property found there, not as connecting this defendant with it.**

Mr. Gulotta : And not the proper foundation has not been laid.

The Court : Mark it in evidence.

Mr. Gulotta : I respectfully except.

(People's Exhibit No. 8 for Identification was received in Evidence. )

Mr. Innes : Now, then, Sheriff Dempsey.

Mr. Gulotta: Just a moment, Officer.

Cross-examination by Mr. Gulotta :

Q. Now, Officer, Mr. Innes showed you a photograph and I noticed you had to use the glass to see what was on the shelf. At the time you picked up your glass to look at that photograph, you didn't know what your answer was going to be, did you? A. What do you mean, I didn't know what my answer was going to be?

Q. You didn't know that the answer was going to be that on the shelf there was a milk bottle, did you? A. Why I knew it all along.

Q. Yes, but nevertheless you took up the photograph, used a strong glass on it, went to the window and after you looked at it, it was then that you said it was a milk bottle. A. Why, I knew all along that it is a milk bottle. I know it is a Sheffield bottle and I know I marked it.

Q. You knew that before you marked--looked at it in the photograph? A. Why absolutely.

Q. And similarly, when you consulted the picture with a thick glass, it wasn't the looking at the picture that determined in your mind there was a grasshopper in it, you can't see that from the picture, can you? A. I thought you might be able to see it with a strong glass that is why I put the glass on it.

Q. You couldn't see it with the strong glass, could you? A. I can't make it out.

Q. And you knew all along, of course, about this

milk bottle and about the grasshopper? A. If the grasshopper was visible by the glass I would have told you about it.

Q. Now, what was the first thing that was done with that bottle after you saw it? A. That bottle was left there until the technicians arrived to dust it for fingerprints.

**Q. Dust it? A. Powder it with the brushes to produce fingerprints.**

**Q. And that was done down at the bungalow? A. It was.**

Q. I see, and then where did the bottle go after that? A. Detective Paola brought it with the bathing suit, and halter straps to me at the office here at St. George.

Q. Yes, and when you got to the office, what did you do with it? A. I marked it, "T. C. " and--

Q. And you will now say that that has been in the station house ever since, will you? A. I will, yes.

Mr. Gulotta : That is all.

Mr. Innes : Sheriff Dempsey.

Sheriff WILLIAM S. DEMPSEY, 121 Wood Avenue, Tottenville, Staten Island, called as a witness on behalf of the People, first being duly sworn, testified as follows Direct examination

By Mr. Innes :

Q. You are the Sheriff of the County of Richmond at the present time? A. Yes.

Q. And you know Samuel Elmore, now, do you not? A. Yes.

Q. Were you present in the District Attorney's Office on the 16th day of August last? A. Yes.

Q. At a time when Elmore made and signed the paper, People's Exhibit No. 5? A. Yes, sir.

Q. And were you present during the time when that paper was read over to him or read by him? A. Yes, sir.

Q. Did there anything occur during the reading of that paper, Sheriff, that brings, it to your mind? A. I don't quite understand the question.

Q. I say, was there some correction made in that paper after it was prepared? A. There was.

Q. What was the nature of that correction?

Mr. Gulotta : I object on the ground that the statement speaks for itself and is now in evidence.

The Court : Are you trying to refresh the Sheriff's recollection? He says he remembers being there, Mr. Innes.

Mr. Innes : Yes. Well, he says he remembers a correction in the paper. I want him to now say what the correction was.

The Court : Let me see what you are referring to.

Mr. Innes : It was made in the typewriting, if the Court please.

( The Court examines the Exhibit. )

The Court : Were you present, Sheriff, when the defendant signed the paper?

The Witness : Yes, your Honor.

The Court : And you saw him sign each sheet of the paper?

The Witness : Yes, sir.

The Court : All right, overruled.

Mr. Gulotta : I respectfully except.

By Mr. Innes :

Q. What was the correction that he suggested? A. When the statement was read to Elmore, he said originally he bought a loaf of bread and a piece of huckleberry pie, rather, he said he bought a huckleberry pie for fifteen cents. When Mr. McKinney read the statement, it was read, "I got a loaf of bread and a fifteen"--

Mr. Gulotta : I object to that on the ground that it is now a statement of something not in evidence.

The Court : I think it is a matter for cross-examination, Mr. Innes, and not a matter for direct examination. The Sheriff says he was there when he signed the paper.

Mr. Innes : All right. Well, I want him to tell what Elmore said about the piece of huckleberry pie.

The Court : I will sustain the objection.

Mr. Innes : All right.

Q. At the time when this paper was taken, Sheriff, was the defendant apparently calm and collected?

Mr. Gulotta : I object to that as calling for a conclusion.

The Court : Overruled.

Mr. Gulotta : I respectfully except.

A. I would say he was.

Q. And did he read the paper himself ? A. He did.

Q. And did you render him any aid or assistance in reading it? A. I did.

Q. What did you do? A. He said he couldn't read without his glasses and I offered him my glasses, he put them on, we asked him if he could then read with them, he said he could, and Mr. McKinney read the statement and he followed him along.

Q. I see, holding one paper in his hand? A. He had the original, I think.

Q. He had the original in his hand? A. In front of him.

Q. And Mr. McKinney was holding a duplicate? A. Right.

Mr. Innes: All right, your witness.

Cross-examination by Mr. Gulotta:

Q. Sheriff, when did you first see the defendant, that is, for the first time? A. Between 11:30 and 12 o'clock on Monday morning, August 16th.

Q. August 16? And by this time did you know whether or not he had been placed under arrest? A. I did not know officially.

Q. I see. Were you notified that Elmore was at the Police Station or Precinct any time before August 16th? A. No, sir.

Q. Did you ever see Elmore before August 16th? A. No, sir.

Q. Did you ever hear that Elmore, on the 13th of August, 1937, sometime in the afternoon, was brought to the 120th precinct? A. I did not.

Q. You did not? And had you known about it you, would have immediately gone over to the 120th Precinct? A. I would not.

Mr. Innes : I object to that as calling for a pure conclusion.

The Court : Objection sustained.

Mr. Innes : I withdraw the objection.

Q. Now, you, of course, know now that Elmore is being tried for murder in the first degree, don't you? A. I do.

Q. And I believe you told me that you did not know when he signed that statement whether he had been placed under arrest or not, is that right? A. When he signed that statement?

Q. Yes. A. I knew he had been under arrest.

Q. Yes, and do you know how long he had been placed under arrest? A. No.

Q. And did you know that he had been placed under arrest on a charge of murder? A. When?

Q. On August 16th, when you witnessed the signing of this statement? A. I did.

Q. And knowing all that, I believe you told Mr. Innes when he asked you, that the defendant was calm? A. I did.

Mr. Gulotta : That is all. One minute, Sheriff.

Q. Sheriff, did you ever take the defendant to the District Attorney's Office? A. I did.

Q. And will you tell me when that was? A. It was between 11:30 and 12 o'clock on Monday morning, August 16th.

Q. August 16th? Was that before the signing of this statement, or after? A. He was taken there before that statement was signed.

Q. Before it was signed? A. Right.

Q. And that was, of course, he had already been arrested? A. He was arraigned in this Court.

Q. And you didn't take him in your custody until when? A. Between 11 :30 and 12 o'clock on Monday, August 16th.

Q. August 16th. And when you took him in your custody, what did you do with him? A. I was requested to take him to the District Attorney's office for further questioning.

Q. For further questioning? And did you take him? A. I did.

Q. And how long did Elmore remain there? A. **'Till about 5:30 that afternoon.**

Q. That is Monday? A. August 16th.

Q. August 16th. And did you stay there with the defendant? A. Never left his presence.

Q. And when he was through about five o'clock, where did you take him? A. To the Richmond County Jail, about quarter to six, between 5:30 and 5:45.

Q. That is Monday night. On Sunday he was at the Richmond County Jail all day, was he not? A. On Sunday when?

Q. On Tuesday, I mean. A. Yes, sir.

Q. And when did you bring him to the Magistrate's Court for the purpose of making an arraignment? A. I don't think he was ever taken there, to my knowledge.

Q. So that he was never taken to the Magistrate's Court from the time you met him at the time of the signing of this statement, is that right? A. Not to my knowledge.

Q. Well, you are the Sheriff of this County? A. That is right.

The Court: He has testified he was arraigned in this Court on the morning of the 16th, when he was put in the custody of the Sheriff.

Q. On the morning of the 16th, and what time was that, Sheriff? A. Between 11:30 and 12 o'clock.

Redirect examination

By Mr. Innes:

Q. And that was on an indictment charging him with murder in the first degree before Judge Cosgrove, in this very room? A. He was remanded without bail in the custody of the Sheriff.

Mr. Gulotta : That is all.
Mr. Innes : All right, the People rest.

Mr. Gulotta : Now, if your Honor please, I am going to ask your indulgence in giving me until, say ten o'clock tomorrow morning for the purpose of making my motion and opening my case.

The Court : No objection to that?

Mr. Innes : Not a bit, I am very glad to accommodate you.

Mr. Gulotta : Thank you, Mr. Innes.

The Court : Gentlemen, we will recess until tomorrow morning at ten o'clock. Now, the instructions which I have issued to you at every adjournment and recess apply at this time. Do not discuss this case with anybody, or even among yourselves, or come to any conclusion in the matter until the case is finally submitted to you and do not read newspapers, if you can avoid it. However, if you do read a newspaper, I do not want you to gather any impression or be guided by anything you see in the newspaper. I have previously instructed you at every recess, at every adjournment, that your decision when you come to make a decision, shall be founded only upon the evidence produced before you. Tomorrow morning at 10:00 o'clock. (Whereupon, at 3:20 P. M. Court recessed until the following morning at 10:00 A. M. )

COUNTY COURT,
RICHMOND COUNTY.
PEOPLE OF THE STATE OF
NEW YORK
Against Indictment No. 55/1937.
Murder 1st Degree. Before:
Hon. THOMAS F. COSGROVE, County Judge, and a Petit Jury.
At the Court House, St. George, S. I. , N. Y. ,
Friday, November 19, 1937, 10 :00 A. M.
APPEARANCES :
Hon. FRANK H. INNES, District Attorney;

JOSEPH A. MCKINNEY, Esq.
   Assistant District Attorney, For the People.
PETER GULOTTA, Esq. ,
WILLIAM C. CASEY, Esq.
   Attorneys for Defendant.

MOTION TO DISMISS.

   Court Clerk Kosman : All manner of persons having any business to do with this term of County Court, held in and for the County of Richmond, draw near, give your attention and you shall be heard. People against Samuel Elmore.
   (Both sides are ready. )
   (Whereupon the Jury was polled and all Jurors answered present. )
   Court Clerk Kosman : People rest.
   Mr. Gulotta : May it please your Honor, the defendants at this time respectfully move to dismiss the second count of the indictment on the ground that the People have failed to make out a prima facie case under that count of the indictment, and on the further ground that facts sufficient to constitute the crime specified in Section 1044 of the Penal Law have not been sufficiently proved to make out a prima facie case, and on the further ground that the people have failed to prove that the deceased died as the result of the violation mentioned in the indictment, Section 2010 of the Penal Law, since it affirmatively appears by the People's own testimony that the deceased died by strangulation.
   The Court : Motion denied.
   Mr. Gulotta : I respectfully except.
   Now, if your Honor pleases, the same motion is made concerning the third count of the indictment, except to substitute instead of Section 2010 of the Penal Law, Section 690, of the Penal Law.
   The Court : Motion denied.
   Mr. Gulotta: The motions are also made with respect to the first and fourth counts of the indictment on

the ground that the people have failed to establish facts, on the ground that they have failed to make out a prima facie case under those counts of the indictment, and on the ground that they have failed to elicit facts sufficient to constitute the crime specified in Section 1044 of the Penal Law, which have not been sufficiently proven to make out a prima facie case.

The Court : Motion denied.

Mr. Gulotta : I respectfully except. Mr. Collins. (No response. )Mr. Steinberg.

Deputy Sheriff : Mr. Collins is here too.

Mr. Gulotta : All right, then, Mr. Collins.

DEFENSE

PATRICK COLLINS, 1559 Richmond Road, Dongan Hills, called as a witness on behalf of the defendant, first being duly sworn, testified as follows :

Direct examination by Mr. Gulotta:
Q. Mr. Collins, will you please talk up loud so that the last juror can hear you? A. Yes.

Q. How long have you lived on Staten Island? A. 65 years.

Q. And how old are you now? A. 69, at the present time.

Q. Do you know a man by the name of Simon Elmore? A. I don't know him by his last name, I knew him by his first name, Sam.

Q. Sam? A. On account of working.

Q. And that person whom you describe as Sam, is he the defendant sitting here? A. Yes, sir.

Q. And that is Simon Elmore? A. Yes, sir.

Q. Now, how long have you known Mr. Elmore? A. I know the man about three years since I worked up that way.

Q. Now, on the 12th day of August, 1937, where were you employed? A. In the W. P. A.

Q. And with any particular project of the W. P. A.? A: Yes, I was a watchman up there.

Q. Watchman. And did your duties bring you at Seaview Hospital? A. Yes.

Q. And did such duties bring you there on the 12th day of August? A. Well, I can't exactly tell the right date.

Q. Yes. Do you remember the day of the week that it was? A. Yes, I remember it was a pay day of the

Thursday.

Q. Yes, of a Thursday. Now then, what time did you get at Seaview Hospital on that Thursday, August 12th? A. Well, I can't--I left the house, I caught the 20 minutes after ten bus coming from St. George.

Q. Yes, and did you see Mr. Elmore on the bus? A. Yes.

Q. And did he ride with you to Seaview Hospital? A. No, he rode with me to Egbertville.

Q. To Egbertville? A. We transferred there.

Q. Transferred? A. Yes.

Q. For another bus? A. Yes, to Seaview Hospital.

Q. To Seaview Hospital. Now, what time did you get to Seaview Hospital? A. I got there the same time as he got there.

Q. I see. And what time was that, Mr. Collins? A. Well, I should judge it was about a quarter to ten.

Q. A quarter to ten. Now, when you got there at Seaview Hospital at a quarter to ten, there is no doubt about it that Elmore was there with you? A. Yes.

Q. Right. Do you know a man by the name of Jack Steinberg? A. No, sir, I don't.

Q. Do you know a man by the name of John Bateman? A. No, sir, I don't.

Q. Do you know Irving Bodaness? A. No, I don't.

Q. Do you know a man by the name of Charles Meyer? A. No sir, I don't.

Q. Do you know Bernard Steger? A. No, sir.

Q. Now, did you go to the Seaview Hospital to collect your pay? A. Yes, sir.

Q. And who was the paymaster there that morning? A. Well, we couldn't tell, because different paymasters every week.

Q. And did you get in line? A. No, sir, I didn't get in line.

Q. Did you go to the pay booth? A. No, we go inside, the watchman is the first man that is paid.

Q. Now, what time did you leave Seaview Hospital? A. Well, as soon as I got paid, I can't exactly say, some days he is there at ten o'clock and some days there at half past ten.

Q. Now, let us restrict ourselves, Mr. Collins, to August 12th. What time about did you leave Seaview Hospital in your estimation? A. I should judge about eleven o'clock.

Q. About eleven o'clock. When you left Seaview Hospital was Samuel Elmore at Seaview Hospital? A. He was in line. He had to get in line to get their money.

Q. And did he remain there when you left? A. Well, that I can't say. We were the first that was paid.

Q. But, it is so that when you left, Simon Elmore was still at Seaview Hospital, isn't it? A. Yes.

Q. And did you leave by bus? A. Yes.

Q. But, Mr. Elmore didn't get on the same bus with you? A. No, sir.

Q. Just one moment.

Mr. Gulotta: Your witness, Mr. Innes.

Cross-examination by Mr. Innes :

Q. You are not positive of the date, Mr. Collins? A. No, sir, I am not.

Q. Except that you know that on a certain pay day-- A. Yes, it happened to be on a payday.

Q. You got on the bus that Elmore was on? A. I got on the bus at Dongan Hills.

Q. And Elmore was on the bus at that time, rode with you? A. To Egbertville.

Q. To Egbertville, there got off the bus? A. Yes.

Q. Took another bus to Seaview and you saw him in line after that? A. Yes.

Q. And you think it was about eleven o'clock that you last saw him? A. No, I should judge it was about twenty minutes to eleven.

Q. Twenty minutes to eleven? A. Yes.

Q. Some time between ten and eleven? A. Some time between ten and eleven.

Q. You can't fix the time so far as that is concerned? A. No.

Mr. Gulotta : One more question, Mr. Collins.

Redirect examination by Mr. Gulotta:

Q. There is no doubt that this is the month , of August that you are discussing, is that right? A. **Oh, it was a hot morning, I remember that.**

Q. Now, how many times a month do you get your pay check? A. Well, our paycheck was changed from one week to two weeks afterwards and that is how we had to go to the second week for our pay.

Q. And this day was payday at Seaview Hospital? A. Yes.

Mr. Gulotta : Thank you.

Recross-examination

By Mr. Innes :

Q. Now, then, Mr. Collins, you were examined by Mr. McKinney in my office, weren't you? A. Sir?

Q. You were examined by Mr. Kinney in my office, weren't you? A. I was examined up in the District Attorney's Office.

Q. Yes. And didn't you tell him that you didn't know whether it was June or July or August? A. Yes, I told him that I didn't know. I know it was a hot morning.

Q. I see, that is all right. All right.

Redirect examination by Mr. Gulotta :

Q. So far as you are concerned now, you are definite that it was in the month of August, are you not? A. I couldn't swear to that, I know it was in hot weather.

Q. How many times did you get your pay in the month of August, if you recall? A. Well, that I can't recollect.

Q. I see. Now, were other people in line getting their pay on that day, is that right ? A. Oh, there was about 75 or 100 men.

Q. Did you know any of the people? A. No, I didn't because I had no business with them, I don't go out there with them.

Q. No one? A. We get paid in the office, see?

Mr. Gulotta: All right.

Now, Mr. Steinberg.

JACOB STEINBERG, 4 School Street, Great Kills, Staten Island, New York, called as a witness in behalf of the defendant, first been duly sworn, testified as follows:

Direct examination by Mr. Gulotta:

Q. What is your age? A. 27.
Q. What is your occupation? A. Painter.
Q. Were you employed by the W. P. A. ? A. Yes, ma'm.
Q. Were you employed by the W. P. A. on August 12th? A. Yes, ma'm.
Q. Of 1937? A. Yes, ma'm.
Q. And did you have occasion on that day to go to Seaview Hospital? A. Yes, ma'm.
Q. Where did you live? A. 4 School Street, Great Kills.
Q. And how far away is that from Seaview Hospital, about? A. Well, with the car it takes me about ten minutes, yes.
Q. Did you go with your car? A. Yes, ma'm.
Q. With your own car? A. Yes, ma'm.
Q. What time did you get at Seaview Hospital? A. At a quarter to ten.
Q. And why did you go to Seaview Hospital? A. To get paid.
Q. To get paid? A. Yes, ma'm.
Q. And do you know Simon Elmore? A. Yes, ma'm.
Q. And how long have you known him? A. I worked with him up there about two years.
Q. Two years. Did you see Simon Elmore at Seaview Hospital? A. Yes, ma'm.
Q. Whereabouts in Seaview Hospital did you see him? A. On a pay line.
Q. Pay line. Were you on the pay line? A. Yes,

ma'm.

Q. Did you finally get your pay? A. Yes, ma'm.

Q. And how much was that, if you remember? A. About forty-two dollars.

Q. About forty-two dollars. Then, having got your pay, I withdraw the question. Were you in line ahead of Elmore? A. Yes, ma'm.

Q. And when you got your pay what did you do, did you go home? A. I went right home.

Q. And did you go home alone? A. Yes, ma'm.

Q. What time did you leave Seaview Hospital towards home? A. Between ten and ten-thirty.

Q. Between ten and ten-thirty. Now, there is no doubt in your mind, is there, that this day was August 12th? A. Yes, ma'm.

Q. 1937, and it was a Thursday, was it not? A. Yes, ma'm.

Q. And it was pay day, was it not? A. Yes, ma'm.

Q. Now, do you know John Stockel? A. No, ma'm.

Q. Do you know the paymaster's name? A. No, ma'm.

Q. Do you know Pat Collins? A. No, ma'm.

Q. Do you know John Bateman? A. Yes, ma'm.

Q. Who is John Bateman? A. He is a painter working up in Seaview.

Q. And he works for the W. P. A., is that right? A. Yes, ma'm.

Q. Did you see a man by the name of Charles Meyer, at Seaview Hospital? A. No, ma'm.

Q. When you left Seaview Hospital was Elmore still on line? A. Yes, ma'm.

Q. He was on line? A. Yes, ma'am.

Q. How many persons ahead of him toward the pay window were you about? A. He was about three in back of me.

Q. All right.

Mr. Gulotta : That is all.

Mr. Innes : Just a question.

Cross-examination by Mr. Innes :

Q. How long did it take you to get your pay there? A. It took me about five minutes to get my pay.

Q. I see. What did you do, sign a payroll? A. Yes, sign a sheet.

Q. And did you get a check after you signed a receipt? A. Yes, ma'am.

Mr. Innes : All right, that is all.

Mr. Gulotta: John Bateman.

JOHN BATEMAN, 229 Beach Terrace, Midland Beach, called as a witness in behalf of the defendant, first being duly sworn, testified as follows:

Direct examination by Mr. Gulotta:

Q. Mr. Bateman, what is your occupation? A. Painter.

Q. And how long have you been a painter? A. 40 years.

Q. 40 years, and how old are you? A. 62.

Q. 62. Now, were you a painter on the 12th of August, 1937? A. Yes.

Q. And for whom were you employed at the time? A. P. W. A.

Q. Did you have occasion to go to Seaview Hospital on that day? A. Yes.

Q. And you are sure that was the 12th of August, are you? A. Yes.

Q. Did you receive a check? A. Yes.

Q. There was a date on that check, was there not? A. Yes.

Q. And the date on it you remember was August 12th? A. No, I don't remember the date on the check.

Q. All right, now, how far away is your home from Seaview Hospital? A. About three miles, I guess.

Q. And how did you get from your home to Seaview Hospital? A. Take a Midland Beach bus to Richmond, transfer to the shuttle.

Q. What time did you leave your home? A. In the morning about ten o'clock.

Q. And what time did you arrive at Seaview Hospital? A. About half past ten, quarter to eleven.

Q. Now, when you got there, did you go towards the paymaster's window? A. Yes.

Q. And was there a line there? A. Big line.

Q. Do you know Simon Elmore? A. Yes.

Q. Was he on line? A. I didn't see him.

Q. Did you see Simon Elmore that day at all? A. No, sir.

Q. Not at all? A. Not at all.

Q. Did you see Pat Collins there that day? A. I don't know him.

Q. Did you see Jack Steinberg? A. No, after he was ahead of me.

Q. Did you see Irving Bodaness? A. No, I didn't see him that day.

Q. Do you know Charles Meyer? A. Yes.

Q. Did you see him? A. I seen Charlie, yes.

Q. No doubt in your mind that Charlie was there? A. Who?

Q. Charlie Meyer? A. Yes, I seen Charlie.

Q. Now, who is the paymaster? A. I can't think of his name. We had a different paymaster every week.

Q. I see. If I told you his name would that refresh your recollection? A. No.

Mr. Gulotta: All right, your witness.

Mr. Innes : No cross.

Mr. Gulotta : Irving Bodaness.

IRVING BODANESS, 14 Avon Place, Tompkinsville, Staten Island, New York, called as a witness in behalf of the defendant, first being duly sworn, testified as follows :

Direct examination by Mr. Gulotta:

Q. Mr. Bodaness, on the 12th of August, 1937, were you at Seaview, Hospital? A. Yes.

Q. What time did you get there? A. Well, it was on a Thursday, getting paid there between ten and eleven.

Q. Yes. And do you know Simon Elmore? A. Right.

Q. Did you see him there that morning? A. Right.

Q. All right, what time did you see him? A. Oh, between ten and eleven.

Q. Eleven o'clock. Did you get your pay? A. Right.

Q. What time did you leave? A. Well, I left, I don't know the time but between ten and eleven--

Q. Between ten and eleven. Well, you say you got there between ten and eleven? A. Somewhere around that time.

Q. And you left between ten and eleven? A. Yes.

Q. All right, now, when you left was Elmore still there? A. Right.

Q. Where was he? A. He was in back of me, about five or more in back of me.

Q. Five in back of you on the line? A. Some where around there.

Q. Now, how long had you known Elmore? A. About the time I was working there, two years.

Q. There is no doubt about it that the man you saw was the defendant here? I say, there is no doubt in your mind that the man you saw is the defendant, Simon Elmore? A. Right, yes I know.

Q. All right. Mr. Gulotta: All right, that is all.

Mr. Innes : Just one question.

Cross-examination By Mr. Innes :

Q. You are not able to fix the time with any definiteness at all? A. No.

Q. It might be near ten and it might be near eleven when you saw Elmore there, is that right? A. Yes.

Mr. Innes : That is all.

Mr. Gulotta: Charles Meyer.

CHARLES MEYER, 49 Townsend Avenue, Clinton, Staten Island, New York, called as a witness in behalf of the defendant, first being duly sworn, testified as follows:

Direct examination by Mr. Gulotta:

Q. How long have you lived on Staten Island, Mr. Meyer? A. Oh, about 27 years.

Q. Do you know Simon Elmore? A. I do, sir.

Q. Did you have occasion to call at Seaview Hospital for your pay on August 12th? A. Yes.

Q. What time did you get there? A. I got there about eleven o'clock.

Q. Eleven o'clock. And when you got there was Simon Elmore there? A. Yes, he was ahead of me in the line.

Q. Now, did you have a conversation with Simon Elmore that morning? A. Not exactly a conversation.

Q. Well, did you swap any words at all? A. Just I said, "Hello Sy".

Q. He said to you-- A. No, I said, "Hello Sy", and he said "Hello" to me.

Q. Does that mean, "Hello Simon"? A. Well, we always called him that since I know him, about 25 years.

Q. And there is no doubt about it in your mind, Mr. Meyer, that the person you saw and about whom you have been testifying is Simon Elmore, the defendant? A. Yes.

Q. All right. Now, what time did you leave Seaview Hospital that morning? A. A quarter of twelve.

Q. Quarter of twelve. Was Simon Elmore still there? A. No, sir.

Q. He had gone? A. He had gone, yes.

Q. What time did he leave? A. Oh, I couldn't' exactly tell you what time he left, it was between eleven and eleven-thirty.

Q. Between eleven and eleven-thirty? A. Eleven thirty because the paymaster--I was way down the line.

Q. All right. Now, there is no doubt in your mind, is there, Mr. Meyers? A. No, sir.

Q. Thank you.

Mr. Innes : Just a question.

Cross-examination by Mr. Innes :

Q. You had no watch or clock, did you? A. No, sir.

Q. You are just giving us your best recollection of the time? A. Yes.

Q. And it might vary half an hour or an hour, might it not? A. Well, I couldn't say that, I couldn't say that it would vary much more than half an hour.

Q. All right, that is all, thank you.

Mr. Gulotta: Bernard Steger.

BERNARD STEGER, 71 Briggs Street, Great Kills, Staten Island, New York, called as a witness in behalf of the defendant, first being duly sworn, testified as follows : Direct examination by Mr. Gulotta:

Q. Mr. Steger, you own an automobile, do you not? A. Yes.

Q. How long have you owned an automobile? A. About 20 years, 22.

Q. Did you own an automobile on August 12th, 1937? A. Yes, sir.

Q. Did you have occasion to drive that automobile to Seaview Hospital? A. Yes.

Q. On the morning of August 12th, 1937? A. Yes.

Q. And did you start from your house? A. Yes.

Q. And how far away is that from Seaview Hospital? A. Well, five miles.

Q. Five miles, and what time did you arrive at Seaview Hospital? A. Well, an average of about ten minutes to eleven.

Q. Ten minutes to eleven. And did you go there for your pay check? A. Yes.

Q. What time did you get your pay check, about? A. Well, it must have been about ten minutes after, maybe five, I can't tell exactly the minutes.

Q. Were you part of this line that had been formed toward the paymaster's window? A. Yes.

Q. Did you see Simon Elmore in that line? A. Yes.

Q. And was he ahead of you or back of you? A. He was in back of me.

Q. And how many persons in back of you was he, about? A. Well, maybe six or seven.

Q. Six or seven, and you told me, I believe, that you got your pay check about what time, quarter after, did you say? A. Not,--well, not a quarter after--about five or ten minutes.

Q. Five or ten minutes after. And when you got your pay check you waited around awhile, did you not? A. Yes, I did.

Q. And did you wait for such time as Elmore got his pay check? A. Yes, sir.

Q. Did you say anything to him about giving him a ride? A. Well, I said, "Hurry up, Elmore, I will take you down to Egbertville."

Q. Egbertville. Did he tell you what he wanted to go to Egbertville for?

Mr. Innes : Oh, I object--I withdraw the objection.

Mr. Gulotta : I will withdraw the question.

By Mr. Gulotta:

**Q. What time did he get in your car about? A. Well, it must have been about a quarter after eleven.**

Q. Quarter after eleven, and you drove, did you? A. Well, I drove him down to Egbertville.

Q. And particularly where in Egbertville? What street? **A. Right on the corner where he gets the bus for Stapleton.**

Q. Yes, would that be Rockland Avenue and Richmond Road? A. Rockland Avenue, it must be it.

Q. Yes. And you let him off at that corner, did you? A. Yes.

Q. And what time was it about when you let him off at the corner? A. Well, it must have been about twenty after.

Q. Eleven? A. Something around that.

Q. All right, now, how long have you known

Simon Elmore? A. Well, I worked with him about off and on maybe a year and a half to two years, I ain't certain because it averaged about that, I would meet him on different jobs.

Q. And the person you saw at Seaview Hospital and the person who came in your automobile and whom you left off at Rockland Avenue, is that Simon Elmore, the defendant? A. That is him.

Mr. Gulotta : Cross-examine.

Cross-examination By Mr. Innes :

Q. This question of time is just your best recollection, isn't it, Mr. Steger? A. Yes, sir.

Q. And it might be before eleven or after eleven? A. Well, it is--the last minute, I know I was at the bank at eleven-thirty in Great Kills.

Q. Eleven-thirty? A. Yes.

Q. That is where you fix the time? A. Yes.

Q. And that is the thing you fix the time on because you were at the bank at eleven-thirty? A. Yes; sir.

Mr. Innes : That is all.

Mr. Casey : Emma Keil.

EMMA KEIL, 600 Richmond Road, Concord, Staten Island, New York, called as a witness in behalf of the defendant, first being duly sworn, testified as follows :

Direct examination by Mr. Gulotta:

Q. Mrs. Keil, do you know Simon Elmore, the defendant in this case? A. I do.

Q. And how long have you known him? A. About 25 years.

Q. 25 years. Do I understand you to say that you now live at 600 Richmond Road? A. I do.

Q. And did you live there on August 12th, 1937? A. I did.

Q. And do you remember that day, do you, Mrs. Keil? A. I do.

Q. Did you at any time on August 12, 1937, see Simon Elmore? A. I did.

Q. Where did you see him? A. Right at my door.

Q. Is that 600 Richmond Road? A. It is.

Q. And what time was it, Mrs. Keil? A. Between eleven and twelve.

Q. Between eleven and twelve. Now, was it towards twelve o'clock or eleven o'clock?

Mr. Innes: Oh, I object to that.

Q. Can you give us anything more definite?

Mr. Innes : That is leading and suggestive, if the Court pleases.

The Court : Objection overruled. Fix the time. As near as you can.

By Mr. Gulotta:

Q. As near as you can, Mrs. Keil. A. Well, I guess it was a little after half past eleven because I have a vegetable man call at that time.

Q. Yes, and you fix the time in that way, do you? A. Yes, between half past eleven and twelve.

Q. Now, you have a place of business, have you, Mrs. Keil? A. I have.

Q. And in what business are you? A. Well, it was a dry goods store, but it isn't any more.

Q. And did you exchange words with Simon Elmore that day? A. I did.

Q. Tell us what words were spoken? A. We bid the time and then I asked him about--

Q. Well, wait a minute, Mrs. Keil. When you say we "bid the time", how was that? A. "Good morning".

Q. You said, "Good morning"? A. Yes.

Q. Did he respond? A. Yes.

Q. What did he say? A. Just "Good morning".

Q. And what after that, Mrs. Keil? A. Then we asked him about his wife's health.

Q. And what did he say? A. He said she was getting along nicely.

Q. Yes. And did he say anything about your health? A. No.

Q. Did he say something about the fact that you

should take turkish baths? To help you out? A. He said it to my brother, not to me.

Q. Was your brother there at the time? A. He was.

Q. And what did he say about taking a turkish bath? A. Oh, "Take a turkish bath and you will be healthy".

Q. Now, you saw him the following day, did you? A. Yes, I did.

Q. And that would be August 13th, is that right? A. I did.

Q. And what time about did you see him on the morning of August 13th? A. Well, it was before noon.

Q. Yes. And some time before noon, did he have a package under his arm? A. Yes.

Mr. Gulotta : May I have that?

By Mr. Gulotta, :

Q. Did the package that he had under his arm look anything like this? A. It was a cement bag.

Q. Cement bag, all right.

Mr. Gulotta : This is referring to People's Exhibit No. 9 for Identification.

Mr. Innes: I note that I remember that it was offered as your exhibit, Mr. Gulotta.

Mr. Gulotta : No, it is marked that way. I will make it my exhibit if you wish.

The Court : Has it been marked in evidence?

Mr. Gulotta : I have no objection.

The Court : That has been marked in evidence?

Mr. Innes : That is my recollection of it, it was marked as Defendant's Exhibit No. 1.

The Court : It is marked for identification. but it is an exhibit in evidence.

Mr. Gulotta : No. 9.

The Court : No. 9 in evidence.

By Mr. Gulotta:

Q. Now, Mrs. Keil, have I asked you everything that transpired when you saw Elmore on the 12th and 13th days of August, 1937? A. Well, all I know is that he **walked down towards Vanderbilt Avenue,** that is all I know.

Q. Was that on the 13th? A. No, that was on the 12th.

Q. After you saw him at the time you have testified to, he walked towards Vanderbilt Avenue? A. Yes.

Mr. Gulotta : All right, your witness, Mr. Innes.

Cross-examination By Mr. Innes :

Q. Mrs. Keil, your recollection of the time is based on, not on examining a clock, is it? A. How do you mean?

Q. I mean did you have a clock to look at to fix the time? A. No.

Q. So you are giving us your best recollection only? A. There was a clock in the butcher store on the corner, but I know I just came--the vegetable man comes between eleven and twelve on that day always.

Q. And you relied on his being there about the same time each day to fix the time? A. Yes.

Q. And you were talking to the vegetable man when Elmore went by? A. Yes.

Q. Now then, on the next day, on the 13th, what do you say as to the time when you saw him there with this cement bag? A. I couldn't exactly tell you the time but I know it was before noon.

Q. Before noon? A. Between ten and twelve.

Q. I see. And--

Mr. Innes : All right, I think that is all.

By Mr. Innes :

Q. In what direction was he going at that time? A. You mean on the 13th?

Q. **On the 13th. A. Well, he went towards Steuben Street. Now, if he went down Steuben Street or across the street, I don't know.**

Q. And he was going in the opposite direction at that time? A. In the opposite direction but I didn't notice what way he went.

Mr. Innes : All right, that is all.

Mr. Gulotta : Thank you, Mrs. Keil.

Mr. Casey : August Charles Baccarezza.

AUGUST CHARLES BACCAREZZA, 16

Waverly Place, Stapleton, Staten Island, called as a witness in behalf of the defendant, first being duly sworn, testified as follows :

Direct examination by Mr. Gulotta:

Q. Mr. Baccarezza, what is your occupation? A. I am a grocery clerk.

Q. For whom? A. A. and P. Tea Company.

Q. And were you in the same job on the 12th day of August, 1937? A. I was.

Q. When you say grocery clerk, what are your duties? A. To serve people groceries behind the counter.

Q. **In other words, you take orders and wrap them up and deliver them? A. Right.**

Q. **Now, did you ever see Simon Elmore in your life? A. Yes, sir.**

Q. **Did you see him on the 12th of August? A. Yes, sir.**

Q. **And where did you see him? A. I saw him in the store where I work.**

Q. **And about what time did you see him? A. A quarter to twelve.**

Q. Now, you were in attendance as a clerk there, were you not? A. That is right.

Q. And did he place an order with you? A. He did.

Q. And can you remember what order he placed with you? A. I don't remember exactly, it was bread and canned milk, things like that.

Q. And such things as that? A. Yes.

Q. Articles of groceries? A. Yes.

Q. **And do you remember how much the bill came to? A. It was approximately $1.40.**

Q. **$1. 40. Did he pay you? A. Not that day.**

Q. **Not that day. Did he offer to give you a check? A. He did.**

Q. Do you remember whether or not it was a check of the W. P. A. ? A. I don't know, sir.

Q. But, nevertheless it was a check? A. It was a check.

Q. Did you cash that check? A. No, sir.

Q. What did you say, if anything, concerning that check when he handed it to you? A. I said I didn't have enough money handy to cash the check and he could pay me tomorrow if he wanted to.

Q. And did you allow him to take the groceries along? A. I did.

Q. Had you known Simon Elmore before that day? A. I did.

Q. And how long had you known him? A. Oh, about six or seven years.

Q. And how long had you known him? A. About six or seven years.

Q. And had he traded in that store before? A. He did.

Q. May I ask you for the time again when he came into the store? A. About a quarter of twelve.

Q. **And what time did he leave the store, about? A. He wasn't in the store more than ten minutes I should say.**

Q. **Ten minutes. So that he left your store approximately around 11:55? A. Right.**

Q. **That's correct? A. That is right.**

Q. **Did he exchange any words with you that day? A. Not that I can remember.**

Q. **Well sometimes they call you "Buck" don't they? A. Yes.**

Q. **And they call you "Buck Jones" sometimes, don't they? A. No, --a little.**

Q. **Do you know the reason for that? A. No, I don't.**

Q. **Did Simon Elmore call you "Buck" on that day? A. Yes, I think he did.**

Mr. Gulotta : All right, that is all.

Cross-examination By Mr. Innes :

Q. Do you remember--now, let's see--young man, isn't it a fact that Elmore was there earlier that morning? A. He was.

Q. What time was he there first? A. About 9 :30 in

the morning.

Q. And did he leave an order at that time? A. He did.

Q. And you had filled it when he came back, is that right? A. Yes.

Q. And that you think was about 11:45? A. Yes.

Q. And you had the order already for him? A. No, he had to wait for it, I didn't have it ready.

Q. Can you remember what he ordered that time? A. As I said before, it was canned milk and bread and things of that kind.

Q. Now, then, do you remember whether or not he ordered clams? A. No, sir, I don't.

Q. Or carrots and peas? A. No sir, I don't.

Q. Would you say that he didn't order or he did order at that time? A. I can't say, I really don't remember.

Q. You don't remember anything that he ordered? A. Just bread and canned milk.

Q. You are giving us your best recollection as to the time, are you not, young man? A. Yes, sir.

Q. You are not positive? A. I am not positive.

Mr. Innes : All right, that is all.

Mr. Gulotta : Thank you, Mr. Baccarezza.

Mr. Casey : Staten Island Savings Bank?

Mr. Gulotta : Mr. Arrington.

ARTHUR ARRINGTON, 5769 Amboy Road, Princes Bay, Staten Island, New York, called as a witness for the defendant, being first duly sworn, testified as follows:

Direct examination by Mr. Gulotta :

Q. Mr. Arrington, what is your business? A. Architect.

Q. And how long have you been an architect? A. About 30 years.

Q. Now, at my request this morning, did you take a look at this map? A. I did.

(Referring to Defendant's Exhibit A. )

Mr. Innes: People's Exhibit number--identify it.

Mr. Gulotta : This is Defendant's Exhibit A. A. It is a map of the property from--

Q. Just take that. A. It is a map of the area of Staten Island from Midland Beach to Fort Wadsworth, bordering on the Bay.

Q. Now, Mr. Arrington, can you pick up Metcalfe Street on that map? A. Yes.

Q. Now, will you take your pen, Mr. Arrington, and put your initials where it says "Metcalfe Street". A. I did.

Q. You have that. Now, will you draw a line along Metcalfe Street to Targee Street? A. (Witness does so. ) It is done.

Q. Now, will you draw a line to Vanderbilt Avenue? A. Yes.

Q. And then to Richmond Road? A. Well, that is at Richmond Road now.

Q. Now, then will you trace that down on Richmond Road to Clove Road, let me see that one moment.

Mr. Gulotta : Where is Metcalfe, you have got that line, this, you should come down here. Now, I will have to ask Mr. Arrington to strike out this line he has made, Mr. Innes.

Mr. Innes : Yes, surely.

Mr. Gulotta: All right, just strike that line out. (Witness strikes line out. )

Mr. Innes : You made a mistake.

Mr. Gulotta : If you will just take here a minute, I can follow it through. Will you draw this line down Targee Street into Steuben? (Witness draws line. )

Mr. Gulotta : And down Steuben Street and down Steuben Street to Hanover Avenue, across Hanover Avenue to DeKalb, across the meadows to Moselle Avenue, Clove Road and Hylan Boulevard is it--down through Clove Road to Hylan Boulevard, down Norway Avenue to Olympia Boulevard. Don't write over this, just wait, for a minute. All right, that is good. In through

Olympia Boulevard to Xenia, across the meadows to Evergreen Avenue, down Evergreen Avenue to the beach, up to here please. All right, now take it back again.

Q. Now, Mr. Arrington, what is the scale of miles on that map? A. It is about a thousand foot to the inch. The paper has shrunken so that it doesn't quite scale that now. There is a scale right on here for my measurement.

Q. But, it is fairly accurate, though, isn't it? A. Yes.

Q. Now, can you measure those lines that you have drawn on that map? A. Yes, sir.

Q. And tell us the distance between the first point and the last? A. It is approximately 15,000 feet.

Q. 15,000 feet. How many miles does that make? A. About 3 miles.

Q. 3 miles plus. A. Three minus.

Mr. Innes : Minus. A. No, three miles minus.

By Mr. Gulotta:

Q. And how much minus? A. Well, probably 600 feet.

Q. 600 feet minus of three miles, is that right? A. Something like that

Mr. Gulotta : Your witness.

Cross-examination by Mr. Innes :

Q. Do you remember that when you were a school boy that a mile contains 5,280 feet? A. That is right.

Q. And 15,000 divided by 5,280 leaves you quite a lot shy of three miles, does it not? A. It would leave about 6, 7, 800 feet.

Q. Yes. That is all.

Mr. Gulotta: Just one moment, if you please, may I have that paper? If your Honor will bear with me a minute. Oh, yes.

Redirect examination by Mr. Gulotta:

Q. Now, Mr. Arrington, I am going to ask you to take this map and locate for me Seaside Boulevard. Have you got that? A. Yes.

Q. Now, will you draw a line from a point on Seaside Boulevard to Sand Lane?

Mr. Innes : Starting where, Mr. Gulotta?

Mr. Gulotta : Starting at about a point at Peter Crane's Hotel.

Mr. Innes : Peter Crane's Hotel I take it is not shown on the map so you will have to locate it otherwise.

Mr. Gulotta: Well, we will have to locate it. Maybe we can agree on that, Mr. Innes.

Mr. Gulotta: Do you know the name of the street?

Mr. Innes : No.

Mr. Gulotta : I don't find it on the map.

Mr. Innes : There is no street anywheres near it.

By Mr. Gulotta:

Q. Now, will you draw a line to Sand Lane, Mr. Arrington? A. From what point?

Q. Can you tell us, Mr. Arrington, about what point in that map Peter Crane's Hotel is? A. I didn't know there was such a place.

Q. Yes. Do you know where Bessi's Hotel is? A. Down near May's.

Mr. Innes : Below May's.

By Mr. Gulotta:

Q. Just below May's, right. A. Just below May's. Now, from this map I couldn't tell. I am familiar with that area too.

Q. Can you locate any street on Seaside Boulevard? A. Oh, yes, McLaughlin must be somewheres around it because I was down there and that is somewheres in the area of that.

Q. All right. Now, where you have put the circle, now would that be fairly accurate? A. I think it would be fairly accurate.

Mr. Gulotta: I think we can agree--all right.

By Mr. Gulotta:

Q. Well, now, if you will draw a line to Sand Lane and draw a line now all the way down to McClean Avenue. A. On Sand Lane?

Q. Will you make that Old Town Road, and then we will get over to the other line later. That is Olympia Boulevard perhaps on that map. A. Olympia Boulevard.

Q. Either that or Old Town Road, I don't know

how it is on that map. A. I can't find any Old Town here. Here is Old Town.

Q. It is above the Railroad? A. I find Old Town Road coming down here to Nugent, and then it breaks off and stops. Olympia Boulevard.

Mr. Innes: Yes, that has been broken in to three streets, Mr. Arrington, Vulcan Street and Olympia Boulevard.

By Mr. Casey:

Q. There is Olympia Boulevard there, that is the line you want. A. Up here to there and then along Olympia Boulevard to here.

Mr. Casey : Yes, that is right.

By Mr. Gulotta:

Q. Have you got that, Mr. Arrington? A. Yes.

Q. All right. Now then, will you continue that line up Old Town Road to Norway Avenue? A. Well, we have that, it comes into the intersection of Norway.

Q. All right. Now, Mr. Arrington, will you give us the measurements there as you did in the other case, will you give us the distance? A. Yes. About 5, 400 feet.

Q. Now, did you estimate what that is in miles or a fraction of a mile or-- A. It is about a mile and--

Q. A mile? A. Mile and a tenth, something like that.

Mr. Gulotta: All right, Mr. Innes, that is all, your witness.

Mr. Innes: I have no questions.

Mr. Gulotta: All right, thank you, Mr. Arrington.

JOHN P. CARNEY, 125 Osgood Avenue, Stapleton, Staten Island, New York, called as a witness in behalf of the defendant being first duly sworn, testified as follows:

Direct examination by Mr. Gulotta:

Q. Mr. Carney, what is your business? A. Sheet metal worker.

Q. Were you employed on the 12th of August,

1937? A. Yes.

Q. And where were you employed? A. B. & 0. Railroad, Clifton, Staten Island.

Q. Now, what is the nature of your work down there, is it indoor work or outdoor work? A. In and out.

Q. In and out. Now, during the course of that day, August 12, 1937, did you at any time see Simon Elmore? A. I did, yes.

Q. How long have you known Simon Elmore? A. 15 or 20 years.

Q. 15 or 20 years. Have you been friendly with him? A. Occasionally met him, talked to him on the street.

Q. Now, did you see him on August 12th? A. I did.

Q. And what time did you see him? A. Between 2:00 and 2:15.

Q. Now, how do you arrive at the hour, 2:00 and 2:15? A. Because I was working on an electric car at the time and I left the job to go up to the tin shop to get something and happened to look at the boss' clock and see that it was 2:00 o'clock.

Q. Now, can you give us a more definite location of the B. & 0. yards, where it is located? A. Where it is located?

Q. Yes. A. Just what do you mean by that?

Q. Well, I know it is in Staten Island? A. Yes.

Q. The B. & 0. yard doesn't mean anything to me. Whereabouts on the island is it? A. Well, I would say it is Clifton, the lower part of Stapleton.

Q. Yes, and near Clifton or the lower part of Stapleton? A. Right.

Q. All right, that is all right. Now, did you talk to Elmore that day? A. Just waved my hand and said "Hello, Sime".

Q. "Hello, Sy"? A. "Hello, Sime".

Q. Did he say anything to you? A. "Hello Jack".

Q. Did he have anything with him that day? A. I couldn't say, I only gave him a glancing look.

Q. Now, is there any doubt in your mind that the

person that you saw at the time, at that place, was. Simon Elmore, the defendant here? A. Yes.

Q. Is there any doubt? A. No, sir.

Q. All right.

Cross-examination by Mr. McKinney:

Q. Mr. Carney, you didn't look at your watch when you saw Elmore, did you? A. No sir, I didn't look at my watch, I looked at the boss' clock before I left the shop.

Q. And you figure then, it was about 15 minutes or so after you looked at that clock that you saw Elmore walking through the yard? A. Well, I wouldn't say any more than 15 minutes.

Q. I know, but you figure, or you calculate it was about 15 minutes or so after you looked at the clock that you saw him? A. No, I wouldn't say it was 15 minutes, I would say it was about 5.

Q. Well, now, didn't you, in answer to Mr. Gulotta's question say that you saw Elmore between 2:00 and 2:15? A. That is right.

Q. And so that it was sometime in that period? A. That is right.

Q. It might have been 15 minutes after two? Or it may have been one minute? A. That is right.

Q. So that you just calculate the time to be that? A. That is right.

Q. Is that right, that is your best recollection? A. Right.

Q. Now, you remember being in the District Attorney's office, Mr. Carney? A. Yes, I do.

Q. Do you recall what day that was? A. A week ago Tuesday.

Q. And there you spoke to somebody, is that right? A. Yes, sir.

Q. And that party was myself? A. Yes, sir.

Q. Now, after you spoke to me--question withdrawn. You gave me certain information as to what time you saw Elmore on August 12th, is that right? A. Yes, sir.

Q. Now, did you talk to anybody from August 12th, from that day, which was November 9th, down to date, concerning the time you saw Elmore? A. Not that I think of.

Q. You didn't talk to anyone at all? A. Not that I think of.

Q. Did you ever talk to a Mr. McKittrick? A. Oh, yes, that wasn't since I seen you.

Q. That wasn't since you saw me? A. No.

Q. Did you talk to him before that time? A. Before that when I was served with the summons.

Q. And how long before? A. Oh, I beg pardon, I did talk to Mr. McKittrick. He served me with a summons after I was talking to you.

Q. Yes, and that was after November 9th? A. Yes.

Q. Now, did you have any conversation with McKittrick? A. No, sir.

Q. Did you have any conversation at all concerning the time you saw Elmore? A. Not at the time I didn't.

Q. And at any other time did you have any--A. On investigation, I did, yes.

Q. And tell us what this conversation was concerning the time? A. The conversation was, did I see Mr. Elmore on that day.

Q. Yes. A. And just what time, and that is all there is to it.

Q. Was there anything said about making that time closer to one o'clock? A. Not that I can think of.

Q. You are sure of that? A. I am positive.

**Q. You are sure Mr. McKittrick or someone else didn't say to you, change the time from 2:00 to 2:15 to 1:00? A. No, sir.**

**Mr. McKinney: That is all.**

[Ed. Note: Could this question be the reason the jurors asked about their power to recalculate time if they thought was witness was mistaken? This will become an important question in the closing arguments and appeal.]

Redirect examination by Mr. Gulotta:

Q. Mr. Carney, did you ever speak to me about this case? A. No, sir.

Q. Did you ever speak to Mr. Casey about this case? A. No, sir.

Q. Did you ever speak to Mr. Fogler, of my office, about this case? A. No, sir.

Q. When Mr. McKittrick came to see you, did he represent to you that he was investigating this case for us? A. He didn't say anything about it.

Mr. Gulotta : All right, thank you.

Recross-examination, by Mr. McKinney:

Q. Nevertheless, Mr. McKittrick spoke to you concerning the time you saw Elmore, didn't he? A. He just asked me the time.

Q. Yes. And he served you with a subpoena to appear as a witness for the defense? A. Later on, yes, I also told two detectives in the Master Mechanics' office at the time.

Q. The Master Mechanics, that is two detectives down at the yard? A. Yes, sir.

Q. Down at the B. & 0. where you work? A. Yes, sir.

By Mr. Gulotta:

Q. And did you tell them the same time you just told this court and this jury? A. Yes, sir.

Mr. Gulotta: Thank you.

Mr. McKinney : That is all.

Mr. Casey : Mr. Harris.
Deputy Sheriff: He is not here yet.
Mr. Gulotta : Louis DaLecy.

LOUIS DA LECY, 116 Broad Street, Stapleton, Staten Island, called as a witness in behalf of the defendant, being first duly sworn, testified as follows :

Direct examination by Mr. Gulotta:

Q. Mr. Da Lecy, what is your business? A. Tailor.

Q. And have you a place of business on Staten Island? A. Yes.

Q. And where on Staten Island? A. Stapleton.

Q. Well, do you know the name of the street? A. Street?

Q. Yes. A. It is Broad Street, yes.

Q. Broad Street? A. Broad Street.

Q. And what is the number? A. 116.

Q. 116. And did you have that tailor shop on the 12th of August, 1937, did you have the same shop? A. Same shop, yes.

Q. Same shop? A. Same place, yes.

Q. And how long have you had that shop? A. 30 years.

Q. 30 years. Do you do alterations? On men's clothes? A. Yes.

Q. Do you make suits also? A. Yes.

Q. And repair suits? A. Everything.

Q. Do you press suits? A. Yes.

Q. You press suits too, Mr. Da Lecy? A. I press suits too.

Q. Now, do you know Simon Elmore? A. Well, I know he came in my store.

Q. On that day, August 12th? A. Yes, that day, yes.

Q. And what time did he come in your store? A. It was about half past two or three o'clock.

Q. Three o'clock. And what did he come into your store for? A. He came for to bring a pair of pants to make short.

Q. To make short? A. To make short, yes.

Q. And was that a new pair of pants? A. New pair of pants, yes.

Q. And do you know where he had bought those pants? A. Yes, Harris.

Q. Harris, is that Edward Harris the pants man? A. Yes. He send me on my place.

Q. You mean Mr. Harris sends all alteration work

to you? A. Yes.

Q. In other words, Mr. Harris, sells the finished products ready made? A. Yes, it is made.

Q. And when there are alterations needed, he sends them to you? A. He sends to me, yes.

Q. Now, what kind of pants did Elmore bring in? A. It was a blue with stripes.

Q. Blue with a stripe? A. Yes.

Q. And do you remember the material? A. Sure.

Q. What kind of material was it? A. Well, cheap stuff.

Q. Cheap stuff? A. Cheap stuff, yes.

Q. All right. Now, how much did you shorten those pants, do you remember? A. I don't know.

Q. But, you did shorten them, didn't you? A. Yes, sure.

Q. And did he wait for the pants? A. He was waiting, yes.

Q. And how long did he wait for these pants? A. Oh, about ten minutes.

Q. Ten minutes? A. Yes.

Q. And did you charge him for it? A. Oh, sure.

Q. How much did you charge him? A. A quarter.

Q. Twenty-five cents? A. Twenty-five cents.

Q. How long did all that take from the time he came in? A. That was ten minutes, it took.

Q. A matter of ten minutes? A. Yes.

Q. Did Elmore have any bundles with him? A. No.

Q. He did not have anything? A. He didn't have anything.

Q. But, he had the bundle that he was carrying the pants in, is that right? A. Yes.

Q. Or was it the pants itself? A. Just the pants itself.

Mr. Gulotta : Mr. Elmore, stand up.

Q. Now, Mr. Da Lecy, is that the man that--A. Yes, that is the man.

Q. Is that the man? A. Yes.

Q. All right, now, did he wear those pants, did he change them in your store? A. No.

(Whereupon the defendant sat down.)

Q. He put them in a bundle. A. Yes, bundle.

Q. And left, paid you and that is all, is that right? A. Yes, that is all.

Q. Now, you have never seen me before in your life, have you? A. No.

Q. And have you ever seen Mr. Casey in your life? A. No.

Q. Or my assistant, Mr. Fogler, in your life? A. No.

Mr. Gulotta: All right, that is all.

Cross-examination, by Mr. McKinney:

Q. Do you know Mr. McKittrick, Mr. DaLecey? A. McKittrick?

Q. Mr. McKittrick? A. No.

Q. You don't know him? A. No.

Q. Do you understand the question? A. Yes, I understand the question.

Q. Well, do you know Mr. McKittrick? A. McKittrick, no.

Q. Were you served with a subpoena to attend here as a witness for the defense? A. Yes.

Q. And who served that subpoena upon you? A. I don't know.

Q. Do you know? A. No, I don't know.

Q. And now how do you fix the time that Elmore was in your store between 2:30 and 3:00 o'clock? Did you look at your watch? A. No, about 3--

Q. Now, did you, --question withdrawn. Was it between 3:00 and 3:30? A. Well, about half past two, three o'clock.

Q. Now, you are sure it was not later than three o'clock? A. I don't think it was any later than three o'clock.

Q. What is the answer? A. I don't think

Q. You don't think? A. No.

Q. Now, what makes you say that you don't think it was after 3:00 o'clock? A. Well, I think it was that time he came.

Q. What was the last time you looked at a watch before 2:30? A. Well, I got a clock just on the front of me, you see.

Q. Now, what time was it when you last looked at that clock on that day before 2:30? A. Well, I not remember, I don't know. I told you about half past two, three o'clock.

Q. And do you remember speaking to me in the District Attorney's office? A. Yes.

Q. And do you remember telling me what time you saw Elmore in your store? A. Sure.

Q. I now show you a paper and ask you if that is your signature? A. Yes, about half past two, three o'clock.

Q. Now, I ask you if that is your signature? A. Yes, that is mine.

Q. And I ask you now to look at this paper and ask you if you saw that whole thing before? A. Yes, you showed it to me, this paper.

Q. And where did you see that paper before?

Mr. Gulotta : Mr. McKinney, would you kindly give me a view of the witness?

Mr. McKinney: I am sorry.

By Mr. McKinney:

Q. Where did you see that before? A. Down here.

Q. When you say down here, do you mean upstairs? A. Upstairs, yes.

Q. In the District Attorney's office? A. Yes.

Q. Did you read that paper over? A. Yes.

Q. And the statements contained in that paper were true? A. Yes.

Q. To your best recollection? A. That is right, yes.

Q. Now, I ask you to read that paper over again to yourself. A. ( Whereupon witness reads paper. ) About half past three, yes.

Q. Have you read the paper? A. Yes.

Q. Now, I will ask you the question once again, could it have been or was it later than three o'clock that afternoon that Elmore was in your store? A. Well, I don't remember to be sure because some people come in my store, I can't tell you just so.

Q. Now then, it could have been after three o'clock, is that right? A. I think, yes.

Q. Yes. And it could have been later than three-thirty that he was in your store, is that right? A. I am not sure because the customer--

Q. It could have been? A. Yes.

Mr. McKinney : That is all.

Mr. Gulotta : Can I see the date of that, Mr. McKinney?

Mr. McKinney : I will offer it in evidence.

Mr. Gulotta : I just want the date. I just want to question on that.

Redirect examination by Mr. Gulotta:

Q. What is the date that you signed this paper, Mr. Da Lecy? A. Well, I am not remember.

Q. What--was it in the month of November, in the month of November? A. November, yes.

Q. That was this month you signed it, is that right? A. Yes this month, sure.

Q. And did a big husky man come to inquire what you knew about the case? A. Yes, he was stout.

Q. And a big man? A. Big man.

Q. Do you know his name? A. No, I not remember.

Q. Did he say his name was McKittrick, he didn't say that, did he? A. I don't know, I don't remember.

Q. All right. Well, now, McKittrick came to see you before you saw that paper? A. Two times came.

Q. And that was before that you signed this paper? A. I don't know.

Q. I will withdraw that and ask it again. A. Yes.

Q. The first time McKittrick came to see you. A. Yes.

Q. That was before you signed this paper, wasn't it? Some time in the month of September? A. I no remember.

Q. But, do you remember that it was before

November 8th? A. Oh, sure.

Q. Sure. Now, then, again the same man, Mr. McKittrick, he came to leave a paper with you, is that right, a subpoena; do you know what a subpoena is? A. Yes, subpoena.

Q. And did he leave it with you? A. Yes.

Q. He brought it to you, didn't he? A. Yes.

Mr. Gulotta: All right, that is all.

Mr. McKinney: That is all.

Mr. Casey : Is anyone from the Staten Island Savings Bank there?

Mr. Gulotta: Your Honor, since we are going along so well, making good time, can we have a recess for five minutes?

The Court : I think so. No objection on the part of the jury, I guess. We will recess for about ten minutes. Do not discuss this case or come to any conclusion in the matter until the case is finally submitted to you and you retire to your jury room.

(Whereupon at 11 :30 A. M. court recessed until 11 :56, when it again reconvened. )

Court Clerk Kosman : People against Samuel Elmore. (Both sides were ready. ) (Whereupon the jury was polled and all jurors answered present. )

MATILDA J. MCKITTRICK, 341 Vanderbilt Avenue, Stapleton, Staten Island, called as a witness in behalf of the defendant, first being duly sworn, testified as follows:

Direct examination, by Mr. Gulotta, :

Q. Miss McKittrick, how long have you lived at the address which you have just given? A. All my life.

Q. Do you know where Metcalfe Street is? A. I do.

Q. And do you know where the house that Simon Elmore lived in is located? A. I do.

Q. Do you know the number? A. No, I don't.

Q. How far away is the house that Elmore lived in from your house-- A. Well, I won't give you the exact--I could tell you it is three blocks up from my home.

Q. About three blocks up? A. About three blocks up.

Q. Now, Miss McKittrick, do you remember the 12th day of August, 1937? A. I do.

Q. And that was a Thursday, was it not? A. It was.

Q. And were you home that day? A. I was.

Q. Do you remember what time you got up that morning? A. Well, around, well, between seven and seven-thirty.

Q. Seven and seven-thirty. And did you have your lunch that day? A. I did.

Q. What time did you have your lunch? A. Well, between twelve and twelve-thirty.

Q. Now, after that, between twelve and twelve thirty after you had your lunch, did you go out in the yard? A. I did.

Q. And did you go to the front lawn? A. I did.

Q. You grow flowers and things, do you not, there at your house? A. I do.

Q. Yes. Now, were you using a lawn mower on that day? A. I was.

Q. At about what time were you using a lawn mower? A. Why, I had used it in the morning and after I came out from my lunch I started to use it.

Q. Yes. And what time would you say that you started cutting the grass on that day? A. Well, I would say between ten and ten-thirty.

Q. I mean after lunch? A. Well, I would say at about twenty to one.

Q. Twenty to one? A. About that, I am not certain.

Q. Now, did you see anybody pass your house that day? A. I did.

Q. Who did you see pass your house? A. Well, I saw Mr. Elmore.

Q. And how long were you mowing the lawn before you saw Mr. Elmore? A. Maybe about five minutes.

Q. Five minutes. Had you known Simon Elmore before that time? A. All my life.

Q. And has he been living in that neighborhood for a length of time? A. Yes.

Q. As long as you have-- A. Well, I don't know if he has been there all the time, I have lived there all the time.

Q. I see. Now, was Mr. Elmore on the sidewalk in front of your house? A. No, he was on the opposite side to my home.

Q. And how far away from where you were standing was he passing by your home? A. Well, whatever the width of Vanderbilt Avenue is, I really don't know.

Q. In other words, the width of Vanderbilt Avenue? A. That is right.

Q. Did he say anything to you from the other side of the street? A. No, he didn't speak to me.

Q. Did you say anything to him? A. No, I didn't.

Q. **And you say that at that time he was passing your house, he was passing on the opposite side of the street, that is approximately what time? A. Well, I would say about, well shortly before one.**

Q. Shortly before one? A. Yes.

Q. And would you now help us out and tell us how shortly before one would it be, five minutes before one or ten minutes? A. I can't tell you the exact time, I had no reason to look.

Q. And what would you say that it was, within a quarter of one? A. I think it was just before one, I just can't tell you the exact time.

Q. About ten minutes to one? A. It may have been closer to ten minutes to one.

Q. It was closer to ten minutes to one than to one, is that correct? A. Yes.

Q. **Now, which way was he walking? A. Towards Clifton.**

Q. Towards Clifton. And is there any doubt, Miss

McKittrick, in your mind that the person whom you saw and whom you have just described is Simon Elmore? A. No, I know it was Simon Elmore.

    Mr. Gulotta : Cross-examine.

    Cross-examination By Mr. Innes :

    Q. Miss McKittrick, James McKittrick is your brother, is he not? A. He is.

    Q. And he is a retired police officer of the City of New York? A. That is right.

    Q. And is now retired? A. That is right.

    Q. And getting a retirement allowance, I assume? A. That is right.

    Q. He is your brother? A. He is.

    Mr. Innes: That is all.

Redirect examination by Mr. Gulotta:

    Q. Miss McKittrick, did you notice whether Elmore was carrying anything? A. **Yes, he had a package in his hand.**

    Q. Did you notice what that package looked like? A. Well, it had a light colored wrapping paper on it.

    Q. Wrapping paper? A. Yes.

    Q. I see. All right.

    Recross-examination By Mr. Innes :

    Q. **He was then walking away from the direction of his home, was he not? A. Yes.**

    Q. And you know that your brother has been doing some investigating of this case? A. I do.

    Mr. Innes: That is all.

    Mr. Casey : Edward Harris. Is Edward Harris here yet? (Witness comes up.)

    EDWARD HARRIS, 152 Broad Street, Stapleton, Staten Island, New York, called as a witness in behalf of the defendant, first being duly sworn, testified as follows:

    Direct examination by Hr. Gulotta:

    Q. Mr. Harris, what is your business? A. Men's

wear business.

Q. And do you sell suits? A. No, sir.

Q. Do you sell pants? A. Yes, sir.

Q. Where is your store located, Mr. Harris? A. 152 Broad Street.

Q. And is that store near the tailor shop of Louis Da Lecy? A. Yes, sir.

Q. You know Louis Da Lecy, do you not? A. Yes, sir.

Q. Do you often send him work? A. Yes, sir.

Q. Do I understand you to say that you have no man who does alteration work on your place? Is that right? A. I have alterations done on my place when my wife is at home and my mother.

Q. But, you didn't on the 12th of August, 1937, did you? A. My wife and mother weren't home.

Q. I see. Now, on that day, some time in the afternoon, did a man come in to buy a pair of pants from you? A. Yes, sir.

Q. And is that man Simon Elmore? A. Yes, sir.

Q. Had you ever seen him before? A. Many a time.

Q. Many a time? There is no doubt in your mind that the man that came in to your shop was Simon Elmore? A. Yes, sir.

Q. Now, did he ask to buy a pair of pants? A. I was on the outside of the store when he came across and he asked to buy a pair of pants.

Q. And did he go into your store? A. Yes, sir.

Q. And then did he proceed to select a pair of pants? A. The first pair he saw.

Q. And did you sell him a pair of pants? A. Yes, sir.

Q. All right. Now, did he try them on in your store? A. No, sir.

Q. Was there something about--something said about alteration? A. Yes, sir.

Q. Yes. And what was said about alteration? A. I told him the pants would be too long for him, I said,

"Here is twenty-five cents, go down to the tailors and he will shorten them for you".

Q. And, did you give him twenty-five cents? A. Yes, sir.

Q. Was that out of the purchase price of the pants? A. Yes, sir.

Q. How much did the pants cost? A. $2.95, and he paid $2.70.

Q. $2.70? And you gave him a quarter and he left your shop? A. Yes, sir.

Q. Is that right? Now, will you give us your best idea, please, Mr. Harris, as to the time of the day Mr. Elmore came into your shop? A. Three o'clock in the afternoon.

Q. Three o'clock? And, how long did this process of the purchase of the pants take? A. A couple of minutes.

Q. A couple of minutes?

Mr. Gulotta: Your witness.

Cross-examination By Mr. Innes :

Q. How do you fix the time, Mr. Harris? A. My mother was going to take a bus at 2:30. I went out with her to see that she got on the bus.

Q. Yes. A. And, I remained outside for about a half an hour and Elmore came from across the street and "Harris", he said

Q. So, you fix it as of the time when your mother left and you remained outside, you know that that is a fact? A. Yes, sir.

Q. The bus was on time? A. Yes, sir, the bus was on time, 2:30, and I have the R. & H. clock right opposite my place.

Q. And you paid no attention to the time, you are just estimating it was a half hour? A. Yes, sir.

Mr. Innes : That is all.
Mr. Gulotta : That is all.
Mr. Casey: Al Miller.

ALBERT WILLIAM MILLER, 20 LaForge Place Richmond, Staten Island, called as a witness in behalf of the defendant, being first duly sworn, testified as follows :

Direct examination by Mr. Gulotta:

Q. Mr. Miller, what is your business? A. Manager for the A. and P.

Q. And were you a manager for the A. and P. on August 12th, 1937? A. Yes.

Q. Now, where is that A. and P. located? A. 207 Broad Street, Stapleton.

Q. In this county? A. Yes, sir.

Q. Now, some time in the afternoon, did you see Simon Elmore come into your store? A. I did.

Q. And did he ask you, did he make a purchase? A. He made a purchase, yes sir.

Q. And did you take the order? A. I did not.

Q. Who took the order? A. One of my clerks.

Q. And what is that clerk's name? A. James McMahon.

Q. Do you happen to know what purchase he made? A. I do not.

Q. Do you happen to know how much it came to? A. I do not.

Q. Now, you have a person by the name of Kelly in your store too, have you not? A. Kelly is my superior.

Q. Superior? And was Kelly in the store that day? A. He was.

Q. As well as McMahon? A. Right.

Q. Now, is there a person by the name of Louis, the butcher? A. Yes.

Q. What is his full name? A. Louis Marut.

Q. Louis what? A. Louis Marut, M-a-r-u-t.

Q. And was he there that day? A. He was.

Q. While Elmore was in the store? A. Right.

Q. Right. Now, was there somebody loading a hand truck on the sidewalk that day? A. Yes, there was.

Q. Who was loading the hand truck? A. Two truck drivers and one of my other clerks.

Q. Now, what is the name of that other clerk who was -- A. James Haley.

Q. And, was he there at the time? A. He was, he was outside the store.

Q. Now, Mr. Miller, can you give us the approximate time of the afternoon when Elmore came into this A. and P. store? A. It was after three o'clock.

Q. Now, can you give us a time that is more definite, how much after three o'clock? A. I can not.

Q. You do know that it was after three? A. It was after three o'clock.

Q. It wasn't after four? A. No, it was before four.

Q. It was before four o'clock, was it? A. It was.

Mr. Gulotta : Your witness, Mr. Innes.

Cross-examination By Mr. Innes :

Q. The nearest you can fix it is sometime between three and four? A. Right.

Mr. Innes : That is all.

Redirect examination by Mr. Gulotta:

Q. Oh, by the way, how long have you known Simon Elmore? A. About seven years.

Q. There is no doubt in your mind, Mr. Miller, that Simon Elmore is the person who we were just discussing as coming into your store, was it? A. That is the same Simon.

Mr. Gulotta : The same Simon. All right.

JAMES MCMAHON, 249 Rice Avenue, West Brighton, Staten Island, New York, called as a witness in behalf of the defendant, first being duly sworn, testified as follows:

Direct examination by Mr. Gulotta:

Q. Mr. McMahon, what is your employment? A. I work for the A. and P. Tea Company as a clerk.

Q. And are you assigned to any particular store on Staten Island? A. Broad Street, Stapleton.

Q. What is the number on Broad Street? A. 207.

Q. Do you know a man by the name of Al Miller?

A. I do, yes.

Q. Do you know where he works? A. Same place.

Q. What is his position there? A. He is the manager.

Q. Do you know a man by the name of Kelly? A. Yes, I do.

Q. And is he connected with the A. and P. ? A. He is a district superintendent.

Q. District superintendent. Do you know a man by the name of James Haley? A. Haley?

Q. Is he connected with the A. and P. ? A. Yes, he is.

Q. And do you know a man by the name of Louis Marut? A. He is also connected with the A. and P. he works there.

Q. And were you likewise with the A. and P. and at that store at that address on the 12th of August, 1937? A. Yes, I was.

Q. And were all these other people whose names I mentioned, were they connected with the A. and P. ? A. Yes, they were too.

Q. Right. Now, what is specifically your work in there, Mr. McMahon? A. I am a clerk.

Q. Clerk, you wait on people, do you? A. That is right.

Q. Now, prior to August 12th, 1937, did you know Simon Elmore? A. Well, I didn't know him very well. I had seen him a few times.

Q. A few times? Did you see Simon Elmore on August 12th, on that day that I am describing? A. Yes, I did.

Q. And did you wait on him? A. Yes, I did.

Q. Yes. Now he made a purchase, did he? A. Yes, sir.

Q. Now, as best as your recollection will serve you, will you tell us what he bought there? A. I can't remember that, I couldn't tell you what it was.

Q. Was it an order consisting of several items? A. Just a few items, it may have been one or more.

Q. A few items. Now, did he buy, as far as you can remember, any oysterettes? A. I couldn't answer that question, because I don't remember.

Q. Did he buy any ketchup? A. I couldn't say yes or no definitely, he may have bought them, I--

Q. Now, on that day, there was a person wheeling a hand truck from the sidewalk into the store, is that right? A. That is right.

Q. And Mr. Miller was on duty, is that right? A. That is right.

Q. That is right? A. Yes.

Q. Now, did you see Simon Elmore come in the store that day? A. I did, yes sir.

Q. And, you told us, I believe, that he, that you gave him an order? A. That is right.

Q. All right, now, what time did you first see Elmore when he came into the A. and P. store? A. It would be some time after three o'clock.

Q. Can you give us a better estimate of the time? A. I couldn't give you the time exactly, because I had no occasion to refer to the time then.

Q. Would you say in your opinion that it was, how far before four o'clock? A. Yes, I imagine it was before four.

Q. Yes, and that is the best you can tell us, is that correct? A. That is the best I can do.

Mr. Gulotta : Your witness.

Cross-examination By Mr. Innes :

Q. It is pure speculation as to time, is it not, Mr. McMahon? A. I know definitely it was after three o'clock.

Q. It was after three o'clock. And, from that time on, you don't know just when it was, is that right? A. Well, I know it wasn't six o'clock or five o'clock, I know that definitely.

Q. I see. Well, some time between three and five? A. I would say between three and four, I wouldn't say between three and five.

Q. But, you are not able to state just when? A. No, sir.

Mr. Innes : All right, that is all.

JAMES B. KELLY, 249 Rice Avenue, West Brighton, Staten Island, New York, called as a witness in behalf of the defendant, first being duly sworn, testified as follows :

Direct examination by Mr. Gulotta:

Q. Now, Mr. Kelly, what is your employment? A. Beg your pardon?

Q. What do you do for a living? A. Assistant Superintendent of the Great Atlantic and Pacific Tea Company.

Q. And are you assigned to any particular store? A. No.

Q. You are supervisor over all the stores? A. No, section, a section of the stores.

Q. And what section is that? A. That is here in Middletown.

Q. And, does that include the store located at Stapleton? A. Yes.

Q. And is that a store where Mr. Kelly worked? A. Mr. Miller?

Q. A Mr. Miller? A. Mr. Miller, yes, sir.

Q. And, do you know Mr. McMahon? A. Yes, sir.

Q. Does he work there? A. Yes, sir.

Q. Do you know Mr. Haley? James Haley? A. Yes, sir.

Q. Does he work there? A. Yes, sir.

Q. Do you know Mr. Louis Marut? A. Yes, sir.

Q. Does he work there? A. Yes, sir.

Q. All right. Now, did you have occasion to visit this particular store on August 12th, 1937? A. I did, sir.

Q. And were you there some time in the afternoon? A. I was.

Q. And at any time that you were there did you see Simon Elmore in the store? A. I did.

Q. Did you know him before that time? A. Yes.

Q. How long have you known him? A. Five or six years.

Q. Five or six years? Now, will you give us your best estimation of the time when you saw Elmore come into that store that afternoon? A. I didn't see him come in, he was in the store when I got in.

Q. Well, tell us the time when you saw him then? A. Just about three o'clock.

Q. About three o'clock? A. Uh-huh.

Q. And, do you know how long he stayed in the store? A. No.

Q. Now, how do you fix the time, Mr. Kelly, that it was about three o'clock? A. Well, I left my office on Corson Avenue to get to the bank with the deposit at three o'clock.

Q. Three o'clock? A. I didn't make the bank on that day, I had to use the night depository, so I figured that it must have been around, just around three o'clock.

Q. I see. Well, now, the reason why you had to use the night depository is because the bank was closed? A. Yes, sir.

Q. Does that bank close at three o'clock? A. Yes, sir.

Q. Now, how far away is the bank from your store? A. It is, well, about a mile.

Q. About a mile. So that, when you got to the bank it was three o'clock, or after, is that right? A. Yes, sir.

Q. And then you had to travel this mile back to the store? A. No, I didn't. That was another --my office, I left to make the bank, then I went to this other store for to do my other work.

Q. I see. Then, did you go from the bank to this store on Broad Street? A. I did, sir.

Q. Yes. And, that is what I am getting at, and how did you travel? A. By automobile.

Q. And, was it your automobile? A. Company car.

Q. Yes, but did you drive it? A. Yes.

Q. So that you drove about a mile from the bank to this store? A. No, it isn't a mile from my office to the bank, I figure about a mile, but it is only three or four blocks--

Q. Yes, well, tell us now what the distance is between the bank and the store where you saw Elmore? A. Four blocks, about.

Q. Yes, and you traveled that distance after the bank had been closed and you made the night deposit, is that right? A. Right.

Q. And did you see Elmore immediately when you went in the store? A. Yes.

Q. What was he doing in there? A. He was standing against the counter, when I passed him, and he said, "Hello, Kelly, " I says, "Hello, Sam, " and that was all. I passed along, did my--called my orders in, and when I got all through he wasn't in the store, no more.

Q. Yes, and that is all you exchanged, he said "Hello, Kelly"? A. That was all.

Q. Did he ever say "Hello, Kelly" before this time? A. Oh, yes.

Q. And did you ever say "Hello, Sam, " before this time? A. Yes.

Mr. Gulotta: All right, cross examine.

Cross-examination By Mr. Innes :

Q. Who did you first talk to about what you have testified to here today, Mr. Kelly? A. To the manager of the store, when it appeared in the papers that Elmore was held, we talked it over and we said, we come to the conclusion, "Weren't we talking to that man yesterday? "

Q. I see. A. And sure enough that is how I recollected it and remembered it that we were talking to him.

Q. Because you saw a news article in some paper? A. Yes.

Q. On the following day, is that right? A. Yes, that is it.

Q. And you then read that you had seen him the day before? A. Yes.

Q. But, it was some time after three because when you got to the bank that was closed? A. Yes.

Q. Isn't that correct? A. Yes.

Q. You don't know how long the bank had been closed, do you? A. No, I don't, no.

Q. And what bank was it? A. The National City Bank.

Q. National City, that is in Stapleton? A. Yes.

Q. On the shore road at the corner of the cross street? A. Right.

Mr. Innes : That is all.

Mr. Gulotta : Louis Marut.

Mr. Innes : Same situation?

Mr. Gulotta : The same situation there, Mr. Innes

ELLEN FELDRAPP, 170 Broad Street, Stapleton, Staten Island, New York, called as a witness in behalf of the defendant being first duly sworn, testified as follows :

Direct examination by Mr. Gulotta:

Q. Miss Feldrapp, do you work? A. Yes.

Q. Where do you work? A. Bakery shop.

Q. And is that bakery shop owned by your mother? A. Yes.

Q. And where is it located? A. 170 Broad Street.

Q. 170 Broad Street. Are you anywheres near the store owned by Edward Harris? A. Yes, in the next block.

Q. Is that a block away? A. Yes.

Q. And are you anywheres near a store owned by a tailor by the name of DeLacy or DaLecy? A. Yes.

Q. How far away? A. Two blocks.

Q. Two blocks away? Now, just what do you do in this store, Miss Feldrapp, wait on customers? A. Wait on customers, yes.

Q. And as I understand it, your mother owns the bakery? Is that right? A. Yes.

Q. And you make your own pies, do you? A. Yes.

Q. And were you on duty on the afternoon of August 12th? A. I don't know about the date, I have been there all the time.

Q. All the time. Well, do you remember more

particularly August 12th, the Thursday? A. Yes.

Q. Do you know Simon Elmore? A. Yes, by seeing him come into the store.

Q. And prior to August 12th, 1937, he had been in your store, hadn't he? A. Yes.

Q. To make purchases of cakes, bread, or otherwise? A. Yes.

Q. Did he come in that afternoon? A. On the Thursday he came in, yes.

Q. On Thursday? A. Yes.

Q. And did he come in to make a purchase? A. Yes.

Q. Can you recall what he bought? A. Huckleberry pie and a loaf of Vienna bread.

Q. Yes, and how much did the huckleberry pie cost, do you remember? A. Fifteen cents.

Q. And how much did the bread cost? A. Eight cents.

Q. And he paid you in cash, didn't he? A. Yes.

Q. Yes. Now, will you give us your best estimate of the time that afternoon when Elmore came into your store? A. I should say about from three to four, some place in between.

Q. Something like that. Now, you are unable to give us anything, any better estimate than that, is that right? A. That is the only thing that I can remember.

Q. And you can only say that it was between three and four o'clock, is that right? A. Yes.

Mr. Gulotta : All right, thank you.

Mr. Innes : No cross.

LOUIS GINNIS, 217 Hamilton Avenue, St. George, Staten Island, called as a witness in behalf of the defendant, first being duly sworn, testified as follows :

Direct examination by Mr. Gulotta:

Q. Mr. Ginnis, what is your employment? A. Pharmacist.

Q. And are you in business here? A. No, I am

employed on Staten Island.

Q. And by whom are you employed? A. Stapleton Drug Company.

Q. And where is that located, please? A. 117 Water Street.

Q. In this County, in this County? A. That is right.

Q. Now, Mr. Ginnis, do you remember August 12th, 1937? A. I don't remember that day as August 12th.

Q. Yes, do you remember a Thursday around August 12th? A. I don't remember any date at all, sir.

Q. I see. Well, do you remember a day in August at any rate, did you see--by the way, were you on duty in the month of August? A. Yes, sir.

Q. And what time did you go on duty? A. Oh, that varies, sometimes one, sometimes two, my hours are not definite.

Q. Yes, but however, according to your statement you were also on duty about two o'clock? A. Yes.

Q. Yes, and you would be on duty every working day in the month of August, wouldn't you? A. That is right, sir.

Q. I mean, except Sundays, --perhaps Sundays also? A. No.

Q. You work on Sundays, you do or you don't? A. I don't work Sundays, sir.

Q. All right. Now, did you see Simon Elmore come into your store? A. I don't know.

Q. You don't know? A. I don't know Mr. Simon Elmore.

Q. Did you have a talk with a person by the name of McKittrick, who represented himself as my investigator in this case, did he come to see you? A. I don't know.

Q. Well, do many people come to see you, Mr. Ginnis, do many people come to see you as a general rule on matters outside of your own business? A. No, sir.

Q. No? A. Did a detective from the police department come to see you? A. Quite a few.

Q. Quite a few? Well, now, did a man, a man who is very well built, over six feet tall, and perhaps weighing

250 or more pounds, --do you remember a man of such-- A. Yes, I do.

Q. And, when did he come to see you? A. If he came by himself, perhaps, I think it was on a Saturday, because I was very busy, and I had no time to talk with him.

Q. That is right. Now, do you remember saying that you had sold Elmore a bottle of Ben-Gay? A. No, sir.

Q. Do you sell Ben-Gay in your store? A. I do.

Q. So far as you are able to say now, you never saw Simon Elmore in your life? A. I don't say that either. I might have seen him and I might not have seen him.

Q. Have you got any records with you here? A. No, sir.

Q. From the store? Let me come back a moment. The men from the police department came when, to your store? A. They came some afternoon, the date I don't know.

Q. Did they ask you for any information concerning the case of Simon Elmore? A. They did.

Q. And did you give them any information? A. I did give them information.

Q. Yes. A. Thought Simon Elmore was the last thing mentioned.

Q. Will you tell the Court and Jury what information you gave them? A. A group of five or so men came into the store, asked me if I were on duty such and such a day, and I said, Yes, I was, and did I remember selling a tube of Ben-Gay on such an afternoon. I said, "I might have and I might not have, " and do I remember, asked me if I remembered waiting on a tall man or elderly man with a scraggly mustache, and I said I might have and I might not have.

Q. I see. Did you say anything over and above that? A. And then they said if you did sell it, did you sell it for fifty-nine cents? And I said, "Yes, sir, I sold it for fifty-nine cents, " and then he said, "Was there any question about the price? " And I said there was a man who did come in and did question the price and did say he used to pay forty-nine cents for it and now, then, I did remember these detectives came in, guarantying the low price of our store, and I said if it was sold for less than fifty-nine cents, saying we would make them a present of that tube, and that was all.

Q. I see. Now, does that conversation recall to your memory the looks of the man who questioned the price of the Ben-Gay? **A. Thinking back on it, I might say he was a timid man.**

**Q. A timid man? Would you say that he was an elderly man? A. I would say that too.**

Q. Yes. Now, suppose you take a good look at Simon Elmore, the defendant in this case.

Mr. Gulotta: Stand up, Mr. Elmore. (Whereupon the defendant stood.)

Q. Did he look anything like him? A. I would say he did look something like him. (Whereupon he defendant sat down again.)

Q. Yes. And, I take it then, when I questioned you before, and I said something about Ben-Gay, a tube or bottle of Ben-Gay was sold by you on that day, is that right? A. Right.

Q. Now, will you give me your best estimate of the time that this happened? A. It would happen between 1:30 and 3:30.

Q. Can you give us anything that is any more definite than 1:30 and 3:30? A. It can't be before because I wouldn't be in the store before, and it can't be afterwards, because I am off the counter doing other work then.

Q. But, you will say, however, in view of your answer that it might have been at 1:30? A. It might have been, yes, sir.

Mr. Gulotta : Thank you.

Cross-examination, By Mr. Innes :

Q. And, it might have been at 3 :30? A. Right, sir. It might have been at 3 :30.

Mr. Innes : All right.

ENRICO BOGGENAO, 256 Gordon Street, Stapleton, Staten Island, New York, called as a witness in behalf of the defendant, being first duly sworn, testified as follows :

Direct examination by Mr. Gulotta:

Q. What is your business, Mr. Boggenao? A. Working down on the dock, longshoreman.

Q. On the dock, and what is your occupation down at the dock? A. Well, I do nothing for a long time. I was sick for a long time, see?

Q. Were you working on August 12th, 1937? A. No, I was working around the house.

Q. Around your house? A. Yes.

Q. You live there? A. Yes.

Q. And, what is the address there at the house where you were working? A. 256 Gordon Street.

Q. I didn't get that. A. 256 Gordon Street.

Q. 256 Gordon Street. Now, do you know where Metcalfe Street is? A. Metcalfe Street is a couple of blocks up, I guess.

Q. Yes. How far away is that from your home? A. Oh, about one, two, about two, three blocks.

Q. Three blocks? A. Yes.

Q. Do you know where Simon Elmore lives? A. No, I don't know the house.

Q. You don't know the place? Do you know that he lives on Metcalfe Street? A. I know he live up the other way, some place, but I don't know the house, only the street.

Q. You can't tell us the house. Now, do you remember August 12th, 1937, doing some work around your house? A. I was doing some work around the house, yes.

Q. What kind of work were you doing? A. I was fixing up the porch.

Q. I have got to get that. A. I was fixing up the front porch.

Q. The front porch? Will you speak up because the last juror has got to get it? A. Yes.

Q. What were you doing on the front porch? A. I was fixing up the front porch because it was all rotten down. I hit it down and fix up the bottom.

Q. And, are you doing that work yourself? A. Yes.

Q. Are you going to put new lumber where you tear down the old? A. No, second hand lumber, I was using him, take them down, use them for the bottom.

Q. I see. Now, sometime in the afternoon of that day, you were working in the front of your house, is that right? A. Yes.

Q. And while you were working in front of your house, or about the house, did you see Simon Elmore pass your house? A. Yes.

Q. What did he have in his hands or arms, if anything? A. He had this bundle, some kind, like paper bag, you know, bundle.

Q. Yes, like a grocery bag? A. Like a grocery bag.

Q. Yes. And, will you tell us now as nearly as you can what time of the afternoon that was? A. Well, I can't say the right time on it. I know it was after one o'clock, around after one, 1, 2, 3, maybe a little before three o'clock.

Q. You can't give us any better idea than that? A. Can't, maybe a few minutes before three.

Q. You can't tell? A. No.

Q. Well, now, did you know Simon Elmore before that day? A. Yes, I never see around here for a little while.

Q. But, you knew. Simon Elmore before? A. Yes.

Q. How long did you know him? A. Oh, I know Sammy for about 15, 16 years.

Q. 15, 16 years? A. Yes.

Q. And did you know that Simon Elmore did painting? A. I don't get you.

Q. Do you know that he did painting work? A. Yes.

Q. Yes. And did you talk with Simon Elmore as he passed, while you were working? A. Yes.

Q. Now, what did you say to Elmore and what did Elmore say to you? A. Elmore was say to me, why don't you fix up the house and give me the job of the painting the house.

Q. Yes. A. And so--

Q. Did you say anything about giving him the job? A. I say, yes, get the job, I say, who is going, who going to get the money to get the paint, buy the paint to give you a job.

Q. At any rate you talked to him for some time, did you, how long a time did you talk to him, about? A. Well, five, ten minutes.

Q. Five or ten minutes? And during that five or ten minutes was he holding this bag on his arm? A. Yes, he was holding the bag on his arm, yes.

Q. Now, the direction in which he was walking was that toward his house, toward Metcalfe Street? A. I don't know where he was walk, **I seen him go up straight, Broad Street up to Gordon.**

Q. Now, he called you Joe, didn't he? A. Yes.

Q. And, did he call you Joe on that day, did he call you Joe? A. He called me Joe that day, yes.

Q. And, your name is not Joe, is it? A. No.

Q. Is it Enrico? A. Enrico.

Q. And, you remember that that happened on August 12th, do you? A. Yes.

Mr. Gulotta: All right, cross-examine.

Cross-examination By Mr. Innes :

Q. How do you fix the day, Mr. --how do you fix it as the 12th of August? A. I was fixing the house as it was bad, you know, the top, the upper porch, it was.

Q. Did you always do that on the 12th? A. And, it was a bad thing, --no, I was do it, I was working there two day on the 11th and the 12th.

Q. How do you know it was the 11th you started? A. I know because I know when I come out of the Hospital and my first day, I do the work, I do on Friday.

Q. I see. The first work you say you did was

Friday? A. It was Friday, yes, the 13th.

Q. Friday, the 13th? A. Yes.

Q. And, that is the day you saw Elmore? A. The day before.

Q. The day before? A. Yes.

Q. When did you, the first work you say you did was the 13th? A. Yes, my first work I do down at the dock was the day of the 13th.

Q. Oh, I see, that is when you went to work on the dock? A. Yes.

Q. And, you came to the Hospital? A. I was on the hospital a couple of months, you see, I was just doing a little work around the house.

Q. I see. Well, anyway you say he had a grocery bag in his hand? A. Yes.

Q. You didn't look at any clock, did you? A. No.

Q. And you are just guessing when you tell us the time that you saw him there? A. That is all.

Mr. Innes : That is all.

Mr. Gulotta: That is all. Now, if your Honor please, I am pretty well run out of witnesses for the present. I think I have done pretty well calling as many as I have. I would ask your Honor for a recess until 2:00 o'clock.

The Court : All right. Gentlemen, we will recess until 2:00 o'clock. Do not discuss this case or come to any conclusion in the matter until the case is finally submitted to you and do not read any newspapers during the lunch period.

(Whereupon at 12:44 P. M. Court recessed until 2 :00 P. M. )

AFTERNOON SESSION. Friday, November 19, 1937, 2 :00 P. M.

Before : Hon. THOMAS F. COSGROVE, County Judge.

Appearances : Same as before.

Court Clerk Kosman : People against Samuel Elmore.

(Both sides ready.)

(Whereupon the jury was polled and all jurors answered present.)

Mr. Gulotta : May it please your Honor, I subpoenaed a number of witnesses, the majority of whom I put on the stand this morning. I felt that we made some good time in the examination because of the cooperation of the District Attorney. But, I also find that some of the witnesses that we have subpoenaed are not here today, so therefore we must work during the weekend in order to get them here Monday morning.

In view of that fact, may I respectfully ask your Honor to take a postponement until Monday morning at 10:00 o'clock and further ask that full instruction be given by the clerk to the witnesses for the defense to return at that time.

The Court : No objection to that?

Mr. Innes : There is no objection. I am anxious to complete the trial but Mr. Gulotta has been so very, very nice that I am unable to resist his appeal at this time.

The Court : All right. Instruct all witnesses to come back Monday morning. All witnesses in court.

Court Clerk Kosman : All witnesses for the Defendant will appear here next Monday morning without further notice or subpoena.

The Court : Gentlemen, we will recess until Monday morning at 10:00 o'clock. The instructions which you have received at previous recesses apply now. Do not discuss this case or come to any conclusion in the matter until the case is finally submitted to you and until you retire to your Jury room. 10:00 o'clock Monday morning.

( Whereupon at 2 :15 P. M. Court recessed until Monday morning at 10:00 A. M.)

Court Clerk Kosman : All manner of persons having any business to do with this term of County Court, held in and for the County of Richmond, draw near, give your attendance and you shall be heard. People against Samuel Elmore.

(Both sides are ready.)

(Whereupon the Jury was polled and all Jurors answered present.)

JOHN TECHKY, 29 Warren Street, Stapleton, Staten Island, New York, called as a witness in behalf of the defendant, first being duly sworn, testified as follows:

Direct examination by Mr. Gulotta:

Q. Mr. Techky, what is your business? A. I help my father, bar tender.

Q. And is your father's name Alex? A. That is right.

Q. And does he own the business? A. He does.

Q. What kind of a business is it? A. Saloon business.

Q. And where is that located? A. That is in Warren Street, 29.

The Court : Will you speak up louder?

Q. Speak up a little louder please. Now, do you know Simon Elmore, the defendant? A. I do.

Q. And how long have you known him? A. I have known him pretty long, not so long.

Q. How long would you estimate? A. Well, about two years, I imagine.

Q. Two years. Now, do you remember the 12th day of August, 1937, sometime in the afternoon? A. I do, sir.

Q. Were you on duty at your father's place of business? A. I was.

Q. And your duties consisted of what? Waiting behind the bar? A. Waiting behind the bar, that is right.

Q. All right. Now, did Simon Elmore come into your saloon that afternoon? A. He did.

Q. And did anyone come in with him? A. No, just alone.

Q. Now, did he have anything to drink? A. He did.

Q. What did he have to drink? A. Just beer.

Q. And how many beers did he have? A. I imagine about four or five.

Q. Four or five. Now, when you noticed that Simon Elmore came into your saloon, did you notice that he had a package in his hand? A. He did.

Q. And was that the ordinary type of grocery package? A. Yes, white bags, they were.

Q. Yes. Now, what time of the afternoon of that day was it that Simon Elmore came into your saloon, about what time, Mr. Techky? A. Well, it was between three and four o'clock, I imagine.

Q. Between three and four o'clock, and how long did he stay? A. About twenty minutes.

Q. Yes. Now, when he left did he bid you the time of day? A. He didn't.

Q. To say good-bye or anything? A. He said, good-bye, yes.

Q. He said good-bye and you said good-bye to him? A. So long.

Q. And that was all? A. That is all I could remember.

Q. Was there any conversation during the time that he was having the beers? A. There was, I think, I can remember, yes.

Q. Do you remember what the trend of this conversation was? A. Well, he was talking about painting in the back room.

Q. Paintings, and that is all that you talked about? A. That is all I could remember of.

Q. All right, thank you.

Cross-examination by Mr. Innes :

Q. You were--you have no time piece in the place, you didn't observe the time? A. Yes, we have--I didn't observe it, no.

Q. You don't know what time it was? A. No.

Q. It might have been later than four but it is your best recollection between three and four? A. Between three and four, yes.

Mr. Innes : That is all.
Mr. Gulotta: Thank you, Mr. Techky.

SADIE ELMORE, 37 Metcalfe Street, Stapleton, Staten Island, New York, called as a witness in behalf of the defendant, first being duly sworn, testified as follows :

Direct examination by Mr. Gulotta:

Q. Now, Mrs. Elmore, you are the wife of the defendant, Simon Elmore, are you not? A. Yes.

Q. And how long have you been married to him? A. 16 years.

Q. 16 years. Now, you have some children, have you? A. Yes.

Q. How many have you? A. Two.

Q. And their names, please and ages? A. Dorothy is 18, she is the daughter of my first husband, and Sybil is, Samuel Elmore's child.

Q. Sybil is how old you say, Mrs. Elmore? A. 13.

Q. And she is the child by Simon Elmore? A. Yes.

Q. Now, prior, shortly prior to August 12th, 1937, what was Mr. Elmore's occupation? A. He was a painter in the P. W. A.

Q. And he worked continually up to and including, not including, up to the 12th of August, 1937? A. Yes.

Q. Now, do you remember the 12th day of August, 1937, Mrs. Elmore? A. Yes, I do.

Q. Now, the night before that, Mr. Elmore slept at his home, did he not? A. Yes.

Q. And on the morning of the 12th, he got up in his home, is that right? A. Yes.

Q. Do you remember what time he got up that morning? A. Well, he always gets up about seven o'clock.

Q. And after he got up, shortly after seven o'clock, did he change the bath for the bird? A. Yes, he always does that.

Q. Yes. And did he on that morning? A. Yes, I think so, I am not quite sure about that.

Q. And did he take care of a few other chores around the house that morning? A. Well, I didn't pay much attention to that.

Q. Did he go out to the garden to look at his tomatoes that morning? A. Yes.

Q. You remember that as a fact, don't you? A. Yes, that is true.

Q. Now, about what time did he go out to the garden to look at his tomatoes? A. I should say about nine o'clock.

Q. Now, he had had breakfast before nine o'clock had he not? A. Yes.

Q. And I believe he prepared the breakfast that morning, did he not? A. Yes, because he usually prepares, gets his own breakfast ready.

Q. As a general rule he does prepare the breakfast for the family, doesn't he? A. No, not for the family, for himself.

Q. Now, he went out, did he not, that morning. About what time did he go out? A. No, I don't remember that, I don't think, he was only in the yard.

Q. I see. Do you remember him going out at any time that morning? A. No, because it was pay day, see, and he had to go to get his pay.

Q. Yes, but you know he went to get his pay, don't you? A. Yes, ten o'clock.

Q. And would you say he left some time around ten o'clock? A. Yes, because he must do that in order to get his pay because they don't pay if they are late.

Q. And this was a Thursday, was it not, Mrs. Elmore? A. Yes.

Q. Now, knowing that he was going after his pay, you gave him directions to buy some groceries did you not, that morning? A. Yes, I gave him an order for the A.& P.

Q. And was that a written order or a verbal order? A. No, written.

Q. Who wrote it down? A. I did.

Q. Now, do you remember what you wrote down on that order? A. Well, a few of the things because we always get them every two weeks.

Q. Well, give us such things as you remember you told him to get. A. A pound of butter, and eggs, and sugar, coffee, the ordinary things that you generally get.

Q. The ordinary groceries? A. Yes.

Q. Now-- A. Oh, there was a dozen clams I asked him to get a--

Q. All right, dozen clams? A. Yes.

Q. And had you told him that clam chowder would be prepared with these clams? A. Of course. Because that is why I got the clams.

Q. That is why you got the clams. Now, do you remember about twelve o'clock, Mrs. Elmore? A. Yes, because we have lunch at twelve.

Q. And was Mr. Elmore home for lunch? A. **Yes, five past twelve he came in the house.**

**Q. About half past twelve? A. No, five past twelve. I always have the lunch ready right on time, twelve o'clock.**

Q. Oh, now, what did he do with the clams shortly after he got home? A. Well, we had lunch first.

Q. Yes, first you had lunch and do you remember what that lunch consisted of? A. It was very light.

Q. Very light. Now, then, after that, did he do something with reference to the clams? A. Well, he always opened the clams for me.

Q. Yes, and did he open them on the 12th day of August, 1937? A. Yes, he did.

Q. All right. Now, did he do anything else before going out? A. Well, I had asked him to get some vegetables for the clams and there was very little, because--some places you don't get very many vegetables, so I said, "Will you go down to the garden, get me some carrots, for clam chowder, " but he didn't do that. I think he just left two carrots so I went on preparing the chowder. He just opened the clams.

Q. So that he opened the clams and prepared the vegetables? A. No, I did, he just opened the clams.

Q. And he was there while you did it, is that right?

A. Yes, no he went down into the yard to get some bags.

Q. All right. Now, have you ever heard of a neighbor of yours by the name of McKittrick? A. Yes.

Q. And do you know where her house is? A. On Vanderbilt Avenue.

Q. Yes. Now, can you give us an estimate of the distance between your house and Miss McKittrick's house? A. I should say it is about five minutes walk.

Q. Five minutes walk. Now, do you have a clock in your home? A. Yes.

Q. And where is that clock, if you know? A. On Sybil's desk.

Q. Yes, and was that near where you were having your lunch? A. Oh, yes, it is right there.

Q. Yes, and from time to time and between twelve o'clock, while you were having your lunch and after that, did you consult that time piece? A. Yes, I am very accurate in things I do. I know about every few minutes what I do.

Q. Yes. Then, what time in your best opinion, Mrs. Elmore, did your husband leave after opening the clams and after having lunch and after all that was completed, what time did he leave your home? A. Ten minutes to one.

Q. Ten minutes to one? A. In other words 12:50.

Q. Did I understand you to say correctly, do I understand you correctly when I interpreted your answer as saying that the difference between, or the distance between your house and that of Miss McKittrick's, is about a five minutes walk? A. Yes, that is what I should say.

Q. Now, then, he came back sometime in the afternoon, didn't he, while you were still at home? A. Well, Sybil and I didn't leave the home.

Q. You stayed at home? A. Yes.

Q. All day, did you? A. Yes, but I asked him to get other things down in Stapleton.

Q. Yes. And what did you ask him to get down in Stapleton? A. You see he didn't get the check cashed in Oscar's in the A. and P., so therefore he has to go to the bank and cash it.

Q. Yes. A. So I, he said, "Is there anything else you want? " And I said, "Yes, there are a few things I have forgotten in the order, so, as you are going down to Stapleton, you may as well get them for me."

Q. Yes. A. So, he said, "Give me a list, and I will get them." So I wrote the list out of just a few things.

Q. Now, can you give us any of the items that you wrote out on this second list, Mrs. Elmore? A. Yes, I said he needed a pair of working pants.

Q. Yes. A. And he had to take them to the tailors to have them shortened, and I asked him to get two boxes of oysterettes for the chowder. There was bread at the bakers, and a huckleberry pie, and then he would have to go for Ben-Gay from the drug store.

Q. Now, Ben-Gay, what is this Ben-Gay, Mrs. Elmore? A. I had been in the draft and got a stiff neck and it is good for rubbing.

Q. Rubbing, and it aids colds and such? A. Yes, it heals, it is very good.

Q. Yes. Now, does that come in a tube or in a bottle? A. In a tube.

Q. In a tube? Now, coming back to the afternoon, I understand you to say that you did not leave your home that day? A. No, Sybil and I did not.

Q. And your daughter remained at home with you? A. Yes.

Q. Is that right? What time did Elmore, your best recollection of the time, what time did Elmore return? A. Four o'clock.

Q. Four o'clock, and when he returned did he have the tube of Ben-Gay that you had asked him to get? A. He had everything I had asked him to get.

Q. Yes. Now, can you remember what the price of that tube of Ben-Gay was? A. I think it was forty-nine cents, it had it on the box.

Q. Forty-nine cents. All right. Did he have the oysterettes with him? A. Yes, --oh, I had forgotten--

Q. And he had, had he not, the full order? A. Yes, everything.

Q. Do you remember what that order came to? A. No, I don't really remember, I didn't pay much attention to that.

Q. All right. Now, when he got home at four o'clock, what did he do, if anything, that you remember? A. Well, Sybil was hungry, that is how I know it so definitely, it was four o'clock, Sybil was hungry and she said, "Mother, can't we have supper early, I am hungry." I said, "Sybil, it is so early," I said, "if you will wait a few minutes, papa will be home, it is only four o'clock," and as I said that, he came up the stairs with the things and we ate the huckleberry pie.

Q. Now, in the 16 years that you have been married, Mrs. Elmore, did you or your husband, Simon Elmore, ever own an automobile? A. Never.

Q. Did you ever see your husband drive an automobile? A. No, I don't think he could.

Q. Do you know of your own knowledge that he does not drive an automobile, is that correct? A. Yes.

Q. And you don't, do you? A. No.

Q. And your daughters don't, do they? A. No.

Q. All right. Now, when he left your house at 12:50 on the day of August 12th, 1937, did he walk toward McKittrick's house? A. I didn't see where he went.

Q. I see. All right. Now, did you have supper that evening? A. Yes.

Q. And what time did you have supper? A. Well, we weren't very hungry, so we had it about half past five.

Q. Yes. So after that, did Mr. Elmore stay home or did he go out? A. He stayed home.

Q. He stayed at home? Did he make a call, did he make one call about six or half past six? A. Yes, it was Thursday and he had to report to Mrs. Wardell.

Q. All right. Now, Mrs. Elmore, when your husband went out at 12:50, did he take anything with him from the house? **A. Yes, he took some bags that he had been saving for the fish man.**

Q. And how many bags were there, about? A. Oh, there were quite a few.

Q. Did he trade those in for the fish, or was that to carry the fish in? A. No, you see the man has a boat somewhere down in Stapleton, and he, I suppose the poor fellow can't afford to buy bags, so my husband, I think he used to give him fish for the bags.

Q. Yes. Now, when he came home about four o'clock, as you have told us, did he have the fish with him? A. Yes.

Q. And sometime between four and half past five, did he fix that fish up for bait to be used? A. No.

Q. To be used the next day? A. He put it in the ice box.

Q. He put the fish in the ice box? A. Yes.

Q. Now, the next morning, the next morning, the 13th of August, 1937, did he go to the ice box for that fish? A. Well, I told him I didn't like the smell of them, would he take them out of there, and he said he didn't want to go crabbing.

Q. Yes, but finally on the morning of the 13th he left the house with certain crabbing pots, didn't he?

A. Well, you see he didn't want to go crabbing, and I couldn't understand why all of a sudden, all the week, he had been telling me he wanted to go crabbing and I couldn't understand why all of a sudden he wanted to refuse, because that is one thing he likes to do is crab, so I said, "I can't understand what is the matter with you, you don't want to go crabbing, you bought fish and I have given you sixty cents for carfare, why don't you want to go?" He said, "I don't want to go. "So, I said--it wasn't an argument--it was just a few words over it. I said, I was going to New York and I didn't see why he wouldn't go crabbing, so he said, "I just don't want to go, that is all. "

Q. Yes. All right, now, Mrs. Elmore, he came back from Mrs. Wardell's, didn't he? A. Yes.

Q. What time? A. Well, he was in the kitchen, I didn't really pay any attention, he wasn't very long.

Q. Yes. Would you say that about seven o'clock he was home that night? A. Yes.

Q. I am now talking of August 12th, of course. A.

Yes.

Q. And, you have a radio in your home, have you not? A. Yes.

Q. And did you listen to the radio that night? A. I did, Sybil did.

Q. And, did Mr. Elmore? A. No.

Q. So far as you know, where did he go? A. He was in the kitchen.

Q. In the kitchen? And, do you remember what time he went to bed? A. Well, at nine o'clock Sybil wanted a drink of water and I said, "I will get you the drink of water." So I went to the kitchen to get the drink of water, and he was sitting on the end of the couch and he was looking very strange, I didn't know what was the matter with him, he looked as if he was in a--I don't know what I would call it, sort of a--as if his mind was far back, or something, so I said to him, "Why don't you go to bed?" He didn't answer me, so I got a drink of water and I took it to Sybil. I couldn't understand this funny mood that he was in, I had never seen him in a mood like that before, I seen him in all kinds of moods, but this was something different. So, he was sort of sitting there thinking. So then, a few minutes after I went out, and he was in bed.

Q. And, he went into his own bed, did he? A. Yes.

Q. And later on you went to bed that night, yourself? A. Yes, at ten o'clock I went to bed.

Q. Just one moment. Mrs. Elmore, there is no doubt in your mind that when your husband returned at four o'clock, he was home continually until he went to Mrs. Wardell's? A. Yes, that is right.

Mr. Gulotta : All right, Mr. Innes.

Cross-examination By Mr. Innes :

Q. Mrs. Wardell is a probation officer, is she not, in the Magistrate's Court?

Mr. Gulotta : Just a minute, I object to that as incompetent, irrelevant, and immaterial.

The Court : It is a question of cross-examination.

Mr. Gulotta : I respectfully except.

The Court : Overruled.

(Stenographer, repeats the question as follows :

Q. Mrs. Wardell is a probation officer, is she not, in the Magistrate's Court? ")

A. Yes.

Q. Connected with the Second District? A. I think so, I am not quite sure of that.

Q. You know her, don't you? A. Oh, yes, I have known her for quite a while.

Q. And, the defendant was then on probation on your complaint against him, was he not? A. Yes.

Mr. Gulotta: Just one moment. I object to that and I move to strike out the answer as irrelevant, incompetent and immaterial.

The Court : Overruled.

Mr. Gulotta: Question of character is not in issue at this time.

The Court : Overruled.

Mr. Gulotta : I respectfully except.

Q. Now, you tell us, Mrs. Elmore, that on Tuesday night Elmore was, seemed to have something on his mind, is that correct? A. Tuesday, no, I don't--

Q. On the night of the 12th, you say you went in the kitchen and he was sitting on the couch? A. That was Thursday.

Q. Thursday? A. Thursday, yes.

Q. That is the 12th? A. Yes.

Q. You didn't interrogate him as to why he was in that mood? A. No, it was, it sort of worried me.

Q. I see. Mr. Innes: That is all, if the Court please.

Mr. Gulotta : Thank you, Mrs. Elmore. Mr. McKittrick.

Deputy Sheriff : He is not here.

Mr. Casey : Dr. Schwartz.

Mr. Gulotta: I know, your Honor, Dr. Schwartz is on his way. He should be here any moment. In view of that, those are the only two witnesses we have left, your Honor, Mr. McKittrick, who is around here, I am sure, and Dr. Schwartz, then we will rest our case.

Mr. Casey : Here is McKittrick.

JAMES W. MCKITTRICK, 341 Vanderbilt Avenue, Stapleton, Staten Island, New York, called as a witness in behalf of the defendant, first being duly sworn, testified as follows :

Direct examination by Mr. Gulotta:
Q. Mr. McKittrick, you were formerly with the police department of the City of New York, were you not? A. I was.

Q. But, you are no longer connected with that Department? A. I am not.

Q. Have you been doing some investigation for the defense in this case? A. I have.

Q. And, did you serve all the subpoenas in this case? A. I did.

Q. That were served? Now, in the course of your investigation, did you receive instructions to serve a subpoena upon a fellow by the name of Edwards? A. I did.

Q. And who is he connected with? A. With the P. W. A., which is in charge of the Treasury Department at the Court House in Castleton Avenue.

Q. And, did you serve such a subpoena on him? A. I did.

Q. And when did you serve it? A. About the 10th, let me see now, 16th, I received them--about the 18th day of October.

Q. For his appearance here on Friday? A. No, I beg your pardon, let me change that, about the 10th of October.

Q. For his appearance on the 17th? A. For his appearance on the 17th.

Q. And when you served that subpoena, did you serve him personally? A. I served him personally.

Q. And where? A. At the Court House in Castleton Avenue, West Brighton.

Q. At the same time that you served this regular subpoena for the appearance of Mr. Edwards, did you serve a subpoena duces tecum? A. I did.

Q. And, you know what duces tecum means, don't you? A. To produce the records, if any, to the Court.

Q. All right. Now, is this the original of the subpoena that you served? A. It is.

Q. Your affidavit of service is not on here yet, is it? A. It is.

Q. Is it on here? A. A copy of it has been signed by myself, it is on the back.

Q. All right. Now, did you have a conversation with Mr. Edwards concerning a certain W. P. A. check issued to Simon Elmore? A. I did.

Mr. Innes : That is objected to, if the Court please, as not the best evidence and incompetent, immaterial.

The Court : He has laid the foundation by proving he has subpoenaed him and he is not here. I will allow it.

Mr. Gulotta : That is the purpose, your Honor.

By Mr. Gulotta:

Q. What was the conversation?

Mr. Innes : I object to that, no foundation having been laid for this.

A. I asked Mr. Edwards if he would look at his records and ascertain whether or not a check had been paid to Mr. Elmore on August 12th, 1937, at the Seaview Hospital.

Q. Yes. A. He did look at his records. He informed me that Mr. Elmore received a check and he gave me the serial number of that check. The check was for $31.70.

Q. How much was that amount Mr. –

A. $31. 70.

Q. And, did you say that he gave you the number of that check? A. He did.

Q. You don't have the number of that, do you? A. I believe on another copy I have, yes, the number was 18206089.

Q. Now, with relation to the production of that check, did you speak to anyone else in New York City? A. I did.

Q. With whom did you speak? A. Mr. Doherty, the Assistant Distributing Clerk of the Treasury Department at 111 Eighth Avenue, New York, New York.

Q. And, when did you speak with Mr. Doherty? A. At 11:46 A. M., November 20th, 1937.

Q. All right, now, did you have a talk about this check with Mr. Doherty? A. I did.

Q. Give us the conversation.

Mr. Innes : Same objection as before, if the Court please, as to the other conversation.

The Court : This is merely to account for the failure to produce a check.

Mr. Gulotta : That is the situation and only.

The Court : I will allow it.

A. I informed Mr. Doherty of what my mission was at the P. W. A. Headquarters of the Treasury Department, and I requested that he use every influence to let me have the check or a photostatic copy of the check. He instructed me that the United States Government forbid the photographing of checks or the photographing of money, but that he would use his influence with the Treasury Department at Washington where the check was at the present time.

Q. All right. So that he told you that that particular check, the number of which, and amount of which you have given, is now at Washington, is that right? A. At Washington.

Q. Now, in relation to this check, did you call at any bank in Staten Island? A. I did.

Q. And what bank did you call at? A. Staten Island Savings.

Q. And, when did you call and whom did you see? A. I saw one of the clerks there and I asked the clerk if he remembered--

Mr. Innes : Oh, the same objection--A. One of the tellers at least.

Mr. Innes : --as before, if the Court please, no question about the teller being available as a witness. I submit the conversation is hearsay.

The Court : Objection sustained.

By Mr. Gulotta:

Q. Did you ask the person with whom you spoke whether or not it was possible to obtain any record of the cashing of that check without first having the check in your possession?

Mr. Innes : Same objection as before to the last question.

The Court : You are referring now to the bank teller.

Mr. Gulotta : Bank teller.

The Court : I will allow it.

A. The bank teller informed me that he was unable to identify the check unless he saw the check. His initials would be on the back of it.

Mr. Gulotta : Your witness, Mr. Innes.

Mr. Innes : That is all.

Mr. Gulotta : Dr. Schwartz. I believe, your Honor, that this Dr. Schwartz's testimony is quite important to the Court, so therefore will you give him sufficient time to arrive, a short recess?

The Court : All right. We will take a recess, gentlemen. You may go upstairs, do not discuss this case or come to any conclusion in the matter until the case is finally submitted to you and you retire to your Jury room.

(Whereupon at 10:42 A. M. , Court recessed until 11:18 A. M. )

Court Clerk Kosman: People against Samuel Elmore.

(Both sides were ready. )

(Whereupon the Jury was polled and all jurors answered present. )

Mr, Gulotta : Mr. Schwartz.

HARRY SCHWARTZ, 467 Central Park West, Manhattan, New York City, New York, called as a witness in behalf of the defendant, first being duly sworn, testified as follows:

Direct examination by Mr. Gulotta:

Q. Now, Mr. Schwartz, what is your business or profession? A. I am a chemist and toxicologist.

Q. And are you connected with the City of New York? A. I am.

Q. At the present. time? A. I am.

Q. And you have been connected with the City of New York as such since August 12th, 1937, have you not? A. That is right.

Q. Are you in association with Dr. Goettler, the City Toxicologist? A. I am.

Q. Now, how many years have you been a chemist?

A. For the past 18 years.

Q. And what part of that time have you been employed by the City of New York as such? A. The whole time.

Q. The whole time? A. Yes.

Q. Now, sometime on the 17th day of August, 1937, did you receive various articles of clothing from Detective Cosgrove? A. Yes.

Q. And what articles of clothing did you receive? **A. At the laboratory was received a man's trousers, made of a brown and white mixture, a man's imitation silk undershirt, a men's blue and white striped shorts, and a men's handkerchief.**

Q. Now, then, did you proceed to make a chemical analysis for blood? A. I did.

Q. And when did you make that chemical analysis? A. The tests were not done until on or about November 10th.

Q. November 10th? Now, you were served with a subpoena by the defense here this morning, were you not? A. Yes, sir, I have it here.

Q. And, did you bring the articles of clothing with you? A. No, they were turned over to the police.

**Mr. Gulotta : Is the District Attorney in a position to produce them?**

Mr. Innes : I am, sir.

**( The District Attorney produces some clothing. )**

**Q. Now, I show you various articles of clothing and ask you whether or not that is the clothing that you have just described? A. Yes, they are.**

Mr. Gulotta: These are offered in evidence by the defense.

Mr. Innes : No objection. Of course, they haven't been connected up, but don't make any point of that at all, Mr. Gulotta.

Mr. Gulotta : Thank you.

(Clothing referred to was received in evidence and marked Defendant's Exhibit B in Evidence. )

By Mr. Gulotta:

Q. Now, did you, Mr. Schwartz, or Dr. Goettler, at any time receive instructions from the District Attorney of this County to make such an examination? A. It came through the police department.

Q. The Police Department? Now, will you tell us the result of your examination? Did you discover evidence of blood on that clothing, or not? A. No.

Q. Now, how do you make this chemical analysis of clothing, Mr. Schwartz? A. First of all, the garment is taken and questioned, and a careful examination is made as to the color of the stains and its location, which appeared to be blood. Then they, a description of the stain is made and a portion of the stain is removed and dissolved in what is known as saline, to which is added certain chemicals, and we get certain colors. These are known as the non-specific tests for blood. Then, the next test is to take a portion of the dissolved stain and place it under a microscope and try to identify the cells, which may be white or red blood corpuscles, and the last test is to identify the hemoglobin with the use of the spectroscope with which we get the D.E. bands which appear in the spectrum, in front of the spectroscope it gives a certain band and the blood gives a certain band in the spectrum. The last test is the specific test, after all the tests have proven positive, that it is blood, we next test the suspected material for human blood and that is done by a serum which we have immunized from a rabbit with human blood and then we take some of this immunized serum from the rabbit and bring it in contact with the suspected stain, after it has been dissolved and we get a cloudy precipitate between the two liquids and if such appears we say that the material or stain originally contained human blood.

Q. Now, Mr. Schwartz, is that method which you have described a recognized test? A. It is recognized tests.

**Q. And, as I understand it, you have told us that the analysis revealed the presence of no blood? A. That is correct.**

Mr. Gulotta : Thank you. You may cross-examine.

Cross-examination By Mr. Innes :

Q. Now, Mr. Schwartz, your records indicate when this clothing was received at the City Toxicologist's Office? A. Yes.

Q. What date was that? A. On or about the 17th of August.

Q. August. And, your test was not made until November 10th? A. That is correct.

Mr. Innes : That is all.

Mr. Gulotta : Just one moment.

Redirect examination by Mr. Gulotta:

Q. Mr. Schwartz, you said that you received that clothing on the 17th of August? A. Yes.

Q. And, the test was not made until November 10th? A. Yes.

Q. Were those articles of clothing continually in the possession of the City Toxicologist? A. Yes, in our office.

Q. Yes. Now, would there be any difference in the test that you made, whether made on August 17th or

November 10th of the same year? A. Absolutely none.

Mr. Gulotta : None, thank you. That is all, Mr. Schwartz, thank you. That is the defendant's case, if your Honor please.

The Court : Defendant rests?

Mr. Gulotta, : May I now ask your Honor, as I think the District Attorney and I and yourself have decided that we sum up tomorrow morning. May I make my motions tomorrow morning?

The Court : Does the District Attorney rest, the People rest?

Mr. Innes : The people rest.

The Court : Both sides rest? No objection to that?

Mr. Innes : Why, I feel that this case has not proceeded with the expedition that it ought, but I have no objection, if the Court feels that the interests of justice could be served by--

The Court : I do not know how it could have proceeded any faster, Mr. Innes.

Mr. Innes : No, I know we have done fairly well, I am agreed to say, not that I am saying, it in a boastful manner at all, but--

The Court : Well, if there is no objection, you can sum up tomorrow morning.

Mr. Gulotta : May I have tomorrow morning for motions also? It won't take me but a minute.

The Court : Gentlemen, we will recess until tomorrow morning at ten o'clock. Do not discuss this case or come to any conclusions in the matter until the case is finally submitted to you and you retire to your jury room. Please do not form any impressions from any newspapers that you read. I won't say that you shouldn't read newspapers, but if you do, do not form any impressions from them. Your impressions must be arrived at solely from evidence produced before you in court. Tomorrow morning at ten o'clock.

(Whereupon at 11 :24 A. M. , court recessed until the following morning at 10 :00 A. M. )

## Motion to Dismiss

Court Clerk Kosman: All manner of persons having any business to do with this term of the County Court, held in and for the County of Richmond, draw near, give your attendance, and you shall be heard. For trial, People against Samuel Elmore.

Mr. Innes: Ready.

Mr. Gulotta: Ready.

(Whereupon the Jury was polled and all jurors answered present.)

Mr. Gulotta: May it please your Honor, the defendant at this time respectfully moves to dismiss the indictment on all the counts set forth at the close of the People's case. On the further ground that the testimony and evidence in this case fails to establish the crime charged in the indictment, on the ground that the testimony and evidence introduced in this case fails to satisfy the provisions of Section 1044 of the Penal Law and on the ground that the People failed to make out the cause of action contained in the indictment.

The Court: Motion denied.

Mr. Gulotta: I respectfully except. Now, if your Honor pleases, may I respectfully ask the Court at this time to instruct the Jury that your Honor's denial of my motion is merely a denial of a matter of law with which the Jury has no concern and which has no indication as to any findings as to the facts raised in the issue in this trial.

The Court: Motion granted. The Jury will be so instructed.

SUMMATION BY MR. GULOTTA--FOR DEFENDANT.

Mr. Innes: I assume that is a part of your Honor's charge anyway.

The Court: I beg your pardon.

Mr. Innes: I assume that would be a part of your Honor's charge anyway.

The Court: Yes.

Mr. Gulotta: May it please your Honor, Mr. Foreman, Gentlemen of the Jury, we have come to a close of the trial in this action. I naturally realize what a job that has been for you and naturally you must realize what a job that has been for me.

I think that everyone agrees in this case that we have gone along all right, no bickering between counsel. The Court, I think I can truthfully extend my thanks too for his demeanor during this case and also Mr. Innes. If you have noticed it, we got along very fine.

Now, at the outset, Gentlemen, I want to say this. I am in deep sorrow because, principally because, of two persons in this case and you must believe me when I tell you that I mean that sincerely and truthfully and without any color. I feel sorry for the parents of this little girl, Joan Kuleba. You of course, those of you who have children realize it and I retained you on the Jury even though the question was asked, have you any children. In my opinion that places you in a better position to share with me my sorrow at this time. And having children of my own, I certainly am in a position to judge.

But, we didn't start the trial of this action by soliciting your sympathy, in other words, we came here with a case, and I told you at the outset what I was ready to prove, as well as the People told you what they expected to prove. Now, if you will recall what I told you and what I asked you at the beginning of this trial, that places you in a position to realize more than myself that I stuck strictly to what I told you I was going to prove, and as sorry as I was and I told you in the beginning, yet we have law, we have order, there is justice and of course, justice must be done. Simply because a crime is committed, I asked you at the outset, is no reason why somebody should forfeit his life unless by a jury of his fellow men and beyond a reasonable doubt, that man is found to be the man who committed the crime in question.

Now, there is an indictment in this case with four counts, and I am not going to read the counts to you, but briefly, it describes the manner in which this crime was committed. The People must stand on that indictment. And the law says that they must also stand upon the bill of particulars that they give us, that is the defense, in which they set out, set out the manner in which the crime was committed, the time when the crime was committed, the place where the crime was committed. If they fail to bring it before any one of those three items, they have failed in their case.

And as to each count of the four counts in the indictment, they say, "The assault described in said indictment was committed on the 12th day of August, 1937 between the hours of 11:00 A. M. and 4:00 P. M." which is a stretch of five hours. "The said Joan Kuleba died on the 12th day of August, 1937 between the hours of 11:00 A. M. and 5:00 P. M. The alleged crime was committed in an abandoned bungalow in the marshland at the foot of Burger Avenue, Dongan Hills at approximately 500 feet west of the corner of **Warren**".

Now that is what they say with regard to the time, the place and the manner in which this crime was committed.

Now the State, I say to you, must prove that these things occurred beyond a reasonable doubt, without you forgetting, while you are considering the reasonable doubt, that presumption of law, that presumption of innocence, which even now, Elmore enjoys. And you cannot deviate from that course until you have gathered for deliberation in your jury room, and I have great faith in you Gentlemen, that when you promised me that that was the situation, that you will do exactly that, and without any doubt about it.

Now, let us concern ourselves with that date, that memorable day, August 12th, 1937, and more particularly with the hours between 11:00 A. M. and 4:00 P. M. What has the prosecution proved concerning that day? For one brief moment, I want to forget the confessions, because I am corning back to that, and I am going to now present to you exactly what the people relied upon in order to establish that a crime was committed on that day between those hours, **and I think you agree with me when I say that the most important witness, the witness relied upon by the State to identify the Defendant was that man William Flick, who worked on route 2, Villa McClean Avenue, and I now consider him as a defense witness,** he is the minute man, he sees all and he knows all, he is the eyes and the ears of the world, that man. And I have a justification and a proper one for saying that.

First he said in his testimony when he took the stand and when a man tells in minutes, usually you don't make a mistake about minutes, but if I say between let us say, 3 and 4, then of course, you give that witness credit for the latitude that he allows his memory, but this man doesn't, this man first said, between 1:00 P. M. and one minute after 1:00, and that is exactly what he said, because when he was asked the question:

Q. And would you fix the time that you saw this man and the little girl ? A. Between 1:00 and 1:01 minutes after 1:00 in the afternoon.

Now, that is very singular when we deal about minutes and seconds isn't it, because later on, when asked again by the District Attorney: "And you say it was shortly after 1:00 o'clock? A. Beg pardon, I made a mistake, it was between 1:10 and 1:11 and I was due at the terminal at 1:15.

Now, there is the situation that you have concerning Flick. Here is a man that is driving a bus and he sees something peculiar, he is driving at the rate of five miles an hour, but having seen something peculiar, he slows down to two miles an hour. If it was peculiar enough, the ordinary man, the cautious man, the reasonable man, would stop his bus after all, if it is peculiar enough and a little girl is involved, he only had five passengers in the bus, he could have stopped. **So that it wasn't so peculiar as he makes it out.** When **he thought it was peculiar, was the next day when he started to read the newspapers.** That is when he first knew it was peculiar, although when I asked him, he said yes, it appeared to me to be peculiar.

And so he slowed down to two miles an hour and testified that he had these people under observation for a minute to a minute and a half. Now what does he say? He said for the first half a minute, "I saw the back of Elmore's head and I saw this little girl two or three feet in front of Elmore." He couldn't tell the color of the bathing suit, because when I asked him, and I might say at this point, Gentlemen, that I am not here to make any dramatic address, because the day for dramatic addresses is past but we want common sense and that is why I must consult this record, this is a record of the trial. **He was asked this question by Mr. Innes, "It was a red bathing suit, something on that style? A. I can't exactly say it was that color" And then Mr. Innes: All right, that is all." That is as far as he would go with regard to the color of a red bathing suit. Do you remember when I asked him about, "Well, was it all red?" He said, "It may have been, or it may have been some other color. I can't tell". I said, "Could part of it be blue? Well, he said, not blue, but some other color."** Well, now, for a half a moment he saw the back of this man's head and then he passed at two miles an hour and the next day he formulates the opinion, after seeing Elmore, with no one around him, that that was the man he saw, the face of the man he saw and without any doubt about it.

Now, what does he say about the little girl, this man who sees so much. He says this: Question by Mr. Innes. "Q. You didn't notice anything on her feet then? A. No, I couldn't get a view of her feet because of the grass."

Well now, he testified that there was a sidewalk there, he testified that this girl was walking two or three feet in front of this man, I asked him about the sidewalk, he said, well it is maybe not cement, but certainly it is ashes. That is not my recollection, Gentlemen, because I covered that point and I asked him sometime after that, "Q. And is that a concrete sidewalk? A. No, it is, I think, it is ashes, I am pretty sure it was ashes." Now, that goes to show the type of testimony that you have. He couldn't see the little girl's feet because of the fact that there was grass on the sidewalk. He is so sure there was a sidewalk. He is so sure that that sidewalk consisted of ashes and yet, he could see everything else.

Now, this observation was made in one minute to one minute and a half, for a half a minute he saw the back of his head, a half a minute he observed through the glass. Now, Gentlemen, I am going to ask you in fairness to the defense here, to make this calculation yourselves. He said, and it is in the record, "That in one and one half to two minutes after he had passed the point where he said the defendant and the little girl were, he covered a distance of 40 to 50 feet while he was looking through that glass." That is after passing. Now, what is that computation. The computation is that in two minutes, he went 40 feet. Well, we will give him the figure he mentioned first, 40 to 50 feet. If that is so, in one minute he would go 20 feet, in 60 minutes he would go 1200 feet and you know what that means, Gentlemen, that a fraction which is exposed in this way, 1200 feet over 5280 feet, which make our mile, means that he was going at a quarter of a mile an hour and that is exactly what it means mathematically, not two miles per hour.

Now, let us assume and give him the benefit of a doubt that he deserves as a witness. Suppose he was going two miles an hour and he covered that distance, it merely means that that 40, that 40 feet that he went, must be multiplied by 8 and the result is that in two minutes he would have gone 320 feet. What does that mean. It means that when he passed these two persons, whoever they were, he couldn't have seen anything that would have permitted him to make positive identification, he would have been going too fast for that, and I asked him, could you see the man's face after you passed him through the mirror. What was his answer? His answer was, "No, I couldn't see that, I didn't see a thing, I only saw his face as I came abreast of him". On the other hand, he didn't see the little girl's face and she is walking ahead of some person and if he saw through the mirror at all, he would have recognized the head of the girl facing him.

Now, I want to go over with you for a short moment the observations that this man Flick made, and I say it is important. He saw a girl in a red bathing suit. He saw a man, he saw that this man had no hat, he saw that this man was wearing a dirty gray pair of pants, he saw that he was wearing a white shirt, he noticed that she had blonde hair, he noticed that she had curly blond hair, he noticed that the man had a mustache, he noticed the distance between the girl and the man, and he noticed an object that the defendant was carrying, he says, an object which was from 10 to 12 inches long and he noticed ashes on the sidewalk.

Now, Gentlemen, reasonable men as you are, can you notice driving a bus after he testified that his instructions were that he is to look in the direction he is going, is it possible to make all of these observations, all that he says happened that day? **When he went to the Police Station this day, he found out certain things he was talking to people, they told him certain things and he made that knowledge his own, but he didn't testify about conversations or he didn't testify about a frame of mind that he was enjoying the next day, he testified that he saw those things as that bus passed going at 2 miles an hour.**

Now, I am going to distinguish in fairness, in fairness. I am going to distinguish another People's witness whom I think is a truthful witness and I believe every single word she says. Contrast this testimony of Flick with Selma Goller. Selma Goller is a young girl who knew this little girl for a period of three years. And certainly it is in the testimony that Flick never saw this man before. What does she say? After knowing this girl three years. Here is what she says: "Q. Now, you have known this little girl for about 3 years, haven't you? A. Yes. Q. And did you talk to her? A. What is that? Q. What is that? A. She called me. That is how I remembered seeing her. Q. She spoke to you? A. No, she just said Hello, called me my name and said Hello". And then, "Q. This is by me, you don't remember how she was dressed, do you? A. No, I don't."

Now, if anyone wants to talk about a red bathing suit and how clearly red is distinguishable, even in a small size bathing suit, Selma Goller was there, knew the girl, said Hello, not like a bus driver driving past at 2 miles an hour, Hello, and the little girl ran by and she was right in front of her father's place, the Silver Wave. What happened? She is unable to tell you Gentlemen how that little girl was dressed. Now, mind you if she could tell you that, she would be only too pleased to tell you, she would come here and say, yes, I saw her go by but she was not about to say.

And I want you Gentlemen, if you will, to contrast this with Eagle-eyed Flick. There is no doubt about him.

Now you remember if Flick is so good at remembering faces and details, you will remember Flick's testimony concerning the fact that he had 5 passengers aboard, and I asked him whether or not through that glass it is possible to see some of the passengers that are seated in the rear of the bus. He testified that there were 5 passengers, but I asked him whether at least he could tell us whether these passengers were at least men, women, or children and what did he say? "Q. And I understand you to testify definitely that as you **could state now, you don't know whether they were men, women or children, is that right? A. Yes."** Now, here is a man that sees persons come in and out of his bus, men, women and children. I don't so much criticize him because of the fact that he is unable to tell you Gentlemen whether the 5 passengers were men, women, or children, that isn't it, but I do criticize him when he endeavors to tell you all of the observations which he made in that short space of time, a half a minute, while his bus is in motion with passengers in it. That is not fair, that is not the truth, as men know it.

Now, what about continuing with his testimony for just a short while. He said that the man was carrying something and that that something that he was carrying was an object of glass and he said that it looked something like a pitcher. All right. Now, there is no doubt about that and I don't want any doubt about it, because it was the Court who asked?"Describe the package whatever it was, the size of the package, whether it was wrapped or unwrapped or anything in that connection. A. Well, it wasn't wrapped, it was a thing, an object, I will say about 10 or 12 inches in length and it was glass, whatever it was I can't say whether it was a pitcher or what it was." So far, I should say, so good. But, later on, if he is that definite, why should he change his testimony, if it is a thing that he observed and he is a man that is sure of pretty nearly everything, if that is the case, why is it that on cross-examination, I said, I asked him this question?"Well now, I understand you even at this very moment to express some degree of doubt as to whether or not this object was wrapped up or not. A. It wasn't." **After having told you Gentlemen, because he knew that there was a milk bottle in this case, and that is what I was trying to tell you before, he ventures to say that it was a thing of glass, about 10 to 12 inches.** Well, you know that is about the length of that bottle, 10 or 12 inches, he tells you. I wouldn't know whether it was 10, 15, or 20 inches just like that. (Mr. Gulotta snaps his fingers.)

Now, he don't know whether it was wrapped up or not. Now, how can a man tell you that it is an object of glass if he don't know, in the first place, whether it was wrapped up or whether it was unwrapped.

And further on we now get him to admit, first it is an object of glass, then he doesn't know whether it is wrapped up or not, and now he doesn't know whether there was a package at all, because I asked him, "You couldn't give us any geometric description of it, could you? A. No."

Well, right there, if he could give any geometric description of it, why does he venture of the information that it is 10 to 12 inches in length. And I went on, "Would you say whether it was round or square? A. No, I couldn't say that." Well, if a man can't say whether it was round or square, can he say it was 12 inches long? "Do you know what a pitcher looks like? Yes, I think so. Would you say whether it was long or short? A. Well no, I couldn't say that." And that absolutely will bring out the point that you might have thought a moment ago when I said was it square or round. It could still be square or round and still be 12 inches long on one part of the square or the other, but when I asked him, would you say whether it was long or short, now I am talking about his inches, and he said, "Well no, I don't say that. And Q. Why did you express the opinion to the District Attorney that it looked like a pitcher? **A. Because when I went by it, the man was bent over this way (indicating). Q. Did I ask you how the man was bent over? A. No, but that is why I couldn't see what he was carrying, that obstructed my view from seeing it." He now didn't see it at all, and that is the record, Gentlemen.**

Now, that is part of the State's case, Gentlemen, you heard about an officer Marrinan who took the stenographic minutes as Elmore was talking. You heard of Inspector Lyons and Inspector McGrath. You heard of those people, but I don't think it is so important that I should ask you, well, where are they, since it is so important to have witnesses at the time of the signing, These are high officials of the Police Department, but I will make a point of the signing. Where is Mrs. Budd? Where is Mrs. Budd? I wasn't aware of the fact that the State produced Mrs. Budd, and where does she fit into this picture. Here is a question, while Officer Cosgrove is being examined. "Q. And were you there when a Mrs. Budd was brought in and saw Elmore? A. I was. Q. And did you hear what both Flick and Mrs. Budd said in the presence of

Elmore, what they said in the presence of Elmore? A. I did. Q. What did they say? **A. Mrs. Budd said that she was on the Beach the day before. That was the 11th and that she seen Elmore on the beach, that she was with her grand-children on the beach and she noticed Elmore and her child walking up off the beach or walking from the beach, that she then ran after the child, took her and looked at Elmore. She had something on her mind, she said, and when she came to the station house, on the morning of the 14th about 4:00 o'clock, Inspector Lyons was there, myself, Inspector McGrath, she seen Elmore there and she said that that was the man she seen on the beach the day previous when she was there with her grandchildren." All right. Now they produced Flick ; of course for all I know Flick was more imaginative than Mrs. Budd but Mrs. Budd was not produced.**

Now Gentlemen, what have we? I am going to be as brief as I possibly can because I think that is all I need do.

We have two confessions and I say that we can construe the voluntary nature of that confession or those confessions by looking into the facts and circumstances thereof and every fact and circumstance in connection with those confessions must be taken into consideration. In other words, here is what I mean. **If a man confesses a crime and then the People show you details that he had talked about in that confession and locality shows them, I would say that there was something to that. But, if the Police Department make an investigation and find such as a milk bottle and stuff like that, and then put them into the confession, that part of the confession becomes as erroneous as the part where the man says I did it and there is no doubt about that.**

[Ed. Note: Viewers of "Making a Murderer" and "Scenes of a Crime" and "Paradise Lost" will know exactly what Mr. Gulotta is getting at.]

Now, Elmore got to the Station House sometime before 4:00 o'clock. I think that there is no speculation about that, and I mean 4:00 o'clock on the 13th day of August, 1937, because a question was asked and I want to refer also to the record. "Now what time did you get to the station house? I think about 4:00 o'clock that afternoon". That is Cosgrove. "And when you got there, who was present in the room with Samuel Elmore? A. Assistant Chief Lyons, Inspector McGrath, Detective Murphy, Detective Brannon, Sergeant Hilderbrand, they were all in and about the office there", where they had this man in the station house.

Now what happened, when was the first confession obtained by the State here? Well, the date of it is, to my recollection, August 14th at 5:45 P. M. How long after he was at the station house at 4:00 o'clock, I am not even quibbling about how long before 4:00 o'clock he was at the station, but how long after 4:00 o'clock, August 13th, is this 5:45, August 14th. **Gentlemen that works out to be more than 26 hours afterwards.**

Now another question. **When was he placed under arrest? We find that that is the following day at 12:30, August 15th. That, Gentlemen, is 45 hours after the detention.** Now why do I mention that. Because various people are brought in in the meantime, Mrs. Budd and Flick and if it was on Flick's identification that they finally decided to arrest Elmore, then I feel sorry for any Gentleman that would find himself at any time in a similar place.

When was the second confession signed. He is now under arrest, he has already signed a confession, so we go to the next confession wherein we permeated with the greatest of details and that has details in it. That was signed on the 16th day of August and it was signed on the same day that the defendant was arraigned in this Court before Mr. Justice Cosgrove. What have we got there Gentlemen?

We have a situation here where we believe that that shouldn't have been done that way and we urge that at the time. It is not within my privilege to tell you what the law is but I think perhaps you will forgive me for a moment if I tell you that I have some right to mention what I think the law is, having also in mind, as I told you in the beginning, that if I am wrong in the law, then also listen to what the law is from the lips of the Judge, and in that connection, Gentlemen, while I am at it, I want you to know that if I am wrong in any fact which I am presenting to you now, and I am trying to talk from the record, then don't apply the fact as I remember it, please apply it as you remember because you are going to decide on this case and not I.

**But section 165 of the Code, however, does say, "The defendant must in all cases be taken before the Magistrate without unnecessary delay and he may give bail at any hour of the day or night".** That is if it is not a capital crime, the last part where he may give bail.

Now I construe Gentlemen, that when Elmore was taken into custody on the 13th day of August, 1937, he was being detained by the police and so far as my construction on the situation is concerned, he was a defendant, and I say to you, that plenty of hours passed, this was a Monday morning now when that second confession was signed and when he was arraigned before this court.

Now, I want to look at the first confession for a moment and I think I have it here, wherein that confession says this, and something is wrong somewhere, Gentlemen. He says in his confession, **"I met the girl down at the foot of the Beach near Crane's Thursday, August 12th, 1937, about 2:00 o'clock P. M. and took the little girl along for a walk, along Old Town Road, just where the bus driver says."** Now, just tarry a moment. If Flick is right about his time and if the State is right about this confession, I couldn't even ask you that because that is an impossibility. If they rely on Flick about seeing Elmore with the girl at 1:10 to 1:11. Certainly their own confession which they extracted says, **"I met the girl at 2:00 o'clock."** So that, did Flick see something before it actually happened.

Now there is just a little something in that first confession, which I think is worthy of note, because Flick testifies undoubtedly not between 1:00 and 2:00, Flick testifies between 1:10 and 1:11 and there can be no mistake about that, between 1:10 and 1:11. He knows that. He knows that even though there is no clock in the bus, he knows that even though he says, and it is right here that he didn't consult a watch but he knew according to the schedule that he was travelling in view of the fact that he was expected at the terminal at 1:15, that it must have been between 1:10 and 1:11. Of course maybe bus drivers once in a while are able to do that, I don't dispute that at all.

Now, on page 82 of this book here, here is what we have. "I strangled the child about from 2:00 to 3:00 o'clock. In that same confession, that is the first one. I strangled the child about from 2:00 to 3:00 o'clock". Now Carney, our own witness, saw Elmore at the B. & 0. yard at from 2:00 to 2:15, and how is he sure that he saw Elmore at from 2:00 to 2:15. He wasn't driving a bus, Gentlemen. "Q. Now did you see him on August 12th? A. I did. Q. And what time did you see him?"? This is Mr. Carney's testimony, Gentlemen. "A. Between 2:00 and 2:15. Q. Now how do you arrive at the hour, 2:00 and 2:15? A. Because I was working on an electric car at the time and I left the job to go up to the tin shop to get something and happened to look at the Boss's clock and see that it was 2 o'clock."

Now, is Carney lying in this case. Is there such a man on the face of this earth that would go to court and testify on behalf of a man when in his own mind there must be a doubt as to this man's guilt or innocence. Is there a man with a character who would let a crime like this go unpunished by coming here and lying about it. Why, that is impossible. All right, now forget Carney for a moment and I will come back to our own side of the case in a moment.

You see we produced about 18 or 19 witnesses and you know most of them and all of them, I asked a good many of them whether they ever met me. I never talked with any of those witnesses. I never seen them before, any one of them. Would they all come here and lie about a situation of this kind, or is it because Flick has a flare to play an important part in this case and the next day say, yes, I think I did see something. **He might have, but according to the record he never saw Elmore at 1:10 to 1:11. That is an impossibility.**

Now then, in the second confession that we have, there is another singular proposition which I have picked out of this record and this is on the question as to whether or not he was ever seen by Flick. "I then proceeded along Gordon Street to Osgood Avenue, through a lot to Targee Street, which is in back of the laundry, up Targee Street to Roff Street, through another lot to Metcalfe Street and then to my home where I arrived at 1:30". All right. That is in the confession. Now did Mrs. Elmore come here and lie when she said that Elmore got home at 12:00 o'clock with the clams and with the greens and that they had luncheon together and their little daughter and that after lunch at 10 minutes to 1:00 he went out and at five to one was seen again by McKittrick, by Miss McKittrick whose house was a five minute walk and she saw him at 5 minutes to one. Now figure that out whether this could be possibly right. I am trying to show you the things in the confession which are impossible and they are impossible. How could he be at the place where this crime is supposed to have been committed if that is the situation. "I left the groceries on the tubs and came out again and walked out up Metcalfe Street, along Targee Street, along Vanderbilt Avenue, right straight across Steuben Street to Hanover Avenue and went down Clove Road having crossed over the side of the hills at Moselle Avenue, across the boulevard in back of St. Mary's cemetery and walked down Old Town Road across to Olympia Boulevard, went through the meadows to a wagon path and walked that down and went across the creek, out on the beach."

And yet Carney saw him at 2:00 to 2:15. How long do you suppose it would take to walk that distance from Elmore's house down to where this bungalow is. A distance of practically 3 miles. He doesn't drive an automobile, and this is very singular.

Do you remember Flick saying something about that his starting time, his starting time from the Ferry is 12:50 and that about 1:00 o'clock, about 1:00 o'clock he was at Vanderbilt Avenue. That is the way he has his time schedule, and that at 10 minutes after 1:00, or 11 minutes after 1:00 was on Norway Avenue near Scott Avenue. **Now, if there is any truth to this, certainly Flick would have gotten to that spot before Elmore because Elmore was walking all the time and there can't be any doubt about that. So that that situation is impossible.**

**Now you consult that map, and I had Mr. Arrington here, an architect, and he traced the course that Elmore was supposed to have taken and there is a line there and it starts where his initials appear, and it traces the streets where the defendant said in that confession where he went, how he went to this bungalow, and he says that it is about three miles, and that is the reason why I had Arrington come here to testify to that situation, because of the impossibilities here.**

Now, here is another singular thing while we are talking about distances. "And we walked along the beach and came out the path the other side of Sea Side Boulevard in back of the bungalow near Bessi's."

Now you Gentlemen had a little visit there and the Judge and the defendant, counsel for both sides were there and you now visualize the spot, as you looked at it from the other side, you visualize how distant from that spot where you stood that bungalow is situated and Elmore in this confession said, or I should say rather that he put his signature over what it says, "And we walked along the beach and came out the path the other side of Sea Side Boulevard in back of the bungalow near Bessi's. I walked with her up Sand Lane to Old Town Road", mind you, **"I held her little hand while walking to Sand Lane.** During the period that we walked through Bessi's to Sand Lane the only conversation I remember was going to take a walk, we walked up Sand Lane to Old Town Road near the corner of Old Town Road and Sand Lane. **I went to a candy store and bought her 5 cents worth of candy. The store was located on Sand Lane".**

Now, Gentlemen, what does that mean. He says he walked all the way around and I had a diagram here to show you but since you have visited the scene you know. Here is a man about to commit a crime so he takes a notion that he will walk those streets that are littered up with stores and houses, he will walk past a railroad crossing, he will go around about a way, about a mile and a half, instead of cutting across the marshes and going to that bungalow. You saw that. Well, can that distance be walked the other way? Well, you remember the testimony of Mr. Haff and that incidentally, while I think of it, you will remember the little time I had with him when the defendant was supposed to have come up to him and said, "There is a little girl there." And then when I asked him did he say a child, Mr. Haff said, "yes I think he said both". Now, what is the matter with these witnesses. If they can recall a remark a man made on the 13th of August, 1937, I should think that they would remember it, and that is the possibility, if they don't, because I don't think I would know what the man said, whether it was girl, boy or child, I wouldn't, but Haff knew and what did he say. He said, "I think he said both". Well, you can construe that in any way that you want.

Well now, he said that that portion of the marshland can be walked, there are ditches, there, and you remember him saying, why I can jump over any of those ditches except one wide one, and said well, I suppose you being a young fellow, you can, you can jump over that. He said well, all right I can. But, that is the situation. **The short distance is only a half a mile slight, the other distance is a mile and a half. The long distance there** is a possibility of being seen, the short distance is none. Criminals like to be in dark places when crimes are about to be committed and there is no doubt about that.

**As a matter of fact, I might say to you that the testimony of Detective Cosgrove is that he walked that way and that of course wipes off, I had forgotten that, wipes off any proposition about whether or not it can be walked the short way.**

Now, so long as this milk bottle is here I want to say something about it. Detective Cosgrove says that the milk bottle was at the bungalow and it was on a shelf. He motioned in this manner, certainly no little girl could put it up there the way he motioned, it was on a shelf, but somebody put it up there, somebody that is reasonably tall.

Now I remember when District Attorney Innes showed him the photograph and asked him whether or not he could see a milk bottle on it. You can't see a milk bottle on the photograph and I am not criticizing Detective Cosgrove because I will say for him I think he is one of the cleanest men on the police department, but you know the police department is working, they are working on a case, it is a duty to them and they like to perform it their own way.

Now, what was his testimony about that bottle. He says that that bottle was dusted for prints at the bungalow, because I will tell you how sure they are about. that. "Q. Now, you. saw the bottle down there did you? A. I did. Q. Did you take that bottle? A. I didn't. Q. You didn't believe it significant enough to take it, did you? A. I knew it was significant. Q. But, you didn't take it? A. No, nobody is supposed to touch that bottle but the fingerprint expert. Q. And when you went to the station house you left that bottle there didn't you? A. I didn't. Q. What did you do? A. That bottle was left there until Detective Paola and Detective Martin from the Technical Research Bureau arrived." Now, was there somebody else in this bungalow after a crime was committed that touched that bottle. **If they dusted it for fingerprints, nobody touched it,**

286

then Elmore touched it if he was supposed to be carrying it, and he was carrying it, the confession says so. **If they dusted that means that there is the strongest possibility that fingerprints would be on this bottle, because otherwise why dust it. You may as well dust your clothes. But, they dusted it for fingerprints, definitely so.** Now the bottle is produced. Paola came upon the stand. Did he give you any testimony about fingerprints. Did he give us any testimony of any fingerprints on the bottle. Well now, the fingerprints couldn't be disturbed since they were dusted the specimen was there, no fingerprints on the bottle. You will notice this is a fairly smooth surface but there are no fingerprints on the bottle.

Now, "Q. Now what was the first thing that was done with that bottle after you saw it? A. That bottle was left there until the technicians arrived to dust it for fingerprints. Q. Dust it? A. Paint it with brushes to produce fingerprints." That is the answer that we got.

That bottle in my opinion, Gentlemen of the Jury, had no fingerprints on it. That bottle, Gentlemen of the Jury, if carried by an individual for the distance from Crane's Hotel to this bungalow, the long circuitous route, had had fingerprints on it. **Why do I say that. I say it because Elmore was brought to New York and he was in the lineup and he was fingerprinted and when they dusted this bottle they weren't the fingerprints of Elmore which they got over in New York, but justice must go on just the same.**

Now you must know, Gentlemen, that I have been trying to tell you that these confessions are prepared in such a manner as to embody therein facts which were discovered first before they started to question this man about a confession. You know about the testimony when he is brought to the morgue, over the body of this little girl for whom I am grievously sorry and for her parents, he was then and there asked, "Did you do this." Now, there would be the breaking point of a man if he was a criminal, if he committed a crime and watched this little girl there on the slab in the morgue, that is the time he would break and say yes, I did it. But, he put his hand on that girl's heart and said No, I didn't do it.

Now, we come, Gentlemen, to our side of the case and you must at all times visualize this situation. I have been talking to you about the People's case and you must visualize the fact that outside of these confessions for what reason, as Mr. Innes says, men's minds bend, that the only testimony in addition to that is Mr. Flick, the testimony that perhaps would be effective here, of Mrs. Budd and others, it is not produced.

Now, what is our testimony about this case, why do I come to you and say, "This man is going to have a trial along certain lines" and I said that. And I said that to you when I started, "He is going to have a trial along the lines that if he wasn't there, he didn't commit it" and I am sure that if you Gentlemen decide that he didn't and believe his witnesses, that you have done your duty.

[Ed. Note: If there was a defense opening argument, it was not included in the record on appeal.]

You can't speculate. You can't kill a man because justice must be satisfied even though there is a doubt, only beyond a reasonable doubt. Does Flick's testimony give you a reasonable doubt, Gentlemen? Figure that in your own mind.

Now, I have testimony to the effect that this man, who is now sitting there and who the State claims is a criminal, that it was his habit to get up every morning at 7:00 o'clock and the first thing this criminal would do is change the bird bath, feed the bird, odd chores around the house. Well, let us see what he did on August 12th and let us see how we back it up.

After he had his breakfast, 9:30 to 10:00 o'clock, he left the house and her testimony is that he was going after his pay at Sea View Hospital. She gave him a list of groceries to get and see whether or not later on we will check this up about groceries and about what he was to get, the specific articles that he was supposed to get; see if we don't check that up.

Now, here is a woman and I may as well tell you now, I put her on the stand for the purpose of time and only for the purpose of time. She is not solicitous in any way to her husband, as I could see, because she made the remark, after I got through with her almost, she said, well, on the night of August 12th, he seemed a little, he didn't answer me when I asked him why don't you go to bed. He didn't answer me. Well now, I don't know, the District Attorney may make a point of that, that his mind was disturbed, because he had done something, but I doubt it. My goodness, every Monday morning when my wife asks me for money, I have got a sad look and I don't answer either. Is there anything singular about a man not answering, because his wife asked him a question.

Now then, let us proceed along here. He stopped in at the A. & P. and we have young Baccarezza here to testify to that, and the testimony is 9:10 to 10:00 o'clock, not 12 minutes after 9:00 or 12 minutes to 10:00, it is 9:30 to 10:00 o'clock. The A. & P. is located at Richmond Road and Marie Street. 'He went in there with a list that Mrs. Elmore gave him and he brought it into the A. & P.

Now, we have 10:00 to 10:30, and see if the time doesn't check, a man by the name of Patrick Collins, who met him on the bus. He said that they changed buses at Egbertville and that you will remember is Richmond Road and Rockland Avenue. They changed for a bus, and rode together on that bus to Sea View Hospital. That was 10:00 to 10:30. All right. Some time between 10:00 and 11:00 he was seen at that hospital. Now, I know you Gentlemen will believe that he was at the hospital that morning because the testimony is so clear and so convincing there isn't any doubt about it. Who are the other men that saw him at Sea View Hospital? Well, a fellow by the name of Jack Steinberg. 10:00 to 11:00, Irving Bodaness, Charles Meyer. What were they doing there, all W.P.A. workers, all on the line waiting for their checks. Did they get their checks? The answer is yes.

I am going to show you a little something, Gentlemen, which was a complete surprise to me during the course of this trial. I called certain men whom I knew were there. How do you suppose I knew that these men were there if somebody didn't tell me. And in like manner, the name of John Bateman came to my view and I put him on the stand. I never saw John Bateman in my life and I said, were you up at Sea View Hospital. Yes, what did you go there for. I went up there to get my check. Did you get your check? Yes. Did you see Elmore there. No, I didn't see him.

Now, of course, you might say, well here is a witness who said he didn't see Elmore. I consider that the strongest proof, the strongest proof that the man was there, but it is proof of another color too, the color of proof that we are presenting to you on this trial. The fact that if a man didn't see him, he comes and takes the stand and says all right, I didn't see him.

All right, there was one particular individual who was up there by the name of Bernard Stieger and he says that he was there at 10:50, that is 10 minutes to 11:00 o'clock and that there were 6 or 7 in front of Elmore on line, that he got his check at 10 minutes after 11:00 and he waited for Elmore. He knew Elmore, I asked him, had known him a number of years, therefore it is logical to assume that he knew where Elmore lived. And just consider this for a moment. How did Elmore go when he went to Sea View. He changed at Egbertville, Richmond Road and Rockland Avenue, and when Berney Stieger says, come on, I will give you a ride, where did he take him. He took him to Egbertville, the same corner of Richmond Road and Rockland Avenue. How does Stieger know that it was this time, because from there he went to the Bank to cash his check and he got to the bank at half past 11:00. And that is how he knew.

Now, what did Elmore do. He wanted to go and get his stuff, he had placed an order that morning so he went to get his groceries, left the order, now I will pick it up, I will go home the same way, and did he meet anybody on the way?

I don't know whether you remember that old, kind lady that took the stand, her name is Emma Keil, and she lives and has a place of business at 600 Richmond Road, 11:30 to 12:00, she said, she saw Elmore going by. There is an old woman, it appeared to me she is over 70 years of age, she is certainly not going to lie. She said there was a conversation about the fact that Mr. Elmore said why don't you take turkish baths because they are a good thing for you. And she said that they discussed Mrs. Elmore's health. You will remember that.

How does she know it was that time? Well, she is the kind of a woman that buys her vegetables from a man who comes around in a horse and wagon. She said she was talking to the vegetable man who always arrives at 11:30, those fellows are on your doorstep every day at the same time because they have their customers.

**Now, as he passed Mrs. Keil and said hello, where did he go. He went back to Baccarezza, the first stop that he had made in the morning and Baccarezza is at 568 Richmond Road and the distance between 568 and 600 is not a long distance naturally. This man on the stand testified to that. He said that Elmore offered him a check; I asked him do you know whether it was a W.P.A. check. He said no, I don't. Of course, I can't cash the check. You take the groceries. You owe me $1.40 and he remembers it was $1.40 because Elmore, the next day, came back and paid him, $1.40 for groceries.**

Now, where do we come naturally, after he picked up those groceries. See if that doesn't check. 12:00 o'clock noon he reaches home with the groceries, remembers that he got from the A. & P. with the clerk Baccarezza waiting on him. Brought the clams and opened them, I think they said 13. Mrs. Elmore testified to that. That he fixed the greens, that he had lunch, that he accumulated a number of paper bags and that he left home at 12:50, that is 10 minutes to one.

Now, at that point, Gentlemen, I must say this to

you,--and that is why I always go back to this man Flick. If he left his home at 12:50, could he have been at the place where they say he was at 10 minutes after one. She knows it was 12:50 because there is a clock in the kitchen and she says something about she does things very exact. If my memory serves me right. If I am wrong you will disregard it. So there is a clock in the kitchen and she looked at it and it was ten minutes to one.

I said to her, I said, do you live anywheres near Miss McKittrick and she said, yes, and what is the distance? She said about a 5 minute walk. Does this check up? That Miss McKittrick saw him go by with some bags under his arm, he was walking on the other side of the street at 5 minutes to one. **This is singular, Gentlemen, and don't forget it. At the time that Miss McKittrick saw Elmore, she** [sic] **was walking in the opposite direction to that in which the prosecution says he was walking and there is no doubt about that, the opposite direction. Because he was at Vanderbilt Avenue, and listen, he was at Vanderbilt Avenue at that time and the bus driver was at Vanderbilt Avenue starting at 12:50 from the Ferry here, terminal, St. George terminal, and at about 1:00 o'clock he was at Vanderbilt Avenue after and if Elmore was there at 5 minutes to one, we are led to believe that he beat the bus walking. There is no doubt about that.**

Now, a very important situation. Do you remember a witness by the name of Louis Ginnes. Louis Ginnes was subpoenaed by us, by the defendant, and he is the man who is a drug clerk at Hardy's Drug Store. Now, you will agree with me that this witness was anything but voluntary in his statement. He first told me that he didn't remember Elmore, he didn't remember a sale, he didn't remember a thing because so many people come in and out and he is always on duty, sometimes between 1:00 and 2:00, or there abouts. Was he on duty on August 12th? A. Yes he was. "Q. I see. Now, does that conversation recall to your memory the looks of the man who questioned the price of Ben-Gay? A. Thinking back on it, I might say he was a timid man." At first he said he didn't remember. When I asked him did he talk to the police officer in this case. "A. Yes I did. Did you make a statement. Yes. What statement did you make?" Since now, you don't want to give us a statement, then I went out. Yes. "Q. Now, suppose you take a good look at Simon Elmore, the defendant in this case, stand up Mr. Elmore, I said, did he look anything like this man?

A. I would say he did look something like this man."

Now, Ginnes didn't want to testify in my opinion, Gentlemen, he was backward about it. When I asked him about the time, I said, "But, will you say, however, in view of your answer, that it might have been 1:30" because that was the time I was asking him about. "But, will you say, however, in view of your answer that it might have been 1:30? A. It might have been, yes." And then I thanked him and he went off the stand.

Now, you know Gentlemen, that he testified about making a specific sale on that day, selling somebody some Ben-Gay and he said that a man came in and questioned the price of Ben-Gay. He said as to how a man said why it shouldn't be $.59, it should be $.49, all that, and still he didn't remember him. Whereas, Flick, he could tell you, as soon as he passes him, and he could tell you it was Elmore. This man sold him goods. What did Mrs. Elmore say? I said, "did you give your husband instructions to buy Ben-Gay? A. Yes, I did. And what were you going to use it for?" She said, "that was good for colds I had when I was going to use this Ben-Gay." I said, "do you remember the price of it?" She said something like $.49 or $.59, I don't remember now, but there was a 9 on the end of that number and it is on the record.

Now, Louis Ginnis saw this man at 1:30 in his store. There can be no doubt about it because the other witnesses, testified to other times which absolutely put truth in the very statement that I have presented to you by all of these witnesses, so he must have been there, although at first he says between 1:30 and 3:00 o'clock, but when he came around to it, I said could have been 1:30. Why, I don't blame him for not remembering at all, but could it have been at 1:30. Yes it could. Well, diagnose that very statement alone and give that statement the benefit of the doubt and you will see that it might have been at 1:30 because the witness said so, so that that is the possibility that he was. **He didn't want to talk to me though, because he said he had talked to Police officers first.**

Now, let's go from 1:30 and see where we do go.

We go back to John Carney at 2:15. What is singular in my notation here in addition to what I told you about John Carney is the fact that when I asked him had he told that time to be 2:15 to anyone else, he said yes. I told two detectives that time, 2:00 to 2:15. Is there any doubt about it, it might have been someone else but Elmore, he said no, I have known Elmore a long time. Men that know him come here and say we saw him from 2:00 to 2:15. Will you totally disregard what these witnesses have told you. It is an impossibility in construing the reasonable doubt in this case. Now, follow it along, if you like, 2:15, around 3:00 o'clock he is back in Stapleton. A fellow by the name of Harris comes to court and he testified and certainly there is no doubt about this testimony, he said, "I know Elmore, he came in from about 3 o'clock, how do you know it was 3:00 o'clock, well there is a Rubsam and Horrmann clock, a new clock, down there that they dedicated about a year ago and furthermore, he says, I brought my mother to catch a bus and she had to catch the 2:30 and he came back. When he came back, Elmore was in front of his automobile. What do you want, I want to buy a pair of pants. Did he buy those pants? Yes. What color were those pants. They were blue.

Now, you know this thing about details, details are the greatest things, the most important things in the consideration of a case of this kind. I gave him back a quarter change. So that he could go to a tailor by the name of DaLecy and have the pants shortened. I gave him back $.25 and he gave us the price that he paid for the pants.

Now, what happens here. And this is very important. I naturally looked for the fellow that shortened the pants and I produced him. He says Elmore, on direct-examination, came in about 2:30. Well, you know when it is 3:00 o'clock and you didn't expect to be called, you didn't think that a certain thing was going to be eventful to him, like meeting somebody on the street, why you would disregard it from your mind and then try to think back and sometimes you can't. So he says about 2:30. Of course, that is an honest declaration of his estimation of time without a single doubt about it. But, here is what the District Attorney did. Where a witness says a thing like that, the District Attorney straightened me out on it, without a doubt, because he got up on cross-examination and he says, Mr. DaLecy you signed a written statement, you signed an affidavit, didn't you. He said "Yes, I signed an affidavit." "And in there you put in certain time, did you? Is this your signature?" "Yes, it is." "Well, look at that, what **time did you say in there?" "Well, in that I said 3 to 3:30."**

**Well, that is all right, that checks up all the more. For the moment this man thought it was 2:30, but he can't be wrong, because you cannot have pants shortened if you didn't buy pants first. There is no doubt about that in anybody's mind.**

So that, Harris being correct as to his time, because of the Rubsam and Horrmann clock, and because he brought his mother to the bus, and then had to come back and saw Elmore in front of the store, that shows you that DaLecy had made an honest mistake and there can be no doubt about that.

**Now, why is it then since they got DaLecy's affidavit--you know DaLecy is not an outstanding witness in this case at all, he just fills in the gap that we need, naturally. If the District Attorney went to get an affidavit from DaLecy, why didn't he go and get an affidavit from each of my witnesses?**

**Well, I will answer that for you. I think he did. Because there would be no point of singling out**

DaLecy, because he saw him at 2:30 or 3:00 or 3:30. They did get affidavits from the other witnesses, but they didn't have to use them in the other instances, for the simple reason that the time checked exactly, as the affidavits were sworn statements dictated at the time.

So, in only one instance was an affidavit pulled out of the hat on an honest mistake. Well, he said, "Maybe I did say 2:30, I don't know." So, there we have that situation.

Now, what have we got that afternoon? Can so many people see a man between three and four o'clock,-- and that is what I like about a witness when he says, "I saw him between three and four o'clock." I don't like this definite thing, because I think it is superhuman, and I do think that it is a little too much for any sane jury to give any credence to a man who says, "Why, I saw this happen at so and so." It can't be.

Between three and four. I like that, that is reasonable, that is what I would say, that is what you would say. How could so many people see him between three and four now? When the indictment and the bill of particulars says this crime was committed between 11:00 A. M. and 5:00 P. M. And what do I refer to? I refer to the proposition, gentlemen, that Al Miller works in the A. and P. Store down at Stapleton, Broad Street, Stapleton, and see whether it doesn't check, that after he did all this, and he had the pants under his arm, he goes into the A. and P.

Why did he go into the A. and P.? Because his wife testified that she had given him a second order to fill and he went into the A. and P., Al Miller testified.

Now, the A. and P. men are not here for any purpose, except to aid you in doing justice. We got them here. If the District Attorney wanted to tell you all about this time himself, he could have subpoenaed them. He certainly got affidavits from them, but we had to, because this is our defense, he is only charged with the prosecution, he must make out a case, and beyond a reasonable doubt.

296

Mr. McMahon in the store, Mr. Kelly, the Superintendent of the, all of the A. and P. stores on Staten Island, he was there. Well, he figured around three o'clock, he had been to the bank and he made a deposit; as a matter of fact, he had to make a night deposit, if you recall that matter, because the bank was closed, so he says it was between three and four.

Everybody says it was between three and four. There is no doubt about this A. and P. situation. He went there for a package. Did he get one? Let's see if he got a package. He then went to a store and Ellen Feldrapp is the witness who testified to that, and he bought a fifteen cent huckleberry pie and he bought an eight cent loaf of Vienna bread, that was from three to four, so he accumulated another package.

As he was walking up the road he met a fellow by the name of Boggenao,--you certainly must remember that witness, and he said he saw Elmore walking home with a package, it looked as though it contained groceries, the ordinary package you would get in any store. And did they talk? Yes. They talked about painting the house, because Boggenao was doing, or was getting ready to do some repairs on this house, and apparently after you make repairs with fresh lumber, painting is necessary, he knows that Elmore is a painter, they start a conversation about painting, and what is the situation?

Well, all right, when I am ready, I will give you the job. Now, they knew each other, there is no question that Boggenao saw Elmore there, there can't be, because they are so friendly, and I asked him what did Elmore call you on that day, now? He says, "He called me 'Joe'." He called him "Joe," but I said, "Your name isn't 'Joe,' your name is Enrico." "But," he said, "Elmore always calls me 'Joe'." And there you have got a situation.

Now then, what did I do? Either before or after that, it doesn't make any difference.

John Techky was called yesterday morning. He went into this saloon,--John Techky's father owns it--and he stayed there about twenty minutes. He said he had about five beers. What did he have with him? He had a bag that contained groceries. He had a large bag that contained groceries, and when he left, did he leave with the bag? Yes, he left with the bag. Where did he go? Well, Mrs. Elmore tells us where he went, because she testified that this man got home at four o'clock.

Did he come home with the groceries? Mrs. Elmore answers, "Yes, he got home with the groceries." Did you have dinner? "Yes." And he stayed around the house until six o'clock, he went out and you know he had to go to Mrs. Wardell.

Now, gentlemen of the jury, since I have gotten past five P. M. on that bill of particulars, I am no more concerned. I asked Mrs. Elmore where he went at 6 o'clock. To Wardell, just so as to connect the entire situation. He went to Mrs. Wardell, returned home, she said, and then they went to bed.

She said, "Why don't you go to bed?" He didn't answer, he looked sad. That is the situation. There is no doubt about the fact that he went to Mrs. Wardell to report, because Mrs. Elmore had made a complaint against him. The District Attorney brought that out. He said, "You were the cause why Elmore had to go and pay visits to Wardell." He was what they call on probation. That is, because of a family dispute, between husband and wife, which really doesn't concern anybody in this case, but it was brought out, and he came home and he went to bed, and then the next morning, what happened the next day? I have gone over that situation.

I say to you gentlemen now, as men sitting, as men whom in a short while will deliberate on a man's life, I say to you, gentlemen, and ask the same question of you individually,--do you think that you have enough in this case to take Elmore's life? Do you think that the testimony that we have produced, raises a reasonable doubt in your mind? **There can't be any doubt about it at all. I say to you that if Elmore committed a crime, for goodness sake, when did he commit that crime? It is an impossibility.**

Now, there is no doubt about the fact that when he said in that long confession that he got home at 1:30, that is wrong, and when he said that this crime was committed at 2:00 P. M., that is obviously wrong, there can be no doubt about that. Now, gentlemen, can all of these witnesses that we have produced, can they all be lying in order to save this man's life? Did the testimony strike you as if they came here to save this man's life, but in order to do so, take a false oath to tell the truth, the whole truth and nothing but the truth? The case is too serious for that. I say to you gentlemen, that the People have not proved their case here.

The man who committed that crime, gentlemen, I will say to you, is not in this court room, as far as I know. At least, I will tell you it is not Samuel Elmore. The man who committed that crime might he depraved. The man who committed that crime, in my opinion, must be depraved. The man who committed that crime is not the man who sits there listening to testimony and just saying, "Well, this is the world, isn't it, how easy it is to get in trouble."

Will you tell me the caliber of the human brain, the kind of brain, if you assume for one moment that this man committed such a crime on August 12th, and finally he got home, will you tell me what kind of a mind it is that would go down to this bungalow, knowing full well that there is a dead girl there, knowing full well that a crime had been committed?

Would a man go there just to be locked up? Wouldn't he go to the nearest police station, if he felt sorry for her, and wanted to do it that way? But, the caliber of man that commits that type of crime, is he the man that goes and gives himself up, is he the man that says, "I did it and here is the confessions, all you want of them, because I am the guilty man and I did that thing"?

Oh no, the man who commits a crime of that type, he says, "Well, you have got me and I won't talk. You try me for the crime, you prove it--that is the smart aleck of it. Or, is it the man, 57, going on 58 years of age, who is brought to the station house and he is befuddled, and he sleeps in the station house, and finally they say, **"you better admit, it because we have got this, we have got that, and we have got the other,"** and finally he says, **"All right, I will sign anything."**

How long has a man fifty-seven years of age to live anyhow?

Gentlemen, the man who committed that crime is going to be punished by the great Almighty, and there is no doubt about that--but not Elmore, he didn't do it.

Now, I am going to close in a minute, because my hour and a half is up. I want to tell you something about the way in which this case has been tried, but before telling you that, I want you to know that I cast no aspersions on Mr. Innes whatsoever, because I think he is a gentleman of rank and has shown it to you by the way he has treated me, and I dare say I treated him the same. No squabbles, but it just happens to be that that is the way the case went along.

Now, suppose that he wanted to present the truth, the whole truth and nothing but the truth, and our system of jurisprudence sometimes is that way, that the people produce the things that perhaps tend to hurt the defendant. If it were just so that it was a law that all evidence should be submitted and then let you think it over, then this question wouldn't come up. He, of course, would have done this in that instance.

Detective Cosgrove testifies that there was blood on the underwear of the defendant, and without any hesitation and without any doubt, there was blood there. What was done with these clothing? Well, these clothing were sent over to the office of the City Toxicologist and there they went up there for a chemical analysis.

Well, now, Gentlemen, you know by this time that a chemical analysis was performed, there is no doubt about that. So that, if it had shown the presence of blood, it would have checked up Cosgrove's testimony, and the District Attorney, I should think, doing his duty, as I know he does, would present those articles of clothing to you.

But, since Officer Cosgrove testified that he saw

blood and was definite about it, and since the defense--People didn't offer these clothing to you, or the result of a chemical analysis, I said, "Well, I think I will get them myself." And can you believe me, gentlemen, that when I asked, when I had a subpoena served on Mr. Schwartz, a chemist for eighteen years of the City of New York, I did not know what the answer was, and I stand now and tell you that if that had been damaging testimony to me, and I should be damaged, I want to be damaged, because if the defendant was ever guilty, he should be punished, I should say.

But, what did happen? There is the clothing. The testimony is clear, I think, and you will notice that, I think you will recollect that it was just this and no other: "Q. Now, will you tell us the result of your examination? **Did you discover evidence of blood on that clothing or not? A. No."**

Then it came along, another question was asked: "Q. When did you make this examination?" Naturally, Mr. Innes doesn't ask anything else. He said, "Well, I made it on the 10th of November."

"Well," he said, "that is some time after you received this stuff, isn't it?" So he contentedly sat down and then further, we asked: "Now, would there be any difference in the test that you made whether made on August 17th or November 10th of the same year? A. Absolutely none."

Now, where was that blood? The answer is, "Absolutely none."

And, incidentally, and since this is in evidence you will see sooner or later in your jury room, if you desire to examine **this exhibit, a pair of striped pants, brown and white, from a man who is able to pick up minute details, to call this pair of pants a dirty pair of gray pants, is a little too much, I think.**

Now, we have come to this, Gentlemen. My work in this case is over, it has been kind of strenuous for me to present a case of this kind. Your work is just beginning. You have more work to do than I. You have got to deliberate on this case.

Will you kindly and won't you kindly review the entire sum and substance of the testimony, think why a man would sign a confession, two of them, develop the conditions and circumstances under which that statement was procured. Would a man sign such a confession if he was guilty? Would a man of the character that committed this crime sign such a statement?

Will you keep before you continually, gentlemen, the fact that the State must prove its case beyond a reasonable doubt? Will you keep in mind the fact that you can't be in two places at the same time? I am going to turn you over to Mr. Innes now; who will address you, and I want to say that under the law, I must sum up first.

I have completed my work. I am not allowed to answer. If he says anything to which you want an answer, I urge you to supply your own answer, to supply your own answer. If you think I have done well in this case, I am happy. If I haven't done well, I ask you, gentlemen, to do a better job and acquit this man.

The Court: We will take a few minutes recess, gentlemen. Do not discuss this case or come to any conclusion in the matter until the case is finally submitted to you.

(Whereupon, at 11:36 A. M. a recess was taken until 11:54 A. M.)

Summation by Mr. Innes--For People

Court Clerk Kosman: People against Samuel Elmore.

(Both sides were ready. Whereupon, the Jury was polled and all jurors answered present.)

Mr. Innes: May it please the Court, gentlemen of jury. In the orderly practice of courts, criminal courts, particularly in cases of this nature, it becomes my duty at this time to address you on the behalf of the People.

After the magnificent effort of Mr. Gulotta, on helm of his client, I feel that my duty has been increased, the burden has been cast upon me to clear up some of these matters, and when I heard the magnificent effort of Mr. Gulotta here this morning, I became in a measure proud of my profession.

The defendant's counsel here were assigned by his Honor to represent this defendant upon this trial, and to see to it that he had a fair and impartial trial. I join with him in that respect. I ask nothing more than simple justice, so far as this defendant is concerned, and I want at this time to disabuse your minds of the idea that I am looking for a victim--I ask that summary justice be meted out--that is not my purpose at all.

The People of the State of New York is the Plaintiff in this case that is, society at large, and I, temporarily, am here to represent the People and no one else. I have no interest in any one who is vitally interested in the prosecution of this case. I do not represent the father or mother of this little girl. I represent no relative of their's. I am here solely on behalf of the People whom I do represent and nothing else.

And I want to disabuse your mind of any idea that I have any spleen, any rancor, any feeling of animosity so far as this unfortunate defendant is concerned, because I have not.

I am here to present to you as best I can in my feeble way, the salient points which I believe are necessary for you to consider in this matter.

Now then, we have been here more than a week in the presentation of this case. I feel that you have given me your most earnest attention and I am sure that you will not be misled by anything that the counsel on the other side has said, or anything that I may say that does not comport with your recollection of the testimony here, because you are concerned with the testimony only and you must arrive at a conclusion from that evidence and that alone.

Now then, may I at the outset say that we are concerned with two propositions here. I will read the section of the Code of Criminal Procedure, Section 393; "The defendant in all cases may testify as a witness in his own behalf, but the neglect or refusal to testify does not create any presumption against him."

Now, that precludes me from referring to the failure of the defendant to take the stand in his own behalf. He had that right. He did not avail himself of it, but that does not permit me to comment upon that feature of the case.

**Now then, there is another verse in this Code which is directly pertinent and that is Section 395, "A confession of a defendant, whether in the course of judicial proceedings or to a private person, can be given in evidence against him, unless made under the influence of fear produced by threats, or unless made upon a stipulation of the District Attorney that he shall not be prosecuted therefore, but it is not sufficient to warrant his conviction without additional proof that the crime charged has been committed."**

Now, I have told you before that the defendant, exercising a privilege which was his, failed and refused, or at least did not testify in this case, but, I say to you that he did testify, that his testimony is here, black on white, two confessions, which I shall refer to later on more at length, but those confessions--and I anticipate the Court's charge in that respect--must be corroborated to the extent that a crime was committed, and as to that, there is no dispute in this case.

Little Joan Kuleba was murdered in a cellar in a bungalow away out in the meadows near South Beach. That she was strangled and died of strangulation, there is absolutely no question. That she was violated before or prior to the time that she was strangled, there is no dispute, and the defendant here did not question the fact that that little girl was most brutally murdered in that God forsaken place in that cellar.

**Now then, who did it? That is the question for you to determine. Did the defendant do it? He says he did. I could be quite content to rest upon these confessions alone, but there are other circumstances which tend to corroborate these confessions.**

Now then, let us start at the beginning. Little Joan Kuleba was staying with her aunt, Mrs. Lesandi, in a bungalow at South Beach. On the morning of the 12th of August last, the aunt dressed her in a little red bathing suit and she went out with the aunt's two children to play on the beach.

**The aunt intended to come later on and attend to those children. She did come around about 11:00 or a little after, and possibly 12:00 and little Joan was not there, and she became concerned. They organized a searching party. Some twenty or thirty or more people joined in that search for little Joan. She was not found.**

She was turned in as a missing person and Police Officers and the Police Department was notified and Detective Cosgrove came down to the beach and joined in the search. At some time later on in that afternoon, these little sandals which are here, were found on the beach beside an overturned boat in front of Crane's Hotel and there was sand on them, or near them anyway, and the Police Department came to the conclusion that this little girl was drowned, and they started to grapple for her body in the waters adjacent to the place where these shoes were found.

They were not found by Cosgrove, they were

found by Officer Bohan and by Detective Pagano, and when these were found it caused the Police to believe that this little girl was drowned, and as I said, they were grappling for the body.

Now, we pass on. On the morning of the 13th of August, Haff, who was concerned with some boats at the foot of Burgher Avenue, that part of it that you travelled to South Beach, and you were there, all of you, and Fifth Place, saw a man approach this abandoned bungalow, saw him stop behind it and then saw him crossing the meadows in a zig-zagging way, not direct, but going around and finally coming out at or near where Haff had his boats, and he said that man was Elmore--he said, "There is a little girl that is up in that bungalow that is killed, I want a Policeman." And Haff went out on the beach and got Cosgrove, who accompanied them across the meadows to this bungalow.

And bear in mind, both Haff and Cosgrove say that as Elmore passed the window that was out in the basement in the front of the bungalow, he pointed through that window and said, "There she is."

Now then, Cosgrove describes what he found in that cellar, a most gruesome exhibit--a most horrible crime was committed. Fortunately, we are able to reproduce that scene. Here are two pictures showing the body of that little girl as she laid there dead that morning, Friday morning, strangled, a cord around her neck that penetrated the flesh to a half an inch, as was testified here, and that cord was then passed up around the part of the old broken door, and upon the back was a quantity of brick that held her down.

Her head was about an inch above the cellar floor and she was strangled and died of strangulation.

Now, that is what Cosgrove saw there at the time. Fortunately, we have another picture showing the interior of that cellar and upon it and in that picture, shown upon a concrete shelf in the rear and to the left as you approach from the rear, was a milk bottle containing a grasshopper.

There is the milk bottle, there is the dead grasshopper. All of these things are undisputed. They were there in the basement of that abandoned bungalow away from the place, away from any habitation, a thousand feet or more from the nearest house.

Now then, what did Cosgrove do? He asked the defendant his name, where he worked and all that sort of thing. He got a little history of the defendant and he deemed it advisable to take him for a further examination, and he brought him to the station house here at St. George.

He was questioned during the evening of the 13th and at some time during that morning of the 14th, a Mrs. Budd came to the station house; and just let me read what happened when she got there. "Mrs. Budd came in and saw Elmore" in the presence of the officer?"--What did she say? **Mrs. Budd said she was on the beach the day before,"--that was the day of the 11th--"and that she had seen Samuel Elmore on the beach, that she was with her grandchildren on the beach, and she noticed Elmore and her child walking away from the beach, that she then ran after her child, took her and looked at Elmore. She had something on her mind, she said, and when she came to the station house on the morning of the 14th about four o'clock, Inspector Lyons was there, myself, McGrath, she seen Elmore there and said, 'That is the man' she had seen on the beach the day previous when she was there with her grandchildren."**

Fortunately, her little grand-child wasn't the victim, because she ran up and grabbed that child away from Elmore.

Now, then, reference has been made here to the fact that Mrs. Budd was not called as a witness, and I am going to just confide in you a little bit of trial strategy. She would not be a witness, she could not be a witness, because this happened on the day before, and his Honor will charge you that she could not testify to what occurred on the day before, but I had intended to use her as a rebuttal witness in the event that the defendant took the stand in his own behalf. So much for her.

Now then, Flick came in the station house in the afternoon of that 14th day. He was in the presence of the defendant, and Officer Cosgrove, again testifying, said, "Flick was brought in and he faced Elmore and he said, 'That is the man I seen at Norway Avenue and Olympia Boulevard with a child about 1:10 or 1:12 on the day of the 12th of August at Norway Avenue and Olympia Boulevard',"

Now then, that was in the afternoon of August 14th. Mrs. Budd had been there in the early morning. Flick came in the afternoon, and they both confronted the defendant and what did he say in his confession?

**"I took the little girl along for a walk, along Old Town Road, just where the bus driver says." A little corroboration there. And later on he said: "I was on the beach Wednesday, the woman that identified me told the truth."**

Well, that was the situation on Saturday afternoon at about a quarter past five when I was sent for and arrived at the station house, and you have heard what occurred after that time. I was introduced, I said to Elmore, "Do you want to talk to me?" He started off. I said, "You are lying. I want the truth." And he said, "Well, I did it." No doubt about that at all.

Under no restraint. He has said it to several people, that he was treated like a gentleman in the station house, and he was treated like a gentleman when I was there. Maybe I was a little rough with him, but it burst forth and as he said afterwards, it relieved his conscience.

God, I don't believe he has a conscience. I think he is one of those beastial type of men who hasn't any pity, compassion, or anything that resembles conscience about him. This horrible crime would indicate that he had no feeling whatever, that he was a man who was entirely without pity, compassion, or any of the finer sympathies that go to make up a human being.

Usually where defendants are upon trial, they are not apprehended at or near the scene of the crime. The usual defense is an alibi. That is, that they were not there. If they are caught red handed, or confess, the usual defense is insanity. We are not burdened with that latter defense in this case, because that has not been tendered. I was prepared to meet it if it was, but it is not here before you.

Every man is presumed to be sane until the contrary is proved. I was anticipating that that might he the defense here, but it is not, and you have to assume that he is legally and medically sane, and you have no right to consider him in any other capacity at all, because that isn't in the case here.

But, we have the other defense of alibi, and as opposed to that, we have his two confessions, which are absolutely corroborated in two or three respects, and which he, without any hesitation, signed, and upon the larger one, signed each page.

Now then, there has been quite some testimony here as to alibi. If you will consider all of these witnesses, you will find that they leave a gap, with the exception of two, who I will refer to later on.

Is there any doubt in your minds but that Flick, the bus driver, saw this defendant and the little girl down on Old Town Road, or Norway Avenue, which is the new name for it, near Olympia Boulevard, that he was walking towards the beach? And Flick had a reason for fixing the time, there is no question about that. He was on a route, he was near the end of his route, he was due there at 1:15, and you heard him on the stand.

Didn't he impress you as being open, honest giving you his best recollection? After a most severe and searching cross-examination, was his story weakened? Was it in any way shaken? I say not. I say that Flick was a first class witness, that he, having seen a picture in a paper the day before, as a good citizen, as a conscientious man, felt that he ought to come to the station house and there meet the man who he suspected was the one who he had seen in the picture, and he came and he saw Elmore and he said to me as the last question I asked him, "Is there any doubt?" "Not the slightest particle of a doubt as to my identification of that man."

He was walking along, he had something in his band that he said was glass. Counsel tried to trip him with respect to the glass and referred to the fact that Flick knew that there was some glass in the case, that there was a bottle. There isn't the slightest particle of testimony to indicate that Flick at the time when he identified this man in the station house knew that Elmore had a bottle or something that was glass in his hand.

**But, Elmore himself said--let me refer to that again--"I enticed the child by having a bottle with a grasshopper in it." "That is the bottle that you have here." That was in the afternoon, late afternoon of Saturday, September 14th. There is nothing to indicate that Flick knew that there was a bottle, a grasshopper, or any such exhibit at all, and he told you that the defendant was carrying something in his left hand, which he thought was either a pitcher or something that was made of glass.**

Nov, that, gentlemen, is that part of the case? There is the bottle which was identified as being at the bungalow and the picture shows the bottle standing on that concrete shelf in the rear of that bungalow. Again corroborating the defendant's confession.

Now then, another thing which corroborates this confession. After this paper was signed and witnessed by these four officers, Lieutenant Gifford said, "How did it come that this little girl's feet were so clean, if she walked around as you said she did?" Do you remember what the defendant said? **He said to Gifford, "I took those little shoes off her feet, put them in my pocket, went back to the beach and put them down on the sand."**

Gifford said, "Was there anything around near or where you placed those shoes?" He said, "Yes, they were near a flat bottomed boat that was turned up on the beach." **And isn't that the very place that Pagano and**

**Bohan said they found those slippers? Gifford didn't know that.**

There is nothing in the confession about the slippers, and he was just a little concerned as a good cop should be, inquiring about those slippers, and did he know about it? No, not until the defendant told him. **And that is again corroborative of these confessions.**

**Gentlemen, the Court, I think, will charge you that a confession, if made without any threats, without the fear that is caused by threats, is probably the highest type of evidence, and in this case we needed something more than the confessions, and the fact that this little girl was dead in that bungalow.**

Now, I have just sketchily told you how this crime was committed, how he enticed this little girl into that execution chamber and how he there raped her, he said, forwards and backwards, and the doctor, the Medical Examiner, said, "Yes, she was garrotted, she was strangled, she died of strangulation but there was evidence that she was tampered with, both backwards and forwards, and the defendant in his first confession said, "I molested her, I put the cord around her neck before I molested her and I had intercourse with her in the vagina and the rectum, I put the bricks on her back."

My God, gentlemen, do you want any more than that? Isn't that enough to condemn this man for all time? And here is the other confession, which is five pages long, in which he gives details. I am not going to recite them. These confessions can be taken, if you want them, by you into your jury room and there you can consider them at your leisure, you can consider them for whatever they are worth, and I say that they are evidence of the highest type.

Samuel Elmore signed every page of the larger confession, he signed the one page of the shorter confession. Was he under any restraint? No. Was he threatened? Was he fearful because he was threatened? No. Was there any promise made to him by me of immunity? **You have no testimony to that effect, and I can assure you that there was none.**

I have no feeling in this matter. I wanted to do my duty and I felt that I did when I examined him that Saturday afternoon, and I felt that I had done my duty way beyond the perfunctory way, when that confession was made and signed by this defendant.

Now, gentlemen, I am not going to burden you with a long oration, it doesn't become me. I have presented what is the People's side of the case and now I am going to turn to the other side, the so-called alibi.

Outside of two people, the questions of time are indefinite. Can you remember where you. were ten days ago at 11:00 o'clock in the morning? God, I couldn't, to save my life tell you. I don't believe that any one could call back, is there something that would bring to mind a date? I can remember that there was a horrible collapse two days before on New Street, New Brighton.

This was something that was just, oh, aside and apart from the horror of that, the horror of this thing is enough to shake the intellect a little bit, but I am happy to say that I, on that Saturday afternoon, when I asked him and when he had told us some of the details that were put on the typewriter by Officer Marrinan, that I felt that I had done a good day's work.

The situation at that bungalow--and I was down there--was sickening. The horrible nature of that crime indicated that someone who was absolutely beastial had committed it. The horrible manner in which that little girl was killed was enough to make one's stomach a little upset, and that view in the interior, which is reproduced here, fortunately, for you, is something which, well, passes the understanding.

Now then, counsel has argued to you that because this defendant went to Sea View, called at stores, called at different places on that morning and again later on in the afternoon, indicates that he could not have been at the place of the crime.

Now then, with but two exceptions, there is a break in that alibi and that is supplied by the wife of the defendant, who said that he left at some time--well now, I am not going to--some time about, prior to one o'clock. She is the wife. I didn't want to frog her as to time, I didn't feel that it would be proper or fit to do so. But, she is a wife, he is her husband, and that was a thing that appealed to me at the time when she was on the stand.

But, do you remember what she said about him that night? "I went in the kitchen to get the drink of water for Syble and he was sitting on the end of the couch and he was looking very strange. I didn't know what was the matter with him. He looked as if he was in a--I don't know what I would call it, sort of a, as if his mind was far away, or something." "So, I said to him, 'why don't you go to bed?' He didn't answer me, so I got a drink of water and I took it to Syble. I couldn't understand this funny mood he was in. I had never seen him in a mood like that before. I seen him in all kinds of moods, but this was something different. So, he was sort of sitting there thinking."

**Wouldn't he think of that little girl that he had strangled back in that cellar? Did he have anything on his mind? Did he have enough mind to bring back to him, to his recollection the horrible thing that he had done? God, I say he did, that that was enough, that he had done enough to make a man think and think hard.**

I don't know, I am sure, what sort of a mind that man could have, but he did evince some little pity, possibly, some little conception of the horrible thing he had done, and he was brooding over that very thing that night after he had committed that deed.

Now, these witnesses who are so-called alibi witnesses, are uncertain as to time. Miss McKittrick, possibly I might refer to her, her brother was doing some investigating for the defendant, and while I have no reason to believe that the lady would come here and fabricate, yet there might be a suggestion from that big cop brother of her's, who was formerly in the detective bureau and had retired, that that might have affected her recollection as to time.

Now then, distance has been mentioned. Well, I

don't know, you probably know there is a rapid transit connection between South Beach and Clifton, or Stapleton. He said he walked, but he might be mistaken about that. **There are some things in his second confession that clearly are erroneous as to time, but the capital fact stands out like a sore thumb that in both of them he said he enticed that baby to that deserted bungalow, using the milk bottle with the grasshopper as a lure and that there in that bungalow he killed this little girl.**

Now then, the Court will charge you on premeditation, that is at some time in the commission of this particular crime, he conceived the idea of killing this little girl. Now then, every one--and the Court will tell you--intends the natural course of their conduct, and when he tied that rope around that little girl's neck and drew it tight so that it sunk in a half an inch deep in her flesh and tied it with a black knot, as he said, didn't he intend to kill, and hadn't he prior to that time formed that idea?

Why, I say, there is premeditation there. He had molested this little girl. He had--well raped her, and as he expressed it in the second confession, had back-scuttled, bungholed her--that is the word—and after that, wouldn't he want his victim out of the way? It would seem that that is a perfect reason why he had the desire to kill, and which he accomplished by choking her to death.

Now, gentlemen, I am not going to detain you much longer. I have a duty to perform. You have an active duty from this time on. It is not my purpose to make an inflammatory speech here, it is not my purpose to ask for a victim, but I do ask you that when you consider all of the evidence in this case, there is but one conclusion you can come to.

I am not, as I said before, asking for a victim. I am impersonal in this matter. I am the vehicle by which this man is brought to trial, and if I have made mistakes during the trial, or have been remiss in my duty, charge that up to me, don't permit you to be swayed by any consideration of that kind.

Yours is an important duty. You are now called upon to discharge probably what is the highest duty of a juror and the consequences of your verdict is nothing that you have to do with.

The law of the State of New York has taken that burden from you. Your sole duty is, upon the facts, to determine whether or not this defendant, Samuel Elmore on that Thursday afternoon, killed this little girl, and if he did, that he did it in cold blood, so to speak.

There is no personal satisfaction in me, I am not asking for a victim, I am here representing the People of the State of New York. Society at large is on trial in this case. You are to determine the facts and you are the sole judges of the facts. If I have misstated something it is your recollection which will control.

Do not be misled by anything that I have said, and do not he misled by anything that Mr. Gulotta has said, that doesn't comport with your recollection of what the fact is.

I say, in conclusion, do not be cowardly, do not be afraid, do your duty, and having done that, the People of the State of New York are content. You were drawn from the citizenship of this community. You probably represent a fair cross-section of the good citizens of this community. The People don't ask for a victim here, but, I do say to you, that everything points to the guilt of this defendant, and I want you, when you get to your jury room and you have deliberated and come to a conclusion, that you will ask your foreman to render a verdict of guilty of murder in the first degree. Thank you.

The Court: Gentlemen, we will recess until two o'clock. Do not discuss this case or come to any conclusion in the matter until the case is finally submitted to you. And. please do not read any newspapers. Two o'clock.

(Whereupon, at 12:41 P. M. Court recessed until 2:00 P. M.)

EXHIBITS

People's Exhibit 4.

([Not] Mounted on opposite page.)

562 People's Exhibit 10.

[Ed. Note. "A. This picture was taken in the rear of it, this is the back of the bungalow, and I was taking the picture facing the east."]

564 People's Exhibit 11.

[Ed. Note: "A. That shows the front of the bungalow, looking west."]

566 People's Exhibit 12.

[Ed. Note: "A. That is looking north."

568 People's Exhibit 13.

[Ed. Note: "A. That is looking southeast."]

570 People's Exhibit 14.

[Ed. Note: "A. That was taken from the back of the bungalow in the cellar, showing the front and sides."]

572 People's Exhibit 15.

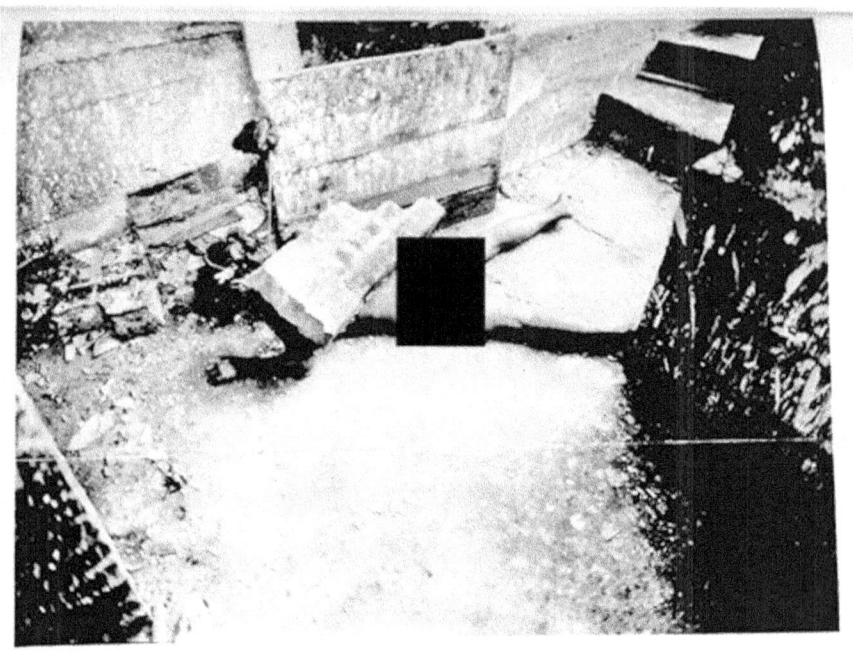

[Ed. Note: The blackout was not in the original.]

574 People's Exhibit 16.

576 People's Exhibit 17.

[Ed. Note: The blackout was not in the original. It looks like the cemented brick came from out of the bottom of the column. If anyone could tell the gender given the body position was an issue during trial. Note how clean her feet are.]

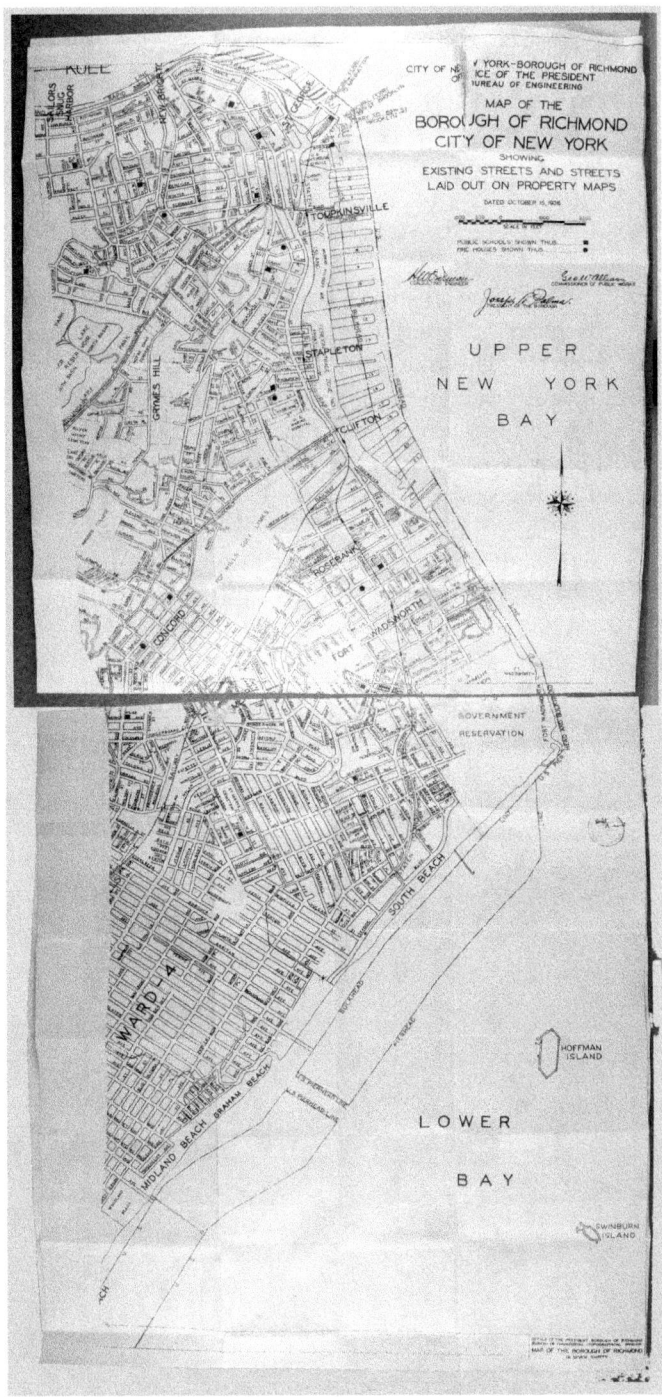

578 Defendant's Exhibit A.

[Ed. Note: Thanks, a big thanks, to the New York State Archives for going to all the trouble of making this map available. The routes are difficult to see because the lines drawn by witnesses are so faded. It is still possible to tell where the bus driver drew the arrow on Norway Ave. and Appleby Ave. There is line drawn to Elmore's home at Metcalf St. It is easier to read in the E-book edition.]

(Mounted on opposite page.)

579
Map

## Stipulation as to Exhibits.

1738

COUNTY COURT,
RICHMOND COUNTY.

THE PEOPLE OF THE STATE OF
NEW YORK,
Plaintiffs,
against
SAMUEL ELMORE,
alias SIMON ELMORE,
Defendant.

1739

IT IS HEREBY STIPULATED AND AGREED by and between the attorneys for the respective parties hereto that the originals of the following exhibits received upon the trial herein may be produced, used and referred to on the argument of the appeal herein with the same force and effect as if reproduced in the case on appeal, and it is stipulated and agreed that the reproduction of the same may be dispensed with:

People's Exhibit 1—Bathing suit.
1740       "    "   2—Sandals.
         "    "   3—Confession of August 14th.
         "    "   4—Photograph (showing northerly side of bungalow with open window).
         "    "   5—Confession of August 16th.
         "    "   6—Piece of cord.
         "    "   7—Bricks.
         "    "   8—Bottle (Milk bottle containing grasshopper).
         "    "   9—Crab pots, hat and bag.

*Stipulation as to Exhibits.*

| | | | |
|---|---|---|---|
| ” | ” | 10—Photograph (showing rear of the bungalow, including outhouse while facing in an easterly direction). | 1741 |
| ” | ” | 11—Photograph (showing front of bungalow while facing in a westerly direction). | |
| ” | ” | 12—Photograph (showing southerly side of bungalow). | |
| ” | ” | 13—Photograph (showing northerly side and rear of bungalow, including outhouse while facing in a southeasterly direction). | |
| ” | ” | 14—Photograph (showing interior of the cellar, facing in an easterly direction). | |
| ” | ” | 15—Photograph (showing position of body, including cord and bricks). | 1742 |
| ” | ” | 16—Photograph (showing interior of the cellar, facing in a westerly direction and including concrete shelf with milk bottle containing grasshopper). | |
| ” | ” | 17—Photograph (showing position of the body from the rear and looking into the cellar). | |

Defendant's Exhibit A—Map.
” ” B—Clothing.

FRANK H. INNES, 1743
   District Attorney,
      Attorney for Plaintiffs.

PETER GULOTTA,
WILLIAM C. CASEY,
      Attorneys for Defendant.

THE PEOPLE OF THE STATE OF NEW YORK, Respondent, v. SAMUEL ELMORE, Appellant

**Court of Appeals of the State of New York.**

277 N.Y. 397 (N.Y. 1938)

THE PEOPLE OF THE STATE OF NEW YORK, Respondent, *v.* SAMUEL ELMORE, Appellant.
Court of Appeals of the State of New York.
Argued March 14, 1938
Decided April 12, 1938
Appeal from the Richmond County Court.
*William C. Casey, Peter F. Gulotta* and *George Fogler* for appellant. *Frank H. Innes, District Attorney* ( *Thomas K. Hall* of counsel), for respondent.

CRANE, Ch. J.

The defendant has been convicted of murder in the first degree for having killed a little girl, Joan Kuleba, on Staten Island (Richmond county) on the 12th day of August, 1937, after or during a sexual assault upon her. It was a revolting crime and one over which indignation against the perpetrator rises as the evidence is read, but yet legal judgment must be kept in the balance and the case examined to determine whether the defendant's life has been forfeited by our rules of law. Twice the defendant confessed, and the confessions were taken down in writing and signed by him after he had read them. Corroboration of these confessions, as required by section 395 of the Code of Criminal Procedure, was provided by the testimony of a man named Flick; the discovery of the child's shoes and the bottle containing grasshoppers caught for the child by the defendant.

There is sufficient evidence if believed to justify the jury in finding the defendant guilty beyond a reasonable doubt, and yet we are obliged to reverse the judgment for reasons which we shall now explain.

There is another side which must be considered in the way the law of this State directs. The jury cannot brush it aside; neither can we say it is of little or no consequence.

On the morning of August 12, 1937, the defendant is alleged to have taken this little girl, Joan Kuleba, from South Beach, Staten Island, to a shack in the meadows or marshes, and there raped and killed her. He tells this in his confession. William Flick, a coach operator for the Staten Island Coach Company, was operating on Norway avenue and Olympia boulevard towards South Beach when he saw the defendant and this little girl walking in the street. She was dressed, all admit, in a red bathing suit. *400400 The time he places as follows: "Between 1:00 and 1:01, one minute after one that afternoon. * * * Why the child looked like she was about six years old to me, a girl would be about six years old, I can't say just how tall or anything she was." He identified the defendant in court as the man.

The confession of the defendant confirms Flick's testimony of this meeting. Both knew each other.

After the assault, the defendant went home according to his story; spent the night, and the next day, Friday, the 13th, returned to the scene of the crime, saw the child was dead, went back to the beach and asked someone to notify the police. When the police came, they found the defendant on the spot, the warning having been given by him.

Leaving out the confession, we have established facts of the death of the child, her body in the shack, and the defendant notifying the police that a murder had been committed. The other independent fact outside of his confession is the testimony of Flick that the little girl and Elmore were seen on the day of the crime in the street some distance from the beach.

The defendant did not take the stand and our law says his failure so to do shall create no presumption against him. (See Code Crim. Proc. § 393.) This always strikes the layman as somewhat strange but such has been the law for many years and we, as well as the jury, are obliged to obey it. In other words, the defendant must be proved guilty by the testimony, or as the case comes to us for a review of the facts, must be proved guilty beyond a reasonable doubt upon the record after a trial according to fundamental rules of evidence.

Thus we have the case — Flick saw the defendant with the child at one o'clock P.M., on Thursday, the 12th. The defendant confesses according to the testimony of the police officers. The defense is, first, that the confession was made under duress or while the defendant was confined in jail or the police station from Friday until *401401 Monday, without being taken before a magistrate as required by section 165 of the Code of Criminal Procedure, and, secondly, that he could not possibly have committed the crime because he was elsewhere at the time — the defense is an alibi.

To the evidence of Elmore's absence we must give serious attention. The defendant's wife says that he was home for lunch between twelve and one o'clock and that he went out thereafter to do errands for her at various stores and returned about four o'clock. The defendant's house is more than three miles from South Beach and as he had no car, and the evidence shows no other means of transportation (except railroads), it would have at least taken the defendant some time to traverse the distance between South Beach and his home on foot. His whereabouts is accounted for by eighteen witnesses, many of whom are merchants or employees having little or no interest in the defendant.

The People's witness Selma Goller saw the little girl on the beach about twelve-thirty "shortly after lunch." At about noon of that day Elmore, the defendant, was seen by Emma Keil and A.C. Baccarezza at a place about three miles from the beach. Baccarezza worked for the A. P. Tea Company and saw the defendant in the store where he worked, apparently in Stapleton. Mrs. Elmore, the defendant's wife, says that he was at home at twelve-thirty-five. As has been said, this was all of three miles from the beach, or the scene of the crime. Mathilda J. McKittrick, who lived about three blocks from Elmore, saw him pass her house on the day of the 12th about twelve-thirty, possibly one o'clock. Louis Ginnis and Enrico Boggenao saw him between one and three o'clock in the afternoon about three miles from the scene of the occurrence. Mrs. Elmore stated that she had sent the defendant after lunch on various errands in and about Stapleton; and the defendant produced the storekeepers and tradesmen to show that he had executed this commission, *402402 and had made purchases in the stores between one and three or four o'clock. For instance, between one-thirty and three-thirty he bought Ben-gay at a drug store from Louis Ginnis. Edward Harris sold defendant a pair of trousers about three P.M., and sent him to Da Lecy to have them altered. Da Lecy altered the trousers between three and three-thirty P.M. Albert W. Miller, James McMahon and James B. Kelly, all of the A. P. Store in Stapleton, saw the defendant between three and four P.M., in the store. Ellen Feldrapp sold the defendant a huckleberry pie and a loaf of vienna bread, between three and four P.M. The defendant had a "few beers" in a saloon between three and four P.M., and was served by John Techky. He had the groceries with him at the time, and arrived home with them about four P.M. We notice that some of these witnesses are quite positive in placing the defendant as far as three miles away from South Beach at the time when the child is alleged to have been taken from South Beach and to have been seen with the defendant at Olympia boulevard and Norwood avenue. Of course all these witnesses may have been mistaken as to the time. It is somewhat difficult to believe that these storekeepers and clerks would be deliberately falsifying about the matter. However, we must remember that the jury were called upon to face an issue and to decide it either for or against the defendant; and if against him, they were to be convinced of their conclusion beyond a reasonable doubt.

Did the evidence produced by the defendant create a doubt as to whether he could have been the man who took the little girl from South Beach around noon of

Thursday, the 12th, and the man seen by Flick with her on the street? That the defendant should have returned the next day to the scene of the crime, and then himself have notified the police of the murder, might also bear in some way upon the consideration of these points. Be it far from us to trespass upon the prerogatives of the jury *403403 or even to suggest or intimate that the evidence does not weigh strongly against the defendant. It does. What we are attempting to explain here so that it will appear clearly is that there was a fair issue of fact for the jury; the guilt or innocence of the defendant was for the jurymen to determine; there was evidence in behalf of the defendant creating a question of fact, and we must, therefore, go further and see whether or not the jury were properly instructed on the law governing their deliberations.

The court was asked to charge the following:

"Mr. Gulotta: May I further respectfully ask your Honor to charge that by section 165 of the Code of Criminal Procedure, the defendant must in all cases be taken before the Magistrate's Court without unnecessary delay.

"The Court: I think I have sufficiently covered that question.

"Mr. Gulotta: I ask your Honor to charge that the violation by the Police of this Statute, that is, Section 165, which calls for prompt arraignment, is a crime under Penal Law, Section 1841.

"The Court: I decline to so charge.

"Mr. Gulotta: I respectfully except. I ask your Honor to charge the Jury that the detention of the defendant in the Police Station from Friday, August 13th, to Monday, August 16th, is a circumstance to be weighed by the jury in determining whether a confession has any testimonial value.

"The Court: I think I have sufficiently covered that, gentlemen." (It was not mentioned.)

The Code of Criminal Procedure, section 165, reads:

" *Defendant in all cases to be taken before a magistrate*

*without delay.* The defendant must in all cases be taken before the magistrate without unnecessary delay, and he may give bail at any hour of the day or night."

In *People* v. *Alex,* 265 N.Y. 192, 194, we said:
*404404

"Here there was delay of almost thirty-six hours. Even where the police, for thirty-six hours, illegally delay arraignment after arrest, for the purpose of obtaining a confession, the confession is admissible, unless `made, under the influence of fear produced by threats, or unless made upon a stipulation of the district attorney, that he (the defendant) shall not be prosecuted therefor.' (Code Crim. Proc. § 395.) Nevertheless, in determining whether a confession has been obtained as a result of a beating, or is voluntary, the circumstance that it was obtained while arraignment was illegally delayed for no apparent reason except that the police needed a confession in order to have competent proof of the commission of a crime, should be considered by the jury ( *People* v. *Trybus,* 219 N.Y. 18.) In every case where there is a substantial question of the voluntary nature of a confession obtained while a defendant is in the custody of the police, and arraignment is delayed, it is the duty of the trial judge, at least upon request of counsel, to charge that any `unnecessary delay' in arraignment is forbidden by law and should be considered by them." "Delay in arraignment does not exclude a confession." ( *People* v. *Doran,* 246 N.Y. 409, 423.)

While there was no evidence of violence used upon the defendant, and there is no claim that he was promised immunity, yet the jury may always consider, in fact must consider, whether the confession has been voluntarily made — that is, has not been produced by fear or under such circumstances and conditions as to lead one to believe that it was not the truth. Even when a confession is admitted in evidence, even when it is conceded to have been made, yet its truth is always a question for the jury and, in determining this, the jury must have all the circumstances surrounding its making. The jurors have the right, therefore, as has been stated by this court, to consider the detention of the defendant from Friday to Monday, while confessions were being taken. In this *405405 case the detention may have had no effect whatever upon the defendant, and all that he said may be true but, nevertheless, this is not for the court, but the jury, to say; in coming to a decision the jurors must consider the continued restraint.

We do not say that we would reverse this case if this were the only error but, coupled with one more serious, we feel that even this cannot be overlooked.

We have stated the evidence and the issue regarding the alibi, in order that the charge to the jury upon this point may also be understood. In a criminal case the defendant never has the burden of proof. The People must prove the case against him beyond a reasonable doubt. In the case of an alibi, naturally he produces his evidence to show that either he is not the man, or else that he could not be the perpetrator of the crime, as he was elsewhere at the time of its commission. If this evidence creates a doubt — a reasonable doubt — in the mind of the jury, he must be acquitted. Never is he called upon to prove his defense beyond a reasonable doubt. ( *People* v. *Barbato,* 254 N.Y. 170, 178, 179; *People* v. *Stone,* 117 N.Y. 480, 484.) This court said in the former case:

"If the proof as to an *alibi* raises a reasonable doubt in the minds of the jury as to whether the accused was present at the place and time where and when the crime was committed, the accused is entitled to have the defense fairly treated like any other defense and is not obliged to establish that it was impossible for him to commit the act charged. If under the evidence tending, if true, to prove an *alibi,* it may have been *possible* for the defendant to have committed the crime, it is still for the jury to determine whether, if the evidence is true, he availed himself of the possibility it afforded. * * * The instructions of the court were too strict in this respect. If the proof as to an *alibi,* when taken into consideration with all the other evidence, raises a reasonable doubt as

406 to defendant's guilt, he is entitled to an acquittal." (See, also, *Brotherton* v. *People*, 75 N.Y. 159, 163.)

As to Elmore's defense, the judge charged:

"The burden of disproving the alibi rests upon the People. If you are satisfied beyond a reasonable doubt with the alibi, and that the alibi covers the time of the commission of the crime; the proof of the alibi, with all the other evidence, may raise a reasonable doubt as to the defendant's presence at the place of crime, and the defendant should then be acquitted." We must not be captious or unduly critical and, although this charge is somewhat confused because of the words. "If you are satisfied beyond a reasonable doubt with the alibi," yet we would pass it, were it not for the clear and definite explanation which the trial judge made in reply to a request:

"Mr. Gulotta: I further ask your Honor to charge that the defense of alibi need not necessarily be established by the defendant beyond a reasonable doubt, but, quite to the contrary, the jury may give to it such credence as in their opinion it should be given.

"The Court: I think I have sufficiently covered that, gentlemen. I informed you that the defense of alibi, like every other defense, may be proved and must be proved beyond a reasonable doubt by the defendant." This is not the law. No matter how strong the evidence may be against the defendant, we cannot overlook such a fundamental error, especially in view of what we have said the evidence shows upon the question of the defendant's whereabouts.

The judgment of conviction should be reversed, and a new trial ordered.

LEHMAN, O'BRIEN, HUBBS, LOUGHRAN, FINCH and RIPPEY, JJ., concur.

Judgment of conviction reversed, etc.

Ed. Note: The caption to this photo is: "Visit Scene of Crime: A New York City Detective, left, escorts Samuel Elsmore [sic], 50, and Chief Inspector John A. Lyons, right, to the deserted cottage where the body of little Joan Kuleba, 4, was found ravished and murdered earlier in the day. Elsmore told police of finding the body, and was being questioned further at a late hour that night. (ACME) 8/13/37.

It is tempting to consider the possibility that Judge Cosgrove believed the alibi defense enough to leave a back door open. There are two reasons for speculating this. 1) He stated in the charge that Elmore was in custody during the interrogation. 2) The charge that proof beyond a reasonable doubt of the validity of the alibi is so fundamentally wrong Judge Cosgrove had to know it was reversible error. These are, however, assumptions. Elmore was retried and again found guilty and sentenced to death. There were no "technicalities" this time on which to reverse the conviction and grant a new trial. Some on the New York Court of Appeals dissented on the grounds of evidence.. Lack of evidence was the argument in 1925 in the case of S.C. Stone for the murders of Nina and May Martin (see *Uncivil Twilight*). His death sentence was commuted to life and his life sentence was once more commuted and he was released from prison.

The opinion of New York's highest court:

COURT OF APPEALS OF THE STATE OF NEW YORK.

**279 N.Y. 691 (N.Y. 1938)**
**PEOPLE V. ELMORE**
**THE PEOPLE OF THE STATE OF NEW YORK, RESPONDENT, V. SAMUEL ELMORE, APPELLANT.**
**COURT OF APPEALS OF THE STATE OF NEW YORK.**
**ARGUED OCTOBER 27, 1938**
**DECIDED DECEMBER 6, 1938**

APPEAL FROM THE RICHMOND COUNTY COURT.
*William C. Casey* and *Peter F. Gulotta* for appellant.
*Frank H. Innes*, District Attorney ( *Thomas K. Hall* of counsel), for respondent.
Judgment of conviction affirmed under the provisions of section 542 of the Code of Criminal Procedure. No opinion.
Concur: CRANE, Ch. J., O'BRIEN, HUBBS and FINCH, JJ. LEHMAN, LOUGHRAN and RIPPEY, JJ., dissent on the ground that the question of fact presented is too close to permit us to overlook the errors committed at

the trial; and RIPPEY, J., dissents on the additional ground that the evidence of guilt was insufficient to warrant a conviction, and the indictment should be dismissed.

COMMUTATION

Thirteen hours before Elmore's scheduled execution, Governor Lehman commuted his sentence to life in prison, swayed by the opinions of New York's highest court and the lack of evidence.

The Colder Case Series

# APPENDIX

What was the argument against allowing the convicted to "get off on a technicality and therefore forbade the highest court of New York to question the verdict? A 1902 Columbia Law Review article explains the reasoning.

## CRIMINAL LAW AND ITS ADMINISTRATION IN THE STATE OF NEW YORK.

ONE of the principal functions of government is the protection of persons and property from crime. The experience of centuries should enable statesmen and jurists to deal with crime with increasing efficiency. New con ditions, however, breed new crimes. The growing density of population in cities and villages, and the increasing pres sure of population upon the means of subsistence make the problem of crime more difficult of solution.

With the procession of the generations there is in this and other lands a constant advance in civilization and refine ment. But yet masses of men in every large community are practically uncivilized. They are covered with but a thin veneering of civilization, and when that is scratched off a savage or barbarian is revealed. These masses are kept in order, not by conscience—not because they want to do right, but by force, the force which is known to be behind the law. When that force ceases to be dominant, brutal pas sions break their barriers and order and safety disappear. This was illustrated in the French Revolution, in the reign of the Commune in Paris, in the Draft Riots of 1863 in the City of New York, and is seen in the savagery so frequently practiced upon Negroes in the south—practiced because there is not force enough back of the law to deal with the situation.

To fit punishment to crime requires great wisdom. Two extremes must be avoided—too much severity and too much humanity. The former brutalizes, shocks the sense of justice, and renders conviction for crime difficult. The latter encourages crime. The sole legitimate purpose of punishment of criminals is the protection of society ; and punishment for this end should be so inflicted as best to reform the criminal and to deter others inclined to crime. Many years ago, Lord Chief Justice Cockburn said : " It may well be doubted whether in recent times the humane and praiseworthy desire to restore and reform the fallen criminal may not have produced too great a tendency to forget that the potection of society should be the first consideration of the law giver." When we notice how the criminal law in our country is administered in many cases, we are sometimes inclined to believe that the great object of the law is not to protect society, but to protect the criminal.

The criminal law has been much ameliorated within the last century. In the early part of that century it was still a capital crime in England to break down a mound of a fish pond whereby any fish escaped, or to cut down a cherry tree in an orchard, or to be seen for one month in the company of Gypsies, or to steal as much as twelve pence. There, less than a century ago, one hundred and sixty crimes were capi tal felonies without benefit of clergy, and somewhat earlier than that a prisoner was not entitled to a copy of the indictment, nor to counsel in cases of felonies. At first he could have no witnesses, but later he could call witnesses but not have them sworn, and yet Blackstone,' speaking of the right of peremptory challenges of jurors, said : " It is a provision full of that tenderness and humanity to prisoners for which our English laws are justly famous."

But while the law was thus harsh and unjust to prisoners charged with crime, technicalities were permitted in the criminal practice which gave them almost their only chance of escape. The omission of some unimportant formality, the absence from the indictment of some unimportant word, the misspelling of a name or of other words, or something else equally frivolous was held to be a fatal defect. Some of these technicalities have been perpetuated to this time, long after the occasion for them has disappeared. One of the old aphorisms of the law, that ten guilty persons had better escape than that one innocent person should suffer, may be worked for more than it is worth, and breed undue caution in criminal trials. In providing for the general welfare—the greatest good to the greatest number—it frequently happens that the innocent must suffer. General laws frequently work hardship to individuals. Private property may be destroyed to stop a conflagration. The smallpox must be stamped out although persons who are well and not exposed to danger from the disease may be put to inconvenience. There is but slight danger that the innocent will be convicted of crime. But their absolute protection cannot stand in the way of the general welfare. The guards thrown around a person charged with crime seem to be ample. His case must first be sifted through a grand jury. He is entitled to a public trial by a jury of his peers, to be informed of the charges against him, to sworn witnesses on his behalf, and to counsel to defend him in capital cases, at public expense in case he is without means. He enters upon his trial with the presumption of innocence in his favor, and the prosecution has the burden of establishing beyond a reasonable doubt every fact essential to the crime with which he is charged ; and he generally has, par ticularly in capital cases, public sympathy in his favor. Our present law is so solicitous for a prisoner charged with murder that it not only requires the public, in case he is without means, to employ and pay counsel for his defense,[1] but in case of his conviction, it gives him the absolute right to

---

[1] Code Cr. Pro. sec. 308. [2] People v. Ferraro, 162 N. Y. 545.

appeal to the Court of Appeals in every case, requiring the county clerk to print the record for that court at public expense ; and it goes still further in requiring the public to fee the counsel who argues his case upon the appeal.[2]

The case reaches the Court of Appeals, usually after a trial which has occupied a month or more, upon a record generally containing a multitude of exceptions taken by astute counsel during the long trial from the empanelling of the jury to the rendition of the verdict. A judge must be very wise and learned as well as very fortunate who upon such a long trial can escape error. How ought such a case to be treated upon appeal ? It is provided in section 542 of the Code of Criminal Procedure that the Court of Appeals shall, in a criminal case, "give judgment without regard to technical errors or defects or to exceptions which do not affect the substantial rights of the parties." Should not a conviction in such a case be affirmed if, upon the legal evidence received upon the trial, the appellate court is well satisfied of the guilt of the defendant, although some illegal evidence was received ? Should not the conviction be affirmed, although competent evidence offered by the defendant was excluded, if the court is satisfied that if such evidence had been received the verdict ought clearly to have been the same ? The Court of Appeals seems to have answered these questions in the negative. The law makers could make the rulings of the trial judge upon questions of evidence final, and when, upon all the legal evidence received and offered, the appellate court can clearly see that the defendant was guilty as charged, what substantial right will be violated by refusing him a new trial? It may well be doubted whether section 542 should not receive a more liberal construction in the interests of the general welfare.

The recent trial of Czolgosz, at Buffalo, was an illustration of what a criminal trial ought to be, and as an example, it cannot fail to be of great value to our country. It was orderly, dignified and brief, and yet all the rights of the defendant were conserved. if he had desired to make a defense and had employed his own counsel, the trial would probably have lasted at least a month, and then an appeal would have stayed the execution of the sentence for several months more, and probably at least a year would have intervened between the crime and its expiation. Thus justice would have been delayed, the general welfare in several ways sacrificed, with the only result to the defendant of prolonging for a few months his worthless life.

In view of modern conditions, particularly in murder trials, it seems to me that some reforms of the jury system ought to be made. I have set forth my views in reference to these at some length in a paper contributed to the Albany Law Journal of January, 1901. I shall close this paper by calling attention to them simply : Amend the constitution so that the trial judge can take a verdict from less than the entire twelve jurors when they are unable to agree, and also from the remaining jurors in the case of the death or serious illness of one or two ; and amend the laws so as to confine the examination of jurors to test their qualifications to sit upon a trial to the presiding judge, leaving to the defendant his peremptory challenges as now. These reforms would leave an innocent person charged with crime all the protection he needs, and would make the administration of the criminal law less burdensome and more certain and speedy. ROBERT EARL.

People v. Wood, 126 N. Y. 249; People v. Corey, 148 N. Y. 476 ; People v. Koernner, 154 N. Y. 355.

www.ingramcontent.com/pod-product-compliance
Lightning Source LLC
Chambersburg PA
CBHW070221190526
45169CB00001B/38